BREAKING
FREE
OF THE
SHAME TRAP

BREAKING
FREE
OF THE
SHAME TRAP

How Women Get Into It
How Women Get Out of It

CHRISTINE BRAUTIGAM EVANS

BALLANTINE BOOKS
New York

Library of Congress Catalog Card Number: 93-14513

ISBN: 0-345-38703-1

Manufactured in the United States of America

Cover design by Kristine V. Mills

First Edition: February 1994

10 9 8 7 6 5 4 3 2 1

In memory of my parents
MARY NASH BRAUTIGAM
HERMAN ARNO BRAUTIGAM
with Love and Gratitude

I would like to thank the following people for their part in making this book a reality:

My writing group, including Beth, Denise, Freida, Laura (in memorium), Linda, Norma, Nancy, and Sylvia—for their honest responses about what worked and what didn't.

My brother and sister-in-law, Richard and Anne Brautigam; Lori Buckley; Libby Coleman; Sylvia Fisher; Allen Fitchen; Wilma Keppel; Arlene Parnay; Sandra Rucker; Susan Stewart; and Linda Ward—for reading early chapters. And my sister, Mary Lois Loe; Mary Riley; Melissa Schwartz; and Merrilyn Scott—for their encouragement.

My women's group, Jann, Judy, Linda, Sandra, and Susan—friends who have been meeting for eighteen years—for sharing their pain and joy as we grapple with the dilemma of being caring women, mothers, wives, lovers, sisters, daughters, grandmothers, and breadwinners, while not giving up our power or authenticity.

Susan Wells for caring and for giving me a safe place to first name my shame, and Michael Sheiner for helping me to rise above shame and become my own person.

Catherine Kamins and Michael Sheiner for their insights into the paths women take as they struggle to become whole—insights that permeate this book.

Dr. Jean Baker Miller, whose compassionate and articulate views on the psychology of women have informed and inspired me.

Landmark Education and Joan Bordow for teaching me about keeping my vision when that seemed impossible.

Judy Semler, my agent, for seeing the potential of the book, for her good ideas, and for ensuring that it landed on the right publisher's desk. Her enthusiasm spurred me on when I became discouraged.

Joëlle Delbourgo, my editor, who aligned herself with my vision of the book, supplied skillful editing, and believed in me; and assistant editor Lesley Malin Helm, for her patience and magical touch.

Judith Searle, vice president of the Editorial Department, who from the beginning believed in my idea, and went far beyond the duties of a gifted editor to become my consultant and partner. Her collaboration and her unflagging support have been invaluable beyond words.

My stepmother, Virginia Corwin Brautigam; my sons, Tom, David; and my stepdaughter, Rebecca; for their love and support. My stepson, Ken, for his patience in teaching me how to use a word processor. How did writers ever manage before computers?

My daughter, Jennifer, for her useful comments and editing, and for giving me the greatest gift of all: a daughter who has a strong sense of self.

My husband, Bob, who never doubted I could do it. He gradually took over meals, dishes, groceries, laundry and didn't complain when I was distracted, grumpy, or unavailable. I have been blessed by his unfailing love and partnership for twenty-six years.

And last my clients, who have allowed me into their lives, who have taught me about shame, about courage, and about strength. It is their willingness to be vulnerable and their commitment to growth that have made this book possible.

CONTENTS

BREAKING
FREE
OF THE
SHAME TRAP

Introduction

Shame has many faces.

If we are mortified at momentarily forgetting a friend's name, we are experiencing shame.

If we compulsively clean house before our mother visits, we are warding off shame.

If our face gets red while lying on our back, legs spread for a pelvic exam, we are reacting to shame.

If we are too shy to speak in front of a group, we are suffering from shame.

If we cover our faces or say "I'm sorry" when we cry, we are hiding our shame.

If we think we're too fat, too thin, too big, or too old, we are contending with shame.

If we envy another's success or fear our own, we are grappling with shame.

If we fail to go after what we want because we don't want to look "unfeminine," we are stopped by shame.

If we consistently put the needs of others ahead of our own, we are ruled by shame.

Shame is the feeling of being unworthy, inadequate, or defective. Though it's accompanied by a sense of being exposed to the unforgiving scrutiny of another person, no one needs to be present to inspire shame in us. We've learned as children to judge ourselves through the shaming eyes of others, and by the time we reach adulthood, we're often experts at shaming ourselves. The loneliness and isolation we feel in our shame testify to our loss of connection with those we most admire and love—those who have rejected, abandoned, criticized, or used us.

Most often we aren't even aware of feelings of being inherently flawed because they're too painful to admit, even to ourselves. Yet unnamed shame lies at the root of most of our troubles. It shapes our identity as women, pervades day-to-day existence, and determines the choices we make in both minor and major arenas.

Small wonder that this disturbing feeling is frequently accompanied by hopelessness. Not only do we believe we are flawed, we are certain we can never change.

We first learn to feel unworthy as children, when our basic needs are not adequately met. Every child needs to feel connected to those important to her, to know she matters as a unique individual, and to develop competence and trust if she is to grow into a woman with a solid sense of self. I am not going into depth about specific types of troubled families such as the alcoholic or workaholic family. There are many fine books available on these subjects. My focus here is on shame issues as they pertain especially to girls and women.

THE POWER OF SHAME IN WOMEN'S LIVES

Our shame is not only rooted in the "dysfunctional" family. It is reinforced by our position in a "dysfunctional" society that historically has considered women less worthy than men. Although I am not able to cover the issue of shame and race (the women I see in my practice are mostly white and middle-class), women of color have a great deal to tell us about the double burden of shame that comes from being both female and nonwhite in our culture.

Since my clients are mainly heterosexual, I have drawn most of my examples from that group. Yet lesbians and bisexual women also carry an extra load of shame that comes from being both female and homosexual in our homophobic culture. They often end up feeling rejected, excluded, and invisible.

Women in our society are particularly prone to shame, with distinct shame-related issues. First of all our male-dominated society views us as second-class citizens, shortchanging us in our schools, our government, and in the workplace. In addition to having less power and opportunity than men, we are demeaned for the way we do things, for the way we think, and for failing to measure up to cultural ideals of youth and beauty. The often-heard comment "Women are the weaker sex" may be a lie, but it's no joke.

In the face of such cultural devaluation *we come to believe there is something wrong with us.*

Although it's easy to blame men for their role in devaluing and disempowering us, we also do this to ourselves and each other—often in ways we aren't even aware of.

Today's woman finds herself caught between conflicting demands. Because society (men, women, and the culture they created together) expects women to take care of others, attempts to expand beyond the role of caretaker, to be assertive, to think for ourselves, to be angry, or to be self-assured often leave us feeling "unfeminine" and ashamed. When we act in our own interests, we risk being called selfish, castrating, or unloving, and we fear our independence will jeopardize our relationships. Yet if we give up too much of ourselves for the sake of preserving these relationships, we love too much or are "codependent." Either path leads to shame.

The quality of our relationships is a dominant concern for women. Self-esteem comes in large part from being connected to others in a meaningful way. When we fail in our relationships, we feel deeply unworthy—because we feel unlovable and because we have failed in the task most central to our identity: to form and maintain relationships.

Poised on the threshold of a society that is slowly changing to give women increasing power in the world, today's woman faces a challenge unknown to her feminine forebears: how to claim an identity for herself yet remain connected to those she loves. Experiencing more freedom than ever before, the modern woman navigates her course through uncharted waters without benefit of a compass or a guide to show her the way.

Becca, thirty-two, juggles being a wife, mother of two, and full-time nursing student. "I feel like it's selfish of me to spend so much time studying. When I'm at the library, I feel guilty that I'm not home with my husband and kids, and when I'm home, I feel like I'm neglecting everybody if I steal a few hours for myself. Plus I still have to keep up with all the housework."

Becca has come a long way from the frightened young woman who first sobbed out her story of being repeatedly molested by a neighbor boy at age eight. Feeling herself to be at fault, she kept her "dirty" secret to herself.

As she grew up, her inferior status became clear when her brothers were encouraged to go to college but she was denied the opportunity. When she complained about the unfairness, her father said to her, "You don't need a college education to be a good wife and mother." She married at seventeen and had two children right away. All during this time she presented to the world a facade of having it all together, hiding her deep humiliation at being an undervalued and abused female and her excessive shame over not being a perfect wife and mother.

Beginning My Own Journey Back from Shame

Although my interest in writing about shame comes partly from working with shame-bound women like Becca, I am also deeply acquainted with the subject on a personal level. I don't plan to dwell on my own story in the body of this book, but I would like to share my experience here. It is my hope that this book will help women better understand why they often act in ways that baffle or defeat them. My goal is to help women move beyond ways of thinking about themselves that keep them psychological second-class citizens.

I was the youngest of three children in my family. There was some physical abuse. Though my father didn't slap my sister and me very often, it happened just often enough to make us duck at the sight of his raised hand, or to run for it when his hand reached to unbuckle his belt (which he never used on us, but who could guarantee this time wouldn't be the exception?). There was confusion: I both loved and feared my father, and I loved and worried about my needy mother. There was hostility: My parents argued continually, and my brother and sister quarreled viciously. It was not a happy home.

My father was often harsh, critical, and easily angered, while my mother was selfless, submissive, and easily intimidated. He drank heavily, and she was chronically ill. Both deeply unhappy, they turned to their children for their unmet emotional needs. While my father favored my sister and rejected my brother, my mother was heavily invested in my brother and rejected my sister. Neither rejected me, because I was a good girl who had (alas) rejected *herself*. Although I never doubted that my parents loved me, I learned that in order to please and take care of them, I would have to deny parts of myself that would burden them further, such as my needs and my feelings.

I always called myself the lucky one, having been born last and able to avoid the damage that comes from being rejected by a parent who resents one's being the other parent's favorite. My brother and sister had taken those slots before I arrived. But deep down I knew I hadn't really escaped, I'd just managed to wear a very convincing mask. I was an imposter, passing for someone who had a solid sense of who she was while feeling empty and unlovable inside.

I also learned about gender shame in my father's house. I understood that women were second-class citizens when I saw my mother sit silently at the unending intellectual discussions, hesitant to express her opinion in spite of her excellent education. I learned that women swallowed their anger and submitted to male authority in all kinds of situations.

I also learned that people can change, as I saw my mother begin to stand up to my father when I was about ten. She taught me that personal growth can be an important and lifelong commitment. And when my father became sober in most of his later years and happily remarried at the age of seventy-four (after my mother's death), I learned that it's never too late to change.

Although both my parents encouraged me to go to college, they didn't mention any career other than nursing or teaching. Even before I graduated college, I married a man who was almost as authoritarian as my father. Too afraid to be on my own, an adult in an adult world, I took the safe way out. I had never been taught that as a female I could have an identity of my own, so I settled for being someone's wife.

Like Becca I had always clung to my false front, the "together" self that I presented to the world. But I constantly feared that some crack would reveal the inadequate little girl inside. And whenever that happened, I was mortified. My sense of shame, I came to realize, was at the core of my being. It controlled not only how I felt about myself but how I related to everyone and everything in my world.

I hadn't known there was any way to see myself except through the lens of shame. I felt scarred and permanently damaged.

I never understood the crucial role shame played in my life until I heard Gershen Kaufman lecture on the subject. Seeing the crowded room, I discovered that shame had touched many other lives as well as mine. Kaufman defined shame as "an invisible wound, a sickness of the soul . . . a feeling of being seen in a painfully diminished way."[1] We become ashamed in our own eyes, he said, as we scrutinize ourselves and find ourselves flawed.

As he described the intense self-consciousness of feeling oneself found out as an imposter, I felt as though he'd been inside my head. Sharing his own struggle, he spoke of shame as an almost inevitable outcome of growing up in a deeply troubled family.

From that point on I was able to see in a new light my feelings of not being good enough. I saw that my deep-seated sense of inadequacy, far from being the result of any natural defectiveness, was simply the price of having been raised by parents who did the best they could but were themselves crippled by shame.

I came away from Kaufman's talk with a feeling of intense relief. Naming the thing, admitting its presence, allowed me to begin healing my shame. For a long time I couldn't shake off my sense of the inevitability of *permanent* scars from being raised in my unhappy family.

Then an amazing thing happened one day when my therapist looked at me intently and said, "Maybe you're not defective." That had never occurred to me before, and it shook me. To allow the possibility of not being damaged was to consider that I might after all be *normal*.

I suddenly felt lighter, freer. *I no longer had to worry about being found out, because I had nothing to be ashamed of or to fear from being exposed.*

My shame had been like a cellar where there bubbled and grew a yeasty mass. Although it was dark and hidden away, I often opened the door to feed it with anything that would confirm my defectiveness. The "stuff" in there never saw the light of day or got checked against reality because I was too scared to face that gooey, smelly mess. It was a substance that could grow only in the dark—and grow it did, to huge proportions. But once the light hit it, it shriveled up and lost its power.

The world looked like a different place from my changed perspective. What I had taken as evidence of my defectiveness (a shattering divorce, my competitiveness, even my messy car) now seemed just part of being human—being me.

I wish I could say that I have banished my shame forever as a result of that intense moment of release; I wish it were that easy. Although my shame continues now and then to sneak up on me unexpectedly, the attacks have dramatically diminished through a lot of long, difficult healing work. I now understand shame, talk about it with others, even joke about it. Rarely do I let it dominate or depress me. I've learned to love myself, shortcomings and all.

Because I now believe in my worth as a first-class citizen, I no longer buy into sexist put-downs or male prerogatives. I value my so-called female ability to be sensitive to the needs of others, but I also respect my own needs and consider them equally valid.

As soon as I acknowledged that shame controlled my life, I was able to recognize it in other women, both clients and friends. This awareness led to a compelling need to write this book, to tell other shame-bound women that *healing is possible.* It is my hope that sharing my own and other women's stories will be instructive, that women will see themselves in these stories and discover ways of freeing themselves from the shame trap. The last chapter is devoted entirely to healing.

Yet to suggest that there are easy or fast answers would be misleading and unfair. Healing takes time and hard work. The journey out of shame is a journey into self—a painful, exciting, and rewarding process, the most significant journey we ever undertake. Along the way we discover we have the ability to cast off our shame and emerge as whole persons, able to love ourselves with compassion for our human weaknesses and healthy pride in our human strengths.

PART ONE

THE
NATURE
OF SHAME

CHAPTER ONE

What Is This Thing Called Shame?

There is a shame that leads to sin,
as well as a shame that is honorable and gracious.
—ECCLESIASTICUS 4:21

"It feels like there's a huge black void out there." Margo, an attractive twenty-five-year-old, was perched on the edge of my couch as if poised for flight. "I've never done any counseling before," she said, "but I can't go on like this. I can't sleep. Sometimes I can't eat and other times I stuff myself—I'm just a wreck." She carefully wiped her tears away with a meek "I'm sorry" and proceeded to tell me a familiar story.

"My parents drank and fought all the time, and I married straight out of high school to get away from them. My boyfriend used to cheat on me when we were going together, but I thought he'd change after we got married. Besides, I didn't think I'd ever find anyone else who'd want me. We'd been married for seven years when I found out he was having an affair with my best friend. It had been going on for a long time, and I was beginning to feel crazy with suspicion. Finally Bill admitted he was in love with her. He moved out three weeks ago. I can barely function without him."

Margo covered her face with her hands and sat in silence for a long moment.

"I don't even know who I am anymore," she said finally. "I used to be my parents' daughter, then I was Bill's wife. Now who am I? My mother always told me I was selfish and that I'd never keep a man if I didn't learn to be more giving. I can hear her now." Margo's voice became a whisper. "Sometimes I wish I were dead."

Margo is one of countless women who suffer from unhealthy shame. Because she believed herself to be unlovable, she accepted the entire blame for her husband's infidelity. She felt certain that no other man would want her. Conscious only of her loneliness, fear, and depression, she felt unequipped to cope on her own, as an adult in an adult world. At the root of all these beliefs and feelings was her intense shame.

Was it wrong for Margo to look at her part in the breakup of her marriage? Of course not. But she didn't have to see its collapse as proof of her unworthiness as a human being.

Her job in healing herself would be to uncover the basic causes of her sense of shame, then replace the shame with love and empathy for herself—imperfect though she might be. Her goal would be to maintain her self-esteem in the face of life's challenges, or at least have faith she would regain it when it was momentarily unavailable.

Where Does Shame Come From?

Like Margo, many of us are afraid others will see us as bad, weak, childish, stupid, or selfish and that we will end up being scorned. Rejection, real or imagined, confirms our inherent sense of unlovability.

These intense feelings of inadequacy have their roots in our past and in our culture. Shame is above all a relationship wound, and our families provide us with our first experiences of unworthiness. From infancy on we depend on the vital connection of love and trust with those most important to us. When the tie with these idols is broken by harsh words, neglect, or abuse, we blame ourselves. When these breaks occur repeatedly, we come to believe there is something wrong with *us* rather than with our parents.

Another source of our shame as women stems from the culture in which we are raised. Most women experience what I call gender shame as a result of being born female in a male-dominated society—a society that uses shame as a way of keeping women subordinate. In subtle and not-so-subtle ways women are often treated as inferior beings.

Many of us learn that as females we are too dependent and too emotional, too flighty to be capable of serious thinking. Qualities such as intuition, emotionality, and the ability to relate to others (which society generally labels feminine) are less highly valued than qualities such as independence, assertiveness, and rationality (generally labeled masculine). Our strengths are discounted: our ability to see both sides of a situation is deemed wishy-washy, our intuition is dismissed, and our desire for connection is considered being "too dependent" or "needy."

When we try to be powerful, we risk shame and guilt for being unfeminine. Because our role has been to be passive and defer to men, we struggle with shame for being competitive and for being successful.

White males, on the other hand, have enjoyed rights and privileges that establish them as superior, and they are encouraged to expand and achieve. Although these men feel deeply ashamed for failure in sports, work, sex, or other activities, they will never know the shame that women experience in being treated as second-class citizens in a male-dominated society.

In general women, more than men, depend on close, positive relationships with others to provide them with self-esteem. This makes us especially vulnerable to shame when we don't get the affection and approval we long for.[1]

Most people in our society believe our role as females is to take care of others, especially males. We are trained as caretakers, and we come to believe our worth depends on performing this monumental task. Our identity is based on the ability to form and maintain relationships. When, like Margo, we inevitably come up short, we feel unworthy and unlovable. Bill's leaving the marriage was proof to Margo that she had failed in the job most important to her identity.

Coupled with these attitudes is society's overemphasis on feminine youth and beauty, which constantly makes us feel that we are never quite good enough. Called the weaker sex, women are considered sex objects—playthings to enhance the male ego. It's no wonder so many women suffer from excessive shame—a double shame that comes not only from being raised in a troubled family but also from being born female in a male-dominated culture.

Although both men and women struggle with shame, women's shame encompasses a wider area and comes partly from different sources. Men are ashamed when they lack power and status—in short when they are too much like women. Women lack power and status and feel ashamed because they *are* women. Yet if they try to be like men, they' are ashamed of being "unfeminine." Either way they lose.

For all the above reasons I believe that women are more vulnerable to shame than men simply because they are women. Our culture defines woman as less than man, giving her a shame-based identity by reason of her birth. I differ with psychiatrist Andrew Morrison, author of *Shame: The Underside of Narcissism,* who recognizes differences between male and female shame yet asserts, "It is a mistake . . . to overemphasize the presence of shame in women."[2]

Although we usually aren't aware of our gender shame, it nevertheless determines much of our behavior.

The Shame Experience

The experience of shame can range from a sudden stab of emotion to a chronic state of being that is based on the belief that we are deeply inadequate.

SHAME AS EMOTION

Shame has its own distinct body language. Picture a small child caught in the act of stealing change from her father's dresser. She hangs her head, avoiding her father's shaming gaze; she is tongue-tied, and she blushes before she runs to hide.

The most significant part of the body is the face, which we hide to avoid revealing our shame. Blushing only makes matters worse, unfailingly calling attention to our shame and our inability to control our emotions.

The importance of the face is revealed by such phrases as "shamefaced," "saving face," or "I couldn't show my face there again." Also, when we fear "losing face," we are concerned with our standing in the "eyes" of others. Since the opposite of shame is pride, to be proud is to be able to look another in the face.

Eye contact is difficult for women who suffer from shame, for the eye is considered the window to the soul and, if gazed deeply into, would expose our core of unworthiness. Sometimes my clients will talk for a whole hour with hardly a moment of eye contact. They are speaking to me yet looking away—anywhere but at my "all-seeing" eyes.

Another common experience of unhealthy shame is its tendency to attack us over the most trivial or unimportant incidents. Running to catch a bus, I drop my purse, and its contents spill out on the sidewalk. As the Scotch tape clatters to the ground and my lipstick rolls away, I feel intense shame for being so clumsy.

Although this incident may seem insignificant, it illustrates how easily shame can insinuate itself into the life of someone who is vulnerable to it. Professor Helen Lynd, in her groundbreaking book *On Shame and the Search for Identity*, describes the nature of this kind of shame: "An ostensibly trivial incident has precipitated intense emotion. What has occurred is harmless in itself and has no evil pragmatic outcome. It is the very triviality of the cause— an awkward gesture . . . a gift or a witticism that falls flat . . . a mispronounced word, ignorance of some unimportant detail that everyone else surprisingly knows—that helps to give shame its unbearable character."

Lynd goes on to describe another common characteristic of the moment of shame: "Because of the outwardly small occasion that has precipitated shame, the intense emotion seems inappropriate, incongruous, disproportionate to the incident that has aroused it. Hence a double shame is involved; we are ashamed because of the original episode and ashamed because we feel so deeply about something so slight that a sensible person would not pay any attention to it."[3]

In other words, we once again end up ashamed of our shame.

SHAME AS IDENTITY

Such intense emotion over seemingly unimportant experiences betrays a core sense of self that is riddled with shame. Eventually, after enough shaming childhood experiences, our feelings of natural shame turn into a belief that we are defective at the center of our being. Shame becomes chronic and maladaptive. *Shame is no longer just what we feel; it has become who we are.* Adding the component of women's gender shame leaves us with a persistent belief in ourselves as inadequate and deficient.

Although the essence of unhealthy shame lies in feeling unworthy in the eyes of others, eventually we take on the job of scrutinizing *ourselves* for faults.

Shame turns us against ourselves, like a cancer eating away at our self-worth, often going undetected while it does its damage. *I believe that most of us are not aware of our deep sense of shame,* so covered is it by other feelings, such as anger, sadness, or guilt.

Faced with so many possibilities of being confronted with our inadequacies, and wanting to appear "normal" or "acceptable," we keep our pain hidden. We hide our deepest selves from others, not only because the experience of shame is so difficult to communicate but because its very nature leaves us isolated and alienated.

Can Shame Ever Be a Good Thing?

Up to now we've been looking at the negative aspects of shame. But not all shame is bad, nor is it possible to rid ourselves entirely of the experience. According to Silvan Tompkins's research on infants, shame is one of the nine emotions humans are born with.[4] Animals instinctively respond with shame, head down, tail between the legs, as they slink away to hide. It is only when we are shamed repeatedly as children that feelings of natural shame turn into a belief about our deficiency as human beings.

Psychiatrist Donald Nathanson discusses the important role of shame in his book *Shame and Pride: Affect, Sex, and the Birth of the Self.* Shame is an automatic response that works to reduce our interest or enjoyment in any activity or interaction at the moment when something impedes it and our attention or involvement has become unrewarding or unsafe.[5] Nathanson claims that *anytime* interest or enjoyment are interfered with we experience shame. In other words, "To the extent that we humans seek pleasure we must experience shame."[6]

Shame also has a socializing function. *Children need to feel some shame and guilt in the process of being raised in order to ensure that they develop a conscience.* This prepares them to live in our society as responsible, law-abiding, and caring individuals. For instance shame keeps most of us from such antisocial behaviors as stealing from our neighbors, slapping someone when we are angry, and running down the street naked. To be "shameless" is "shameful."

To rid ourselves of shame would be, as theologian and analyst Carl Schneider says, "to cripple our humanity."[7] Shame becomes detrimental to our development as human beings as soon as it exceeds the amount necessary for development of a conscience.

Our ability to feel shame makes empathy for others possible. We treat others compassionately because we wish to spare them the feelings of shame we recognize in ourselves as painful. Shame can also make us aware of how we are hurting those we care about, including ourselves. Often it is only after we allow ourselves to feel ashamed that we make necessary changes in our lives.

Shame also plays a vital role in calling attention to social injustice, serving as an incentive for bringing about change. For example racial, ethnic, homosexual, disabled, and other minorities are frequently subjected to shame by the majority. When minorities can overcome their isolating shame, they gain the confidence to speak out. When we can accept our implication in the collective "wrongs" of the human race, we gain compassion and the ability to respond to demands for change.

I have developed the following continuum to illustrate the varieties of shame, from constructive forms on one end to pathological versions on the other:

THE SHAME CONTINUUM

Conscience, social responsibility, humility, empathy, capacity for self-change	Occasional excesses of shyness, embarrassment, self-criticism, Perfectionism	Chronic and incapacitating self-disgust, Paralyzing social fears
Healthy Shame		Pathological Shame

Barbara, thirty-eight, was destroying her family, oblivious of the havoc her drinking was wreaking on her husband and three children. She was accustomed to starting her day with a shot of vodka, then taking a thermos of vodka and tonic with her every day when she left for the high school where she taught. Her family had tried repeatedly to make her see what she was doing to herself, her kids, and her marriage. However, it was only after a loving but powerful confrontation by her entire family and her sympathetic principal that she was able to feel the intense mortification that enabled her to break through her denial. She entered a residential treatment program immediately.

It took healthy shame for Barbara to make a crucial life change, to face the destructive effects her alcoholism was having on herself and her loved ones. Recovery becomes possible for addicts like Barbara when shame helps them realize both that they are powerless over their addiction and that they are hurting people they love.

Healthy shame keeps us humble, reminding us of our human limitations, keeping us from becoming too arrogant. It allows us to admit our mistakes and forgive ourselves. It also encourages us to view the imperfections of others with compassion.

There's a world of difference between Barbara's healthy shame, which enabled her to grow and learn something new, and the unhealthy shame of Margo, which kept her from growing and from having the confidence to build a new life for herself after her husband left her.

Characteristics of Shame-Prone Women

1. **We feel unworthy and inherently defective as human beings.** Our shame is based on the assumption that we are not good enough, that we don't measure up to acceptable or normal standards. We keep our feelings secret, too ashamed even to admit them to another person. We often feel like an outsider.

2. **We feel hopeless.** Since we believe that we are flawed deep in our core, we have no hope of ever attaining a sense of adequacy or wholeness.

3. **We conduct an ongoing critical dialogue with our-**

selves. *Who do you think you are? You'll never amount to much. How stupid can you get? You'd better watch out! Grow up.* Our favorite words are "You should."

Our critical inner voice is powerful in stopping us from being ourselves, risking ourselves, and opening ourselves to others in satisfying relationships.

4. **We give up on our true selves, which we keep concealed inside us.** When we learn early on that we're not acceptable to others, we lose touch with vital parts of ourselves: our *needs, wants, and dreams.* Having discovered that it's too painful to allow ourselves to want or need, we eventually stop even knowing what we want.

The same thing happens with our *feelings,* both positive and negative. Remember how Margo, the woman I described at the beginning of this chapter, apologized and tried to wipe her tears away as soon as they appeared? Unaware of any anger at her husband, she turned her rage against herself. She found both her sadness and her anger unbearable.

As women, many of us learn to disown the ability to think for ourselves. We discover it's safer not to have our own *opinions* or to trust our independent view of things. We allow others to define us, and if, like Margo, we are abandoned, we are left not knowing who we are or how to cope. We fear or can't enjoy success.

5. **We mask our shame and present to the world a facade, fearful all the while of being "found out."** When we abandon those aspects of ourselves that seem displeasing to our parents, we become the person someone else wants us to be rather than who we are. Our true self, sacrificed on the altar of parental approval, is replaced by a false self we think is more likely to please. Of course we end up feeling like a fraud.

In presenting this false front to the world, we live in constant fear of being exposed. In fact we are never able to shake off the feeling that others already know that we are impostors.

6. **We don't like our bodies.** Although cultural pressures make most women anxious about physical imperfections, shame-ridden women are especially disgusted with their

bodies. They are either too thin or too fat, too tall or too short, too flat-chested or too busty. These complaints have little to do with reality—they often come from women who are actually healthy and attractive.

7. **We feel like victims of the circumstances of our lives.** We find it difficult to look at our part in our continuing problems because unconsciously we're afraid that they stem entirely from our own inadequacy. Yet at a conscious level we think other people are responsible for our happiness. As a result we feel powerless.

8. **We have a constant need to control.** Our assumption is that if we can control ourselves, other people, and events, we can avoid such shaming experiences as being wrong, making mistakes, being unprepared, being disappointed, or getting hurt. We often take on the job of fixing or changing people close to us, believing that will make us less vulnerable.

9. **We have troubled relationships and hold ourselves to blame.** Those of us who have been deeply shamed have great difficulty in establishing and maintaining satisfying intimate relationships. In fact since we are usually afraid of being close to another person, we put up roadblocks guaranteed to protect ourselves from further shaming and also from being hurt, abandoned, or swallowed up by an overpowering partner. Yet we are deeply disappointed when these relationships don't work out.

Imagine the predictable problems that come up when two ashamed people—who feel unlovable but act like they've got it together—attempt to have an intimate relationship.

Low Self-esteem and Shame: Two Sides of the Same Coin

Shame and low self-esteem are closely related. I suggest that self-esteem is a concept, or a *judgment* we have about ourselves, while shame is both an *emotion* and an *identity state*. If we endure enough emotionally shaming experiences, we conclude that we are flawed as a person and we end up with a *shame-based identity*. Low self-esteem, based on the painful feelings of shame, lies one step removed from our experience. The *belief* that we aren't good enough, while stemming from shame, is not the same thing as *experiencing* at our center that we are flawed.

Shame Versus Guilt

Shame and guilt are another pair of closely connected states that are often difficult to distinguish. Most writers speak of shame as related to "being," and guilt as related to "doing." While guilt is a feeling of regret about what I have done or not done that hurt someone, shame is a feeling of remorse about my worth as a person. With guilt the major worry is the threat of punishment; with shame it's the threat of abandonment.[8] We believe that people will leave us because we aren't good enough. We think, *No one would really want to stick with me, I'm too unworthy.*

When we feel guilty, we can attempt to make amends, repair the trespass. When we feel ashamed, it seems there's nothing we can do to ease the pain. Morrison suggests that while guilt motivates us to confess, shame motivates us to conceal. The cure for guilt is forgiveness. The cure for shame is "the healing response of acceptance of the self, despite its weakness, defects and failures."[9]

Shame is a more painful experience than guilt, because the self, more than one's behavior, is the target of attack. As psychologist John Bradshaw, author of the best-selling *Healing the Shame That Binds You,* says, "When I feel guilt, I feel that I have made a mistake, and when I feel shame, I feel that I am a mistake."[10]

But I think there is a connection here that Bradshaw does not discuss. I believe that most of us who are shame-based feel ashamed when we have done something we feel guilty about. It's almost impossible for us to simply "make a mistake." For us, making a mistake confirms our belief that we are a mistake. But given the intense pain of confronting our all-encompassing feelings of inadequacy, we focus on the less-painful guilt.

When we talk about our guilt, we often mean our unacknowledged shame. One clue is to ask ourselves, *Does my guilt haunt me, control me, and cause me undue suffering?* If so, it is probably deeply rooted in shame.

Both guilt and shame are related to power in that shame comes from weakness or lack of power, whereas guilt comes from exerting too much power and thereby hurting another.[11] Since to be a woman in our society is to be seen as weak and passive, we bear enormous shame for our position of powerlessness. But because society views powerful women as dangerous or unfeminine, we find ourselves caught in a double bind: *I'm ashamed if I'm weak, yet I'm ashamed if I'm powerful.*

What Are the Opposites of Shame?

To better understand shame, let's take a look at its opposites: pride and empathy.

Nathanson discusses the relationship between shame and pride, two major forces in human life: "The basic feeling of pride stems from the pleasure we achieve in a moment of competence."[12] Feelings of pride begin in early infancy when we squeal with joy at our own accomplishments. A baby's excitement and pleasure in the moment of mastery is further enhanced by its parents' delighted response.

Nathanson believes that we experience shame and pride in the process of normal growth and development; pride is the usual outcome of any accomplishment and shame the result of each failure along the way. He sees shame as the "polar opposite of pride," forming what he calls the shame/pride axis. "It is against this yardstick that we evaluate all of our actions, and along which is strung our fragile and precarious sense of self."[13]

Unfortunately, healthy pride is often shamed out of us by such admonishments as "Pride goeth before a fall." We are more familiar with false pride, or conceit, which serves to hide our sense of inadequacy from ourselves and others.

I knew a man who grew up on a farm, the son of immigrants. Although he was highly successful, he never felt comfortable in society and dealt with his many insecurities by being insufferably pompous at times. Once, to my amazement, he even referred to himself as a "personage."

Sometimes feelings of pride depend more on how others see us than on our own independent feelings of accomplishment. When we fail to earn others' praise and we can't supply it for ourselves, we become vulnerable to shame.

I would like to offer another antonym to shame: empathy. Empathy is the ability to regard others from their perspective with compassion—to enter into their world or experience while drawing on our own experience. Rather than evaluating them, we experience them for who they are.

But why not consider showing a little empathy for ourselves? That, above all, is what we are lacking when we feel shame. Empathy is what was missing from our parents when they shamed, rejected, or intruded upon us. And empathy is what we look for from a therapist. When our therapist views us—our feelings, ideas, needs, wants, actions—with empathy, we learn to treat ourselves compassionately. Only when we become capable of having empathy for ourselves can our healing begin.

Family Shame: The Unspoken Wound

For many women personal shame includes family shame. We may learn early that our family is troubled or harbors "secrets" such as incest, alcoholism, or mental illness. Some families are able to present to the community a facade of health, acting as if everything is normal. Knowing that the family is living a lie adds to their burden of shame. Other families are not able to mask their problems, and they face real or imagined condemnation from the community.

Growing up in a southern small town, Polly felt ashamed of her family. Her father, an alcoholic, was barely able to maintain a law practice. She was continually humiliated by her brother, who dealt with the family problems by being violent and destructive. "When people asked me how I was, or how my family was, I would smile and say 'Fine, thank you,' all the time thinking about last night's fight when all I wanted to do was hide in my room. I was sure I was the only kid in school whose family had problems that bad."

As Polly spoke, we were both aware of the flush creeping up her neck—signaling that her shame was still festering within her.

The conviction of being the "only one" is a dominant theme in shame-prone people, as are deep worries about not being normal.

A common pattern in family shame is the longing to be in another family that we idealize. This may be a family we actually know, or one we've read about or seen on TV. Many of my clients have expressed childhood longings for a "normal" family like the Waltons (though any therapist could see that these television families aren't normal at all, having little real interpersonal conflict or contact).

Polly felt that most of her friends had perfect families. She described her friend Susan's family: "I used to stay overnight at her house and ache to have a family like hers. As she and I would lie in the dark, getting ready to go to sleep, I would ask her to tell me over and over again about the fun things her family did together. She had a real family, not an angry, unhappy family like mine. I kept having this fantasy that they'd adopt me.

"The bizarre thing is that later on—when I was grown up—Susan told me about the problems her family had had with her mom's being manic-depressive all those years."

The Disguises of Shame

How do we recognize a person who bears the hidden wounds of shame? After all, *shame* is practically a taboo word in our society. People are too ashamed of their feelings of being flawed to admit to them. But when we look at their behavior and listen carefully to what they say, we catch shame masquerading in more socially acceptable costumes. For instance it's less humiliating to admit we are perfectionists or embarrassed than to admit we are feeling ashamed.

Shyness occurs when we feel ashamed meeting new people or situations. We're afraid that our lack of social skills will be exposed. Or worse, we feel unworthy to be known. Shy people try to hide by mentally or physically sitting on the sidelines, just observing. Often their silence is misinterpreted by others as critical or hostile. And this may reinforce their feelings of isolation.

Not surprisingly researchers have found that shy people are often lonely, have fewer close friends, and date less frequently than nonshy people. They also earn less money and have more difficulty advancing their careers.[14]

Embarrassment is shame that occurs when we are exposed before others as lacking, foolish, or wrong. When I can't remember a friend's name, I don't just feel embarrassed, I feel inadequate—but it is much easier to acknowledge my embarrassment than my shame.

Self-consciousness often strikes when we are feeling ashamed. We dissect ourselves and conclude that we are defective not only in our own eyes but in everyone else's as well. Our attention becomes painfully focused on ourselves and our feelings of exposure to the watching world. "I feel about two feet tall," one woman tells me.

Performance anxiety is an excruciating form of public shame, resulting from extreme self-consciousness. Perhaps the most debilitating form of shame, it comes from a dread of being exposed when we are exhibiting to an audience our talent or ability. We expect them to evaluate us and find us miserably lacking. Some people would rather stand in front of a firing squad than give an oral report.

Perfectionism comes from the belief that if we do things just right, we can avoid being criticized. Assuming that we need to be perfect in order to be loved, we suffer endlessly from feelings of never quite measuring up. It has been said that a perfectionist is someone who can't stand to make the same mistake once. We fail to realize the utter impossibility of the demand we put on ourselves.

One time as a young wife I was giving a cocktail party. Believing I had to have everything perfect, I had worked myself into a state of extreme anxiety before the guests arrived. You would have thought I was entertaining the queen of England. With my constant worrying about everything being just right, I couldn't even enjoy my guests. I actually believed that if they didn't like my hors d'oeuvres, they wouldn't like me. It helped some to chant under my breath, "I am not my hors d'oeuvres. I am not my hors d'oeuvres."

Arrogance or grandiosity allows shame to parade in a flamboyant costume, which we hope will convince onlookers of our innate superiority. At the same time we hope it will put to rest our own nagging doubts about our adequacy. Though arrogant people often succeed in fooling others into believing they are confident, they may actually be the most deeply wounded of all shame sufferers.

I know a woman who carries about her an air of royalty. She dresses impeccably and has a delightful personality. Men flock to her, yet she is unable to keep a relationship, because she thinks only of herself and demands constant attention. She requires a cadre of admirers at all times to reassure her that she is not the scared and lonely little girl who in her heart she believes herself to be.

Excessive modesty is also an attempt to cover up shame. The inability to accept compliments, constant apologizing, and frequent self-abasing comments all create a refuge for shame.

Envy often stems from shame around what we are lacking and frequently includes resentment. One of my friends is not only broke but overweight and deeply ashamed of her body. Her sister is slim, works out, and looks great. "I wish I could look like her, but I just can't afford to join a club," she tells me. "I know she spends tons of money on herself to get that way."

Confusion and *hurt* are two additional forms of shame. Underlying confusion is the belief that we *ought* to be able to understand something.[15] And in general what we call hurt feelings are actually feelings of shame.[16]

Recognizing all these disguises of unhealthy shame for what they are allows us to begin the hard work of rooting it out of our lives. But first we need to see how these destructive ploys poison our lives—at work, at play, and in our most intimate relationships.

CHAPTER TWO

How Shame
Poisons Our Lives

"If only I had my life to live over," says Tanya, a fifty-five-year-old voice teacher. "I feel like I made some bad decisions along the way." At eighteen Tanya turned down a scholarship at a music conservatory. "I was sure I'd be found out as an impostor if I went there. Instead I went to a state college, where I immediately felt like a misfit. Later I was turned down by my mother's sorority—which just killed me. I was so certain I'd be accepted." This rejection confirmed her deep sense of being flawed.

After she had been away a year, her hometown boyfriend, Ned, urged her to come home. He needed her.

"I lived at home until my parents discovered I was sleeping with Ned. They called me a whore and forbade me to see him, so I moved out. I got a job at Denny's and found a studio apartment. Before long I decided to marry Ned even though I didn't love him. At this point I'd made so many bad decisions, it seemed like

there was nothing left for me. Marrying him gave some meaning
to my life. At least somebody needed me."

The marriage ended in divorce six years and three children
later. Out on her own again Tanya was further shamed by ending
up on welfare when Ned failed to provide child support.

This gifted woman bitterly rues the chain of what she calls
inappropriate decisions. "If I'd had more self-confidence, I could
be a performing artist today," she says. "If I'd had more self-
esteem, I wouldn't have married a man I didn't love." Her enormous musical ability has become a source of shame in itself
because people ask her, "Why haven't you done anything with
your singing? You're so gifted."

In the face of this history of bad decisions, Tanya now finds
herself immobilized. "I don't know what I want in life," she says.

I ask if not knowing could be serving some purpose.

"Well, I *am* terrified of failing. If I don't let myself know what
I want, maybe I don't have to feel my fear."

Tanya's feelings of inadequacy prevent her from acknowledging even what she *has* accomplished: supporting and raising three
healthy children who like to be around her, building a network of
supportive friends, and making a living from her teaching.

How Shame Shapes Our Identity

Tanya speaks about her shame-based identity: "It's like I'm
flawed as a human being. Instead of knowing that sometimes I do
things that are bad and wrong, I believe I *am* bad and wrong. I
just live as an apology." She stops suddenly. "That must be why
I constantly apologize, even when it's not my fault. I don't even
deserve a rewarding life. I feel like I just don't belong. I don't dare
be myself, because people will find out that the real me isn't good
enough."

Like many of us Tanya has given up being authentic in order
to keep her connection to others.

The tragedy of pathological shame is that it causes us to lose
access to our true selves. When, like Tanya, we reject those
aspects of ourselves we've learned are unacceptable to others, we
live half lives, afraid to be fully ourselves. Unfortunately in disowning aspects of ourselves we deprive ourselves of important
inner resources that equip us to live satisfying lives.

When we can't be ourselves, we end up with self-loathing, emptiness, and a pervasive sense of not being real. We grieve over this loss of self. Unable to trust our own inner knowledge, we cast into doubt the validity of our own experience and allow others (especially men) to tell us what we should feel, want, think, and do.

When we ask ourselves *Who am I?* we don't have a ready answer. Instead we usually define ourselves by our affiliations: *I'm David's wife. I'm Sarah's mother.* We put others' needs and interests ahead of our own and find meaning in life by making them our central focus.

Are Women More Prone to Shame?

In our society women have fewer opportunities than men to build a positive self-image. First of all as females we are born into an identity that is shame-based. Our culture defines the ideal woman as passive, not too smart, and ruled by her emotions.[1] When we incorporate these traits into our self-concept, we leave ourselves few choices: We can either continue to accept these characteristics as valid and suffer a negative self-concept or we can break the mold and risk being branded aggressive, domineering, or selfish.

Most of us were raised to believe a woman's most important role in life is that of mother and homemaker. So-called "feminine" qualities of dependence, cooperation, and nurturance are not as highly valued in our society as the "masculine" qualities of independence, competitiveness, and self-assertion.

Paradoxically, although our culture expects a woman to be a caretaker, her need for connection to others leaves her vulnerable to criticism for being "too dependent," being "codependent," or "loving too much."

A woman's self-esteem rests largely on her ability to form successful relationships. And because we have learned that it's our job to be responsible for the success of our relationships, our self-esteem increases when they work well. Failure at this central task usually leaves us feeling deeply defective.

The more we look to our relationships to reassure us of our worthiness, the more vulnerable we are to shame. Success in love is central to our self-esteem. Failure in love—which we define as either rejection or an inability to find and keep a meaningful relationship—leaves us feeling flawed.[2] Of course neither sex likes to lose out in love, but to long for a relationship or to be rejected by a person we love and esteem are especially painful and humiliating experiences for women, who tend to be more dependent than men on what others think of them.

Yet when we do manage to create nurturing relationships, we receive little recognition for our achievements. Even we take our considerable relationship skills for granted. While some of us take pleasure in our ability to create relationships that work, this skill, because it is devalued by society, doesn't enhance our self-esteem the way prowess and performance can for men.

Our inferior position in society does not allow us the same privileges and power men have, and this adds to our shame at being female. We'll be discussing this more fully in Chapter Three.

Two Generations of Family Secrets
Lock Shame in Place

As Tanya's story unfolded, I was struck by the power of shame passed down through three generations. Her mother, Sophie, was twelve when she found out the woman she knew as Mother was really her aunt and that she had been born out of wedlock. Sophie's birth mother, Esther, played the role of "auntie, who lived too far away to visit more often."

Before having achieved a solid sense of her own worth, Sophie fell in love with and married the owner of a jewelry store where she worked as a clerk. His status as a successful local businessman helped ease her feelings of unworthiness and fulfilled her need to be "somebody."

The night her husband confessed he was facing bankruptcy because of his huge gambling debts, her world fell apart. So great was Sophie's shame that she was unable to show her face in her community. She insisted the family move away immediately. The children were never told the reason for the abrupt move, but they sensed something shameful had happened to the family.

True to the unwritten rule that problems aren't to be talked about—a rule most troubled families operate by—Sophie's children, Tanya and her three brothers, kept their questions to themselves. It wasn't until they overheard a conversation among relatives at their father's funeral that they began to put the pieces together.

As Tanya began to heal her shame, her relationship with her mother improved, and she felt safe enough to ask about what had caused that precipitous move.

"All those years I was never sure what was wrong, but I felt somehow *I* must have been the cause of your anger and depression . . . if only I'd been less trouble."

In taking on the responsibility for Sophie's pain, Tanya had taken on her mother's shame as well.

We have seen how the mantle of shame was passed through three generations. Esther's family, in coping with a culture that denigrated illegitimate births, denied Sophie's heritage and guarded Esther's secret. Sophie, ill equipped to handle a devastating marital crisis, never healed the wounds that were to fester into depression in her later life. Tanya, as a member of the third generation, was paying the price for her parents' and grandmother's shame—her deep insecurities kept her from a successful long-term relationship, and she and her mother had continuing conflicts. And so it goes.

Yet honesty and compassion (with or without therapy) can often help to break the cycle of family shame and create new ways of relating for succeeding generations.

How Shame Undermines Our Relationships

Shame determines how we feel about ourselves, and our feeling about ourselves affects our ability to relate to others. A belief that we are unworthy keeps us from loving in healthy ways and prevents us from achieving the nurturing, satisfying relationships we long for.

Intimacy is often beyond the grasp of shame-ridden women, since we don't trust enough to allow ourselves to be seen, certain we are fundamentally unlovable. Or we may think, *I don't dare get too close to my lover, who might see inside me and discover how empty I am.*

This is why many women who feel unworthy end up alone and depressed. Even women who are in committed relationships may find it hard to believe their partners truly care about them. Letting love in is difficult for many of us who feel unlovable.

Without a solid sense of who we are and what we want, it's

difficult to connect with others, and this lack of connection leaves shame-ridden women ill equipped to ask for what they want and to resolve conflict. Feelings of unworthiness erode our personal power. Sometimes we feel we aren't entitled to have more, and sometimes, after years of accommodating ourselves to the wants of others, we may not even know what we want.

Inevitably pathological shame traps us in unhealthy, often abusive relationships and blocks us from acting in our own best interests. We stay for many reasons: We feel we don't deserve better; we blame ourselves; we feel deeply insecure about our ability to survive on our own, both emotionally and economically; and we lack confidence in our ability to find a healthier relationship.

The task of successfully relating to another human being is one of life's greatest challenges. To establish trust and openness, to negotiate inevitable conflicts, to have clear boundaries, even to live easily with another person requires a degree of self-love that the shame-bound woman cannot muster.

The Last-Chance Train

Our shame influences our choice of a mate. If a man wants us, that proves we are desirable, that we matter to someone. Sometimes in our desperation we settle for less than we deserve.

Yolanda, a twenty-six-year-old housewife, was an attractive, gentle person, who had been miserable most of the eight years of her marriage to a man who was verbally abusive.

One day I asked what attracted her to Pete.

She shifted in her chair. "Well, I was very sure none of the guys I really liked would be interested in me, so when Pete proposed, I figured I'd better accept or I'd be single the rest of my life."

I call this the Last-Chance Train, which women leap on because of their terror of being left behind. Of course there were other factors determining Yolanda's choice of a mate, but desperation was surely one of the most powerful.

Several years later I ran into Yolanda and learned she had eventually gained enough self-esteem to leave Pete and was now remarried, to a man more able to love her.

Some women ease their feelings of worthlessness by establishing a relationship in which they devote their lives to taking care of their partners. These women are sometimes called codependents, people whose feelings of worth come from being indispensable to their partners, no matter how badly they are treated. They may be married to alcoholics, workaholics, or abusive men whom they tolerate for many complex reasons. Perhaps, like Yolanda, they feel they don't deserve better, or, like Tanya, they build up their self-esteem through knowing how much the other person really needs them.

I sometimes wonder how useful the term *codependent* really is. It implies a lack of compassion for a woman's basic social situation and slaps her down for doing what our culture has taught her: taking care of others, putting her needs last, gaining an identity through her man, and (in many cases) being economically dependent. In an effort to empower women who want to make changes in their relationships, let's not shame them with a label that further undermines their already shaky self-concept and ignores the powerful cultural influences on their behavior.

Caution: Being Female
May Be Dangerous to Your Mental Health

Although shame often does its damage unobtrusively, it is a crucial component in most psychological pathologies. I would even argue that women's special vulnerability to shame causes them to be more prone to depression, anxiety attacks, and eating disorders.

The heavy emphasis on youth and beauty in our culture and our inevitable failure to live up to these impossible ideals add to women's psychological problems. Equally damaging is the belief that we need to reject our natural selves in order to please others. It is during adolescence that girls become especially vulnerable to two shame-based disturbances: eating disorders and depression.

Eating disorders are clearly women's diseases. Although we don't know all the factors that give rise to eating disorders in women, we do know that a woman's obsession with her body and food serve to conceal feelings of being flawed and unlovable. I will discuss eating disorders more fully in Chapter Ten.

Shame and Depression

Worries about appearance also play a crucial role in the onset of depression in adolescent girls. Recent studies show that around age twelve, girls have higher rates of depression than boys.[3] Why would this be? One study found that not feeling attractive, low self-esteem, and a diminished sense of effectiveness played a more significant role in adolescent girls' depression than in boys'.[4]

Helen B. Lewis believes that shame is at the root of most depression, a condition she describes as characterized by feelings of worthlessness.[5] Most experts agree that the rate of depression in women is almost twice that in men.

Margo, the woman at the beginning of Chapter One whose husband had left her for her best friend, was clearly in a shame-fed depression when she came to me, although her shame went unacknowledged.

"It was basically my fault that Bill left the marriage. I feel like a failure. I'm also depressed because I don't think I can cope by myself. I guess I have a problem with my self-esteem. I suppose I should be angry at Bill, but I'm not. I'm angry at myself for not being a better wife."

Although shame is not at the core of all depression, I believe it plays a greater part than most of us realize. Although experts have traditionally (since Freud) considered anger turned inward as the cause of depression, many are now emphasizing the role of self-esteem and shame in this often debilitating state.[6]

In my experience anger turned inward and low self-esteem are closely connected in women's depression, and both have a strong relationship to shame.

Let's briefly take a closer look at the role of internalized anger. I believe that the anger behind depression has its origins in anger toward someone who hurts us, dominates us, or abandons us. Because anger is unacceptable for women in our society, and because it threatens loss of love or even retaliation, we are frightened and ashamed of our anger. Consequently like Margo we turn it against ourselves, blame ourselves for being unlovable, for asking for too much, for failing in the relationship, for being helpless. And like Margo we become depressed.

I agree with those who conclude that depression frequently is the end result of a chain of shame-related emotions beginning with feelings of failure, weakness, helplessness, inferiority, and/or loss of love, leading to low self-esteem and ensuing shame.

What about women specifically? I think women become depressed when they feel powerless, both in their relationships and in the world. *I see many depressed women who are in relationships where they have limited power* and/or who are ashamed of their inability to be in charge of their lives.

"It's depressing that I can't define for myself what I want and need. Besides, I don't feel any control over my life," Margo says.

We can also agree that loss of love (be it emotional or physical abandonment) can be a shaming and depressing situation at any age. We miss feeling special, appreciated, loved, and supported; we also blame ourselves for being unlovable.

But when a woman's relationships are failing, I believe she confronts additional feelings of shameful inadequacy that arise from her *failure* or inability as a woman to carry out the task assigned to her by society that establishes her strongest sense of self: the task of creating a good relationship. Because interpersonal relationships are usually more important to women than to men, women tend to blame themselves when their relationships aren't working, and this makes them more susceptible to depression and underlying shame.

Most male theorists stop short of flushing out what I consider to be the central cause of female depression: *loss of connection or relationship both to important others and to self.* Traditionally loss of love is viewed as losing only something we are used to receiving, such as support and affection. What I am speaking of goes beyond that to include loss of connection—a sense of relatedness that allows us to be in mutually supportive, empathic contact with another person, in which we are not only nurtured but we also nurture in return and *both partners grow in the process.*[7] When this is consistently missing in our lives, we can suffer a chronic, shame-based depression. Simply having a relationship doesn't solve the problem. There are probably at least as many depressed women whose relationships are unnurturing and not mutually enhancing as depressed women who lack a relationship entirely.

Finally, missing from most discussions of shame and depression is what I consider the most crucial component: our relationship to ourselves. When we chronically deny our feelings (especially unallowed anger and deep psychic pain), when we put our needs and

wants last by accommodating the needs of others—in short when
we fail to take care of ourselves—we become vulnerable to a
shame-related depression stemming from loss of self.

When Margo was able to begin to connect with herself, feel her
anger, assert her wants and needs in the divorce settlement, and
take charge of her life, her depression lifted.

Anxiety: A Shame Reaction?

Anxiety attacks, another shame-related disorder, afflict many
more women than men. In spite of having a predominant fear
component, anxiety attacks are also a response to internalized
shame. And they in turn create a shame of their own.

Ginny, a thirty-four-year-old licensed vocational nurse, was
referred to me by her doctor because of crippling anxiety attacks.
"I go to work most days," she says, "but I often can't stay the
entire day. I'm afraid to go to the mall, can't bear to stand in long
lines. I have to sit near the exits at movies or restaurants. In fact
I'm staying home more and more. I spend a lot of time in bed with
the covers over my head waiting for the panicky feelings to go
away."

"For a long time I was too scared and too ashamed to get help.
I thought there was something terribly wrong with me—that
maybe I was even crazy," Ginny later told me.

Ginny had been the oldest of five, with a chronically ill mother.
Her role growing up had been to take care of everyone's needs,
and she was still at it. But now it was making her ill. "I can't seem
to say no to all the demands on my time and energy. I'll drop
whatever I'm doing to respond to the slightest request from a
relative or friend. The few times I've said no, I've had incredible
guilt and shame."

When Ginny first came to me for therapy, it was clear that she
had lost touch years ago with wanting anything for herself after
her mother had repeatedly shamed her for being selfish.

As we worked together, it became evident that feelings of deep
inadequacy were at the root of her anxiety. She had never dealt
with the early-childhood traumas that created her shame. She
also felt profound conflict between taking care of others and
taking care of herself. After a lifetime of putting her own needs
last, she was angry, but her anger stayed out of her awareness

because she was too terrified and ashamed to express it. Instead she had anxiety attacks.

Learning to value herself without shame and guilt eventually allowed her to balance concern for others' needs and wishes with a healthy concern for her own.

How Shame Undermines and Disempowers Us

Diane, forty-five, a bright and energetic woman, believed she wasn't very smart because she had flunked out of college. For years she held back from applying for jobs at her level of ability. Finally, when she was able to overcome her feelings of unworthiness, she applied for and landed a challenging job that she finds enormously gratifying.

Not only does shame thwart us in our attempts to achieve, it can rob us of the joys of success. I know a woman who as a senior in college entered a poem in a statewide contest. When she won third place, she couldn't enjoy the good feelings because she was haunted by the thought, *There must be something wrong with me that I didn't get first place.*

Shame even undermines our physical health, since it creates more stress than we can handle, increasing the likelihood of back problems, headaches, high blood pressure, certain allergies, and heart and kidney problems. Dr. Hans Selye, in his famous book *The Stress of Life,* says that "many common diseases are largely due to errors in our adaptive response to stress, rather than to direct damage by germs, poisons, or life experience."[8] Considering that we hold in our bodies unexpressed feelings such as resentment and anger, worry and fear, self-hate and shame, it's not surprising that the stress caused by containing these emotions can cause the body to break down.

Avoiding Shame Can Be Costly

When we look at the high costs of excessive shame, we need to include the price we pay when we try to protect ourselves from experiencing this debilitating state. Our defenses against shame control and constrict us. Perhaps, like Sophie, we withdraw from others to avoid painful feelings of humiliation. Or perhaps we avoid getting involved in a relationship because we fear being rejected. Or we lash out at others to ease our feelings of self-contempt.

Or—even though we're overburdened at home and at work—we avoid asking for help, not because we're too proud but because we're too ashamed to let others know we can't do it all.[9]

We abuse our bodies with drugs and alcohol in an attempt to ease our emotional pain. Compulsive eaters "stuff" their feelings by stuffing their stomachs instead.

Pathological shame delivers a double whammy. First it creates myriad problems. Then it prevents us from getting help with the very problems it caused in the first place. Healthy shame, in contrast, pushes us toward seeking help by alerting us to the need to make positive changes in our behavior.

Because we have little confidence in our ability to find creative solutions, many of us continue to lead what Thoreau called "lives of quiet desperation." When we don't seek help for our addictions and eating disorders, when we don't report sexual or physical abuse, when we don't deal with our debilitating depression and anxiety, we are held back in part by shame. *We are convinced that our problems prove there is something wrong with us: "If I weren't so sick, bad or weak I'd be able to handle all this like other people do."*

To ask for help and support is to risk exposure as an "inherently defective" person. In the face of these powerful considerations I never cease to be awed by the courage of people who do reach out for help.

Often we are defeated by a belief that we don't deserve a better life anyway: *Should I object to his mistreating me? I probably deserve it somehow.* Or, *Why should I get into therapy? I deserve the life I've got.*

In this chapter we have explored some of the ways shame poisons women's lives. We've seen how it attacks our ability to be intimate, how it limits our capacity to form and maintain healthy, satisfying relationships, how it makes us feel deeply unlovable.

We've looked at the way we pass shame on to our children, either directly or indirectly, forging yet another link in the chain we inherited from previous generations. We've noted the power of shame to lock us into maladaptive behavior, putting our emotional and physical health at risk; how it also deprives us of full self-expression, inhibits our creativity, and robs us of pleasure in our successes; how it affects the choices we make, from minor daily decisions to major life-changing ones; how it limits us, even cripples us.

Now we turn to an in-depth look at how being born female in our society contributes to pernicious shame by keeping women in a disadvantaged position.

CHAPTER THREE

A Woman's Place

*To be born female in this culture means that you are
"tainted," that there is something intrinsically wrong
with you that can never change, that your birthright is
one of innate inferiority.*
— ANNE WILSON SCHAEF

Although both men and women suffer from deeply rooted
feelings of shame, their experience differs in major ways.
Females are born into a culture that places a higher value on
being male. The belief that women are inherently not as good as
men is deeply embedded in the fabric of our culture. The characteristics associated with males (independence, rationality, leadership) are more highly regarded by our culture than the
characteristics associated with females (concern for relatedness,
intuitiveness, cooperativeness). Therefore females, simply by
being born female, struggle with a kind of shame males never face.

Are we aware that we are feeling gender shame? Probably not.
Yet it exists beneath the surface and influences our choices and
actions. Pervasive and insidious, it informs us that we are not
entitled to be treated fairly, to have what we want and need, or
to stand up for ourselves.

Myths That Keep Women Trapped in Shame

Let's look more closely at how the male-dominated social scheme defines women as inferior or defective. If you were to define someone in a way that would keep her from becoming better or more powerful than you, what characteristics would you assign her? You'd probably tell her that she wasn't very smart; that she was endearingly incompetent (not really capable of handling the affairs of the "real world"); that she was dependent, weak, emotional, and childlike. And many women would believe you.

That people do tend to view women in this manner is borne out by the classic Broverman study, in which women were defined by practicing psychotherapists (both male and female) as inherently weak, dependent, and childlike. For instance when therapists were asked to describe the characteristics of healthy men and women, they considered healthy women to be "more submissive, less independent, more suggestible, less competitive, more excitable in minor crises, more emotional, and more concerned about their appearance" than either healthy men or healthy adults. Significantly the characteristics deemed necessary for healthy adults were those associated with masculinity.[1]

And so our society's view of women seems to be predicated on the following myths:

• **Women are naturally passive and submissive.** In many families the man is considered the head of the household, and his word is final. If he says no, he expects his wife and children to comply. Some women still say, "My husband won't let me (go back to school, get a job, stay in therapy)."

• **Women aren't capable of making important decisions.** In the U.S. Senate, women, who comprise over half our population, are only 6 percent. And why else is it that the man always signs on the *first* line of important documents?

• **Women are too emotional and thus too often ruled by their feelings.** "Don't be a sissy" or "Girl!" are insults boys hurl at each other. Or we hear, "Who'd want a woman for president? She's too emotional, unpredictable. Especially on 'those' days."

• **Women don't think logically (except for those few who "think like a man").** Until recently women were routinely refused admission to law school. Such attitudes are reflected at our jobs: "I often come up with good ideas, but my boss can't give me the credit," says Marcia. "Instead he tells me I must have gotten them from my previous boss."

Defining woman in these terms allows man to deny his own flaws as he assigns her the characteristics he's uncomfortable with, a process called scapegoating.

These characterizations of women are degrading, not only in the eyes of our definers but in our own eyes as well. That we even *allow* ourselves to be defined by others adds further to the shame we endure as women. We're so accustomed to being defined as "the weaker sex," we may not even realize how demeaning this description is.

Some men speak to or about us in ways that let us know we possess these demeaning traits:

- "You can never trust a woman."
- "She's a castrating bitch." (Or milder: "a pushy broad.")
- "Don't worry your pretty little head about it."
- "Here. Give it to me. I'll fix it."
- "You don't understand how things *really* are."
- "A woman's place is in the home."

These messages tell us we're are not as good as men, that there's something inherently *wrong* with us, that we lack the qualities necessary to function independently in a man's world. Small wonder that we have grown to believe in this assessment, that we've let these beliefs shape who we become, that we've taken on an identity that is riddled with shame.

How Society Locks Shame
in Place by Disempowering Women

What are the roots of these myths? Of course they don't arise out of nowhere—they have been part of our culture for centuries. Perhaps they stem from male puberty rites in which the young man had to devalue the realm of the mother in order to enter the world of the father.[2] Certainly the Judeo-Christian tradition has regarded women as unclean and inferior to men.

Women have been treated as property, to be sold, beaten, or used in any way their owner desired. The wedding that ends with "I now pronounce you man and wife" is a remnant of the notion of wife as property, to be given away by her father, often in exchange for a handsome dowry.

Thus through the ages society has been set up as a hierarchy: with God (a male) at the top, men next, then women and children. Once women have been persuaded of their innate inferiority through these powerful myths, the male hierarchy provides a second means of keeping women where they "belong." It takes away their power by preventing them from exercising certain rights.

Until recently women in America were denied the right to be self-determining: to vote, to own property, to enter many professions. Power over their lives was wielded by their fathers, then their husbands, then their sons.

Only after years of struggle did women finally win political rights and, more recently, additional economic rights. We can now vote, own property, be corporation presidents, enter prestigious law schools, hold electoral office, even be Episcopalian priests (though not Catholic priests).

In spite of these recent gains women still suffer from unequal treatment and sexist attitudes in a culture where most of the power lies in the hands of white men.

Denise is a tall, blond, recently divorced business executive. "Frank and I are partners with several other people on an apartment building," she told me. "I couldn't believe what happened when the word got out. Frank got a call from the senior partner: 'Should I take Denise's name off now that you two are divorced?' I felt so insulted. Besides, it's illegal. This is a common-property state.

"And then," she went on, "last week I gave a talk to a private group of men who meet regularly for breakfast. Before I spoke, I sat there for half an hour, the only woman among thirty men, listening to them tell dumb-blonde jokes."

Denise and I explored possible ways to handle the first situation. At first she wanted to call and complain, but didn't really want to be, as she put it, a "whiner." Instead she informed the bank loan officer than she was still a full partner. She was also able to refer an out-of-state lender to the other partners, who had been unsuccessfully searching for an additional loan. She felt empowered by the way she handled the situation.

What do we mean by power? It's easy to misunderstand this crucial concept. *Power,* in the sense I'm using it, does not mean power over someone or use of force. It means personal power: the ability to choose and the ability to act in your own best interests, to be in charge of your life. Throughout most of history women have been denied their power and in the process have taken on the shame of the disempowered.

Yet possibly there was a time when women and men shared equal power. Anthropologists have discovered evidence that suggests that in ancient times there were Goddess-worshiping societies, in which men and women were partners rather than one group dominating the other.[3]

Penis Envy or Power Envy?

In this century Freud had enormous influence in keeping women consigned to a second-class position because he believed that women were inherently inferior biologically. From his observations as a male in Victorian male-dominated society he concluded that woman's neurotic suffering was caused in large part by her feelings of inferiority stemming from her lack of a penis. Few women I know have ever expressed the desire for a penis or the feeling of being lacking without one (except when needing to pee in inconvenient locations). Most women, however, *do* want the power and privileges the penis symbolizes.

Remember Margo, the woman we met at the beginning of the first chapter, who was so devastated after her husband left her? Margo is the kind of disempowered woman I see all too frequently in my office—a woman who, suddenly alone through death or divorce, faces the need to make her way in the "real world" with no confidence in her own ability to manage. Her grief at the destruction of her marriage is understandable, but her panic at having to cope by herself is tragic.

Although she was a competent woman, she had never had a chance to learn she could make her own way in the world. She was missing one obvious proof: a paycheck. When she finally mustered the courage to find a job, payday was a thrill.

"My very own money that I had earned my very own self," she told me. "It may be a pittance, but it's a powerful pittance!"

There are other ways we are disempowered in our daily lives. Recently I did all the required paperwork for a loan (and it was extensive), set up and went to meetings with the loan officer, and brought my husband along to sign. Later, when a letter regarding the loan arrived from the bank, it was addressed to my husband alone. I felt insulted at being so completely erased. This kind of thing occurs all the time, yet we hardly notice it, so automatically do we regard the male as the authority in affairs of the "real world." Most women still see themselves as appendages to their husbands, as evidenced by our giving up our names and taking on theirs.

Even among more privileged women, gender still remains an impediment. Amelia, sixty-two, a widow and a prominent doctor, until very recently was prohibited from continuing her associate membership in a private club after her husband died. Although she was given certain club privileges, she was not allowed the right to vote and was never allowed into the male-only bar and grill. Because she was female, she wasn't even allowed to enter the club through the front door.

Female Olympic athletes encounter inequities. For instance in Barcelona, at the Olympic Village, male athletes had rooms overlooking the ocean, while most of the women had rooms facing the street or other apartments. There were more than twice as many male athletes, the ten-member International Olympic Committee executive board has only two women, and men compete in more events, even in such sports as track and swimming, where women aren't allowed to compete in certain distance events.[4] Not until the 1984 Olympics were women finally allowed to run the marathon.

A Woman's Place Is in the Home:
Woman as Server

The male-dominated social structure has found other ways of keeping women "in their place," by determining what roles and functions are acceptable for them to perform. According to psychiatrist Jean Baker Miller, those with power reserve the most attractive functions for themselves, while those without power are relegated the least appealing tasks.

These roles "typically involve providing services that no dominant group wants to do for itself," says Miller. She points out that "these tasks usually involve providing bodily needs and comforts. Subordinates are expected to make pleasant, orderly, or clean those parts of the body or things to do with the body that are perceived as unpleasant, uncontrollable, or dirty."[5]

Miller maintains that one way for the group in power to keep the most valued tasks for themselves is to convince the others that they are incapable of carrying them out, that they are innately inferior. I suggest that shaming another—defining someone as defective or lacking valued capabilities—is a tactic to keep power in the hands of the powerful.

Of Sugar and Spice and Puppy Dogs' Tails: How Families Shape Crucial Differences Between Girls and Boys

Families teach us many essential things that equip us to live as decent human beings. Not all that we learn, however, is healthy and sound. In reflecting the values of our sexist culture, our families teach in a number of ways that females are less important than males. We see our mothers catering to our fathers. We learn the rules that families pass from generation to generation about how girls are supposed to be. We learn that both fathers *and* mothers more often prefer having a boy.

Alex, a fifty-two-year-old criminal lawyer, grew up always knowing that her father wished she'd been a boy, and this knowledge was to her a never-ending source of guilt and shame. "I've dedicated my life to being the son my father never had. I feel like I've been fighting a losing battle for his love," she says. "Why isn't being a daughter good enough?" Her boyish appearance betrays her mixed feelings about being female. Even her successful law career hasn't been enough to gain her father's approval.

As females we are taught from birth to be sweet, simple, and submissive, although there is no evidence that these so-called feminine traits are biologically inherent. But they do equip us for our job, which is to take care of others, to defer to or accommodate others.

Little boys, on the other hand, are expected to be strong, self-reliant, and smart, qualities highly valued in our male-oriented culture. While our role is to quietly take care of others, men's role is to make their way in the world, to achieve and perform.

Women aren't the only ones who pay a price for these constricting learned sex roles. Men also suffer from pressures to measure up to sex-role stereotypes. Their shame stems from not performing well in school, on the playing field, or in bed. While women feel shame for being inferior, men are ashamed of not always being superior.[6] Prowess and performance are what count.

Because boys are taught to be strong and independent, they may have difficulty learning how to express the vulnerable side of their personalities. They also learn to cover up their dependency, although most women can testify to their mates' unacknowledged dependency on them.

Many men are too ashamed to admit being needy or sad. Yet they, too, have emotional wounds, which they may barely conceal from those who know them best.

How Parents Teach Us Our Place

Parents teach children values and conduct appropriate to their gender by a variety of techniques. One effective way of ensuring that we behave suitably is for parents to praise or punish particular kinds of behaviors. This need not be blatant; one smile or frown can communicate volumes about what is or is not acceptable.

Parents scold boys for being crybabies or sissies if they express sadness or fear. They chastise girls for being selfish or bossy if they assert themselves too much or engage in behavior that's too competitive.

Girls learn early on to take care of others: We are given dolls that provide hands-on practice in the art of nurturing. Boys learn to be strong and aggressive: They are given war toys that offer hands-on practice in the art of violence.

The family is structured so that these roles are securely in place

long before we are grown. We learn well our role as women, but
we pay a price in terms of the resentment, depression, and low
self-respect resulting from giving up our needs in order to take
care of the men in our lives.

If we choose to have a career, we consider it second to our job
of being the emotional and physical caretaker of our family. We
usually end up with the burden and responsibility of two jobs.
Although women are angry about the lack of help from their
mates, they also have deep doubts about whether they have a
right to protest. Their consequent ineffectualness in bringing
about real change in these areas only adds to their despair.

It's not just our mother's direct teachings that exert a powerful
influence on us. We also learn appropriate female behavior by
indirect means: observing our mother.

"I learned what it means to be female, all right. I saw my
mother cater to my father," Greta says. "Even though she had a
full-time job, she did all the housework and took care of us. He'd
call her from his living-room chair to bring his coffee, and she'd
drop what she was doing and fetch it. I saw her defer to him on
the big decisions such as buying a car or where to go on vacation."

Our Part of the Bargain

Why today do we still go along with an imbalance of power?
Some scholars suggest that we originally surrendered our power
because males are physically stronger. It's possible we were forced
into submission through threatened or real violence, including
rape. But today there are other, more relevant explanations for
our consenting to such an imbalance, reasons that keep us stuck
in a one-down position.

Although women have successfully managed to tip the scales
somewhat closer to a balance, everyone knows change is slow to
come. Besides the resistance from those who are invested in keeping their power, there is resistance (for many complicated reasons)
on the part of those who lack it. For one thing, in exchange for
accepting our role as the weaker sex we are taken care of and
protected. We feel more secure relying on our husband to be the
primary breadwinner and to take care of us emotionally because
we believe he is stronger and more knowledgeable. Furthermore
we get to enjoy and applaud his successes and achievements, while

remaining immune from the risks involved.

Although men rule the world, women rule at home, overseeing and controlling the daily affairs of the household and managing the family relationships. As one homemaker put it, "I make more decisions in one day than any corporate executive, but I never get any credit for it." We are far more competent than we allow ourselves to realize.

Herein lies a paradox: Most women are seen as weak and incompetent outside the home, while in the home they are responsible for taking care of the man who, on returning from "his" world, drops his competence at the doorstep and turns into a creature completely lacking in domestic skills. Here he is treated as though he couldn't possibly manage to sew on a button, cook a meal, change a diaper, or even find his own glasses. A man's home is his castle. A woman's place is in the home.

We've Got to Be Carefully Taught in School

The family is not the only place we learn that we don't measure up. Before little girls even reach school, they have already learned they are not as important as little boys. How can a little girl feel she is as entitled to an interesting life when her bedtime stories and TV programs are mostly about the exciting things boys do?

The pattern continues when she goes to school. Males outnumber females as main characters in stories, biographies, and folk, fantasy, and animal tales. Games such as "The Farmer in the Dell" teach the proper hierarchy as the farmer takes a wife, the wife takes a child.

Most subjects a girl studies are resplendent with the accomplishments of males. Males make history, are inventors, become president. A boy is continually validated as he learns about explorers or watches an astronaut walk in space. Much is made of our forefathers coming to this country, but the only female patriot mentioned is Betsy Ross, noted for her sewing skills![7]

Our high school English classes reflect these biases. A 1989 nationwide study found that out of ten high school English books assigned most frequently, only one was written by a woman.[8] Even supposedly neutral math books can reinforce negative stereotypes of girls. Problems were often worded in a way that demeaned girls (" 'Susan could not figure out how to . . .' ") and bolstered boys (" 'Jim showed her how . . .' ").[9]

It's easy to see how a girl's formal schooling reinforces negative beliefs about herself. When she was in the second grade, Wilma, who as an adult became a pioneer in the field of genetics, came up with five different ways a math problem could be solved, yet was put down by her teacher, who told her there was only one correct way to arrive at the answer. Susan was discouraged from applying to medical school by her guidance counselor and was encouraged to become a nurse. "You'll end up staying home anyway when you have kids," he told her.

Girls seldom see women running their schools. A recent study of discrimination against girls in education, funded by the American Association of University Women, found that although 72 percent of elementary and secondary school teachers are women, less than 30 percent are principals and less than 5 percent are superintendents. The message is that men are clearly in charge.[10]

Girls still receive less attention from teachers, are often steered into lower-paying professions, and graduate with an education inferior to that of boys. Teachers call on boys 80 percent more often than they call on girls (and not just because boys raise their hands more often), and teachers reward boys who call out answers but chastise girls *for the same behavior* by reminding them to raise their hands before speaking.[11]

It's no wonder that although self-esteem drops during adolescence for everyone, research shows girls suffer most.[12]

College continues the process that erodes a girl's view of herself as a competent person. A study of high school valedictorians found that by the time these outstanding women graduated from college, their intellectual self-esteem had drastically plummeted. Though 25 percent of the men saw themselves as "far above average," not one woman was able to make that claim for herself—this in spite of excellent achievement.

Consider Nan, an extremely bright and confident woman, who was accepted as a graduate student in the field of space research. "When I asked questions in class, I was ridiculed by my professors. When male students asked the same questions, they were taken seriously. I began to feel stupid and lost confidence in my ability to succeed. I was sure something was wrong with me. Eventually I dropped out of school and left the field, a decision that has haunted me ever since."

It's a tragedy that the very institution we depend on to build not only competence but confidence in our young people ends up failing to deliver on the second half of its promise, especially to its female students.

Shame and Organized Religion

We have seen how feelings of unworthiness begin in the family and are reinforced in school. We turn now to our third major cultural institution, organized religion. Our religious institutions use shame as a means of controlling their adherents. God can read our thoughts, we are told; there is no escape from his judgmental eye. Some religions tell us we are born sinful and must constantly work to overcome this condition.

For centuries religious dogma has greatly contributed to keeping women in their place. By scapegoating women, men avoided facing their own shortcomings. While these religious notions about women are not necessarily commonly held today, their influence still permeates our society, leaving women trapped in their shaming mystique.

• **Women are the source of evil.** The Greeks conveniently blamed Pandora for all their troubles. The Bible says it was Eve, the temptress, who brought shame and sin to humankind by persuading Adam to eat the forbidden fruit. Her punishment was suffering pain in childbirth and having to submit to Adam as master.

Tragically the notion that women embody evil led to the murder of hundreds of thousands of women during the witch burnings of the Middle Ages. America had its own witch-hunts in such places as Salem, Massachusetts, during the Puritan era. According to theologian Rosemary Radford Ruether, witch-hunts were used to terrorize women who refused to accept a subordinate role. A handbook for inquisitors hunting witches in 1486 warns that woman is insatiable in her carnal lust. Because she is defective (being born from a bent rib), "she is an imperfect animal, she always deceives. . . . Since women are feebler in body and mind, it is not surprising that they should come under the spell of witchcraft."[13]

In Massachusetts those most often persecuted by the Puritans were personally and economically independent older women, healers, and midwives, whose wifely and child-rearing tasks were behind them—women who weren't docile to clergy and other men.[14]

• **Women are unclean.** According to Judaic tradition a menstruating woman is "unclean" and must take baths of purification. Anyone who touches her or sits on her seat or lies in her bed becomes unclean. After giving birth to a boy she is unclean for seven days and not allowed to enter the sanctuary for another thirty-three days. If she faces the shame of having a girl, then she is unclean for fourteen days and banned for another sixty-six.[15] No wonder some Jewish men still continue the tradition of thanking God that they weren't born a woman!

• **Males are identified with a higher nature (spirituality, intellectuality, culture), while females are associated with a lower realm (body, sex, sin).** The Bible tells us, "[M]an is the image of God and reflects God's glory; but woman is the reflection of man's glory. For man did not come from woman; no, woman came from man; and man was not created for the sake of woman, but woman was created for the sake of man."[16]

Such theology lends support to the notion that the proper sphere for men encompasses matters of culture, hunting, and warfare; for women, bearing and rearing children and carrying out the less valued domestic tasks.

These notions are echoed through centuries of teachings by leading theologians. Saint Thomas Aquinas saw woman as defective because of her lesser capabilities for reason and moral control. Martin Luther said that the wife should obey the husband's rule— it was God's command. While the husband "rules the home and the state . . . the wife should stay at home and look after the affairs of the household. . . . *In this way Eve is punished*" (emphasis added).[17]

• **Male authority and privilege are divine rights.** The Bible tells us, "Christ is the head of every man, man is the head of woman."[18] God is male. Jesus is male. Until recently all power rested in the hands of male clerics.

Today women ministers often find themselves in lower positions, as associates or as youth ministers. If they have full authority, they still have trouble being accepted. A woman I know says, "I encountered so much resistance to there being a female pastor—by both the men and women in my congregation—that, after several years and after much agonizing, I decided I could no longer continue in that capacity."

   • **Males have the right to control women's bodies.** If woman is to be under the rule of man and such submission is sanctioned by organized religion, her body is truly not her own. For centuries she submitted to her husband's sexual advances, she was denied the right to birth control and abortion, and she had no legal recourse when beaten or raped by her husband.

How Advertising and Other Media Exploit Women

Now that we have seen how women's disempowerment has its roots in our families, schools, and religious institutions, let's look at how it is reinforced by society in general. An advertisement tells us, "You might as well give her a gorgeous pen to keep her checkbook unbalanced with. A sleek and shining pen will make her feel prettier. Which is more important to any girl than solving mathematical mysteries."[19]

   It's hard to imagine how any woman could escape feeling degraded at being depicted as so featherbrained as to be unable to balance her own checkbook. Even if we are not aware of these feelings, we can see their effects in the way we view ourselves. I know a woman whose husband gave her the following bumper sticker: HOW CAN I BE OVERDRAWN? I STILL HAVE SOME CHECKS LEFT. This bright and competent woman was proclaiming to the world her stereotypical female ineptness. Would a man even consider putting such a message on his car?

   An essential part of the women's movement has been to raise our consciousness so that we are no longer numb to the wounds inflicted by the insulting attitudes reflected in advertisements. When we begin actually to experience our long-standing pain and debasement, we are motivated to demand change.

   Although women are no longer portrayed in commercials simply as homemakers whose day is made by getting a ketchup stain out of Johnny's shirt, advertisements and other media still reflect and reinforce traditional sex-role stereotyping. Ever notice that it is the voice of male authority that tells us which detergent is best for us or how to have a spotless kitchen floor? Male voice-overs dominate commercials nine to one, even though research com-

missioned by the Screen Actors Guild has proved that women's
voices are just as effective in selling most products. Although the
results of the research were distributed to media and advertisers
in the late eighties, the ratio of male to female voices in commercials is essentially unchanged.

Commercials prey on our guilt for not being the perfect housewife while at the same time they manipulate us into buying all
kinds of products so that we can live up to the male fantasy of the
sex kitten men want us to be. Being a sex kitten while scrubbing
toilets isn't all that easy. Commercials play on our insecurities and
exploit our shame and fears of not being attractive enough to
catch or keep a man, or they capitalize on our anxiety about
growing old and undesirable.

Underlying it all is the assumption that women are somehow
defective. We are supposed to feel ashamed if we have bad breath,
body odor, or wrinkles. We learn to hate our natural bodies,
believing that to be truly acceptable, we must be blemish-free and
skinny. We are encouraged to worship at the altar of beauty,
youth, and sexiness. At the same time our sexuality is exploited to
sell everything from cars to cottage cheese.

Nor are male insecurities immune from exploitation by Madison Avenue. A "real" man smokes Marlboros, has a stunning
blonde on his well-muscled arm, and drives a dashing sports car.

Recent research on the TV gender gap shows that not only are
prominent characters male, outnumbering women three to one,
but programs clearly reinforce male superiority, portraying men
as knowledgeable, interesting, and authoritative while character-
izing women as subservient and relatively unimportant.

Movies further reflect male superiority myths, because they
continue to characterize women as silly, unstable, or dangerous.
A look at current movie billing confirms that we are not exciting
or interesting enough to be the lead as often as men are. Seven out
of ten movies are about men and their exploits.

Worse yet, leading roles often depict successful women as a
"pernicious new breed of bitch goddess," says journalist Anne
Taylor Fleming.[20] Take the movie *Working Girl*, which portrays
women as conniving and unethical (Melanie Griffith) or cold and
bitchy (Sigourney Weaver). Or *Fatal Attraction* and *Presumed Innocent*, in which women murder their sexual rivals. Fleming thinks

these kinds of movies reflect male fears: "That's what you'll get if you give women power."

I was uncomfortable with *Thelma and Louise*, a film that depicts women who become dangerous outlaws when they discover their own power. Written by a woman, the script's glorification of violence may confirm these male fears. Like any oppressed group, women's rage at being kept down is such that when they do attain power, some may become violent.

It helps to understand men's fear of the "bitch goddess" if we realize that one of their few experiences of a woman being power-ful was when they were children and Mother's power seemed awesome.[21] They feel threatened by the possibility that authority in the hands of women may cost them their hard-won positions of power and control. Worse yet, and more importantly, they fear women will abuse their power. Another echo of the old view that women are inherently evil?

Shame in the Workplace

These same male fears about women's ability to handle power pervade the work world. They prevent women from being awarded top positions in the corporate hierarchy. Most men don't want a woman boss. Although women comprise 40 percent of middle management, they hold less than half of one percent of the top highest-paid corporate positions.[22] A "glass ceiling" prevents qualified women from reaching the top levels of management. Just as it pervades most corporations, this hidden barrier also keeps women reporters from anchor positions in the major net-works. Only four of the top fifty TV news reporters are women.[23]

In spite of gains in women's rights, women still earn lower wages than men, even in the same jobs. A woman now earns only seventy-one cents to every dollar a man earns.[24] A female *college graduate* earns the same as a male *high school* graduate.[25] Women often land in positions subordinate to men when they become teachers, nurses, and secretaries—service jobs that call for taking care of others. Their low pay and status attest to the lesser value society assigns to these "feminine" skills.

Meryl Streep rails at the rampant sexism in the movie industry, citing a union report that shows men make twice as much as women. Being rich and famous is no guarantee of immunity from such unfair treatment: Bruce Willis earns $10 million for a leading role while Streep earns $4 million.[26]

. According to Jean Baker Miller, "the vast majority of working women, 80 percent, hold the lowest-paid and most dead-end jobs in this country." Black women are at the bottom of the totem pole because of the double burden of their race *and* their gender.[27]

A double standard applies to behavior of women in the corporate and professional world. "I have trouble being listened to and taken seriously during meetings," Dena, a corporate partner, tells me. "It's okay for men to express their anger (it even seems powerful), but if I get legitimately angry, I'm considered bitchy or castrating. One time the CEO put 'No Hormone Storms' as an item on the agenda the day after I'd gotten angry at him."

An obstetrician is insulted when she decides that a prospective mother needs a cesarean section, only to be questioned by the father: "*You're* not going to do it, are you?" "I *am* a surgeon," she replies.

Women sometimes have trouble allowing other women to claim their power. Corporate and professional women feel unimportant and shamed by secretaries who hedge on services they wouldn't mind doing for a man. A woman who teaches at a university reports that it sometimes takes a week to get something typed. She sighs as she tells me, "I know if I were a man, she'd have done it right away."

Another source of shame arises from women not being paid for their work at home. The message is that motherhood is a job not worth supporting. As social psychologist Nancy Chodorow points out, "Women are expected to be full-time mothers and to work in the paid labor force, are considered unmotherly if they demand day-care centers, greedy and unreasonable if they expect help from their husbands, and lazy if they are single mothers who want to receive adequate welfare payments in order to be able to stay home for their children."[28]

Our insecurity about our ability to survive on our own can add immeasurably to our sense of inherent defectiveness. Harriet Goldhor Lerner writes about the economic vulnerability of homemakers: "The issue is not, nor has it ever been, whether homemaking is more or less valuable than, say, being an engineer. The real issue is that the role of homemaker places many women in a position of profound economic vulnerability. This vulnerability is fueled by high divorce rates, negligible alimony, low or uncollectible child-support payments, and the lack of high-level training and re-entry programs for displaced homemakers."[29]

Even though today the majority of women who work outside the home say they work to supplement the family income, most would choose to work even if the family didn't depend on them for support. They see their work as a source of self-fulfillment. Unfortunately society regards their contribution as meager and their interest as frivolous. "I have to work twice as hard to get half the recognition," says one woman.

When a woman *does* go to work outside the home, she takes on the burden of a second job. Caught between two worlds, her work load increases. She is never sure how well she's doing, since there is no easy measure of her success, no annual review of her job performance. Overextended and unappreciated, today's woman feels deeply inadequate in the face of impossible demands placed upon her.

Under the illusion that she is escaping the drudgery of domesticity by going to work, she finds her tasks still menial and mundane as she types, answers phones, and generally takes care of all the endless details that keep an office, school, or hospital running smoothly.[30] Woman the caretaker at home becomes woman the caretaker at work. Her ability to nurture is exploited as she makes coffee and runs errands for a boss who is usually a man.[31] But at least she gets paid for these services, although not at equal rates.

Although women comprise over half the work force, the shortage of available child care and family leave testifies to the minimal importance given to our dual role as caretakers and breadwinners. It confirms how society undervalues women's abilities and contribution. Women often feel shamed by male co-workers or bosses for leaving work early or coming in late because of a sick child. While we are expected to be nurturers, we even risk losing our jobs if we take too much time off to tend to sick children or ailing parents.

How Do Women Cope with Being One-Down?

Conditioned almost from birth to see women as the inferior sex, some of us go about our daily lives oblivious to the unequal treatment we receive. Or we accept our position as second-class citizens, figuring that we don't really know as much as the men who run our corporations, our country, our schools, and our religious institutions. This choice allows us to be taken care of and to avoid risks we might encounter if we competed with men for an equal share of power, influence, and reward.

We find ways of exercising the power we *do* have that will not threaten or challenge male authority. We become covert, avoiding challenging men in most areas.

We hide.   We hide our strengths, even faking incompetence. Many of us remember the warnings of our mothers: "Don't act too smart. You'll never catch a man that way." Or we avoid challenging male superiority by expressing our abilities with hesitance.

We neglect our needs.   We become experts about other people, while remaining ignorant about ourselves. We accommodate: we cater to our mate, assuming that his work is more important, so he needs the extra rest or the choicest piece of chicken.

We manipulate to get our way.   For example many women, returning from clothes shopping, quickly spirit their purchases to the bedroom and hide them under the bed, to bring them out later one by one. Thus women avoid confrontation with an angry spouse *and* get to have what they want. But guilt and shame underlie their need to hide the evidence that they have made an independent decision to spend money and, worse, to spend it on themselves. Feeling we have to sneak because we can't openly assert our right to make such decisions further demeans us.

We feel unentitled to our wants, needs, opinions, and to fair treatment.   We put up with abuse, both emotional and physical, because we believe we don't deserve any better. Instead we accommodate.

We play the martyr, "guiltifying" others.   These women don't even buy clothes for themselves, but make sure their husband and children are well dressed.

* * *

Women have all too often been shamed and sabotaged in their attempts to be persons in their own right and to shape their own lives. Myths about women define them as inherently flawed. Constricted roles limit them, and restricted rights and privileges keep them second-class citizens. As retired Supreme Court Justice William Brennan once said, women haven't been put on a pedestal, they've been put in a cage.

In the face of this kind of cultural disempowerment, it may take many years—perhaps generations—for women to cast off their gender shame and claim their full powers. The next chapter, in which we examine the childhood roots of shame, can help you begin this crucial process.

The Childhood Roots
of Shame

"I waited for over an hour for my mother to come home so that we could go shopping together," says Tracy, a thirty-four-year-old lab technician battling bouts of depression. "I was only ten, and I was so excited. I'd really been looking forward to this special time alone with her. When my mother finally pulled into the driveway, I was in tears. I told her how afraid I was that she'd forgotten me. My mom said, 'I got stuck in traffic. How dare you accuse me of forgetting you! Just for that we're not going.' "

Neither Tracy nor her mother ever mentioned the incident again. Had Tracy's mother been able to apologize for keeping her daughter waiting, or had she been able later to take the child in her arms and give her a chance to express her feelings of fear, anger, and hurt, the bonds of love and trust could have been restored and Tracy's shame alleviated. But Tracy's mother, a woman who suffered from manic depression, wasn't able to do the necessary repair work.

I asked Tracy what it was like for her as she began daubing at her eyes with a tissue.

"I felt terrible. I ran to my room in tears. She never came in to console me."

As we can see from Tracy's story, shame is above all a relationship wound. Here was a child frightened that something might have happened to her mother to make her late. Instead of being comforted, she was scolded and shamed.

What could she conclude about herself at such a moment? That her mother didn't care about her feelings? That she was foolish to have expected Mother to comfort her? That she should have known Mother would eventually come? That it was somehow her *fault* that Mother was angry with her?

When Tracy came to see me, she had been depressed for many months. Although she was happy in her job, she was married to a man who was verbally abusive. Raised in a family where verbal abuse was common, she didn't believe she deserved any better treatment.

Where did this debilitating belief come from? Tracy's experience with her mother was one of many that taught her to deny her feelings and needs and to conclude she was unlovable.

As we began to explore Tracy's unhappy childhood, her underlying feelings of defectiveness emerged. As she began to feel safe enough to express her deepest feelings, her shame diminished and her belief in herself blossomed. After several years of therapy she learned to stand up to her husband, to call him on his belittling attitudes, and to demand better treatment. When she told him he would have to change or she was leaving, he sought therapy and eventually came to terms with his need to be so abusive.

Tracy had a difficult childhood. Her family was more troubled than most. I've heard John Bradshaw say that 95 percent of American families are dysfunctional. If he's right, then dysfunction must be normal! Though there are problems in all families, if the term *dysfunctional* is to have any meaning, we must reserve it for families like Tracy's, where the parents are unable to adequately meet the basic needs of their children.

Tracy's mother was manic-depressive. Tanya's father was a

workaholic. Ginny's mother was chronically ill. Yet I see plenty of shame-filled women whose parents' limitations were less obvious—parents who simply were so unhappy and troubled themselves, they couldn't successfully instill in their children a sense of self-worth. And then there are women whose parents weren't basically troubled but who, for many reasons, were still unable to raise strong and self-confident children.

As adults these moderately shame-based women fall in the middle of the Shame Continuum we discussed in Chapter One.

What Children Need

Did Tracy's parents set out to teach her that she's not acceptable the way she is? Of course not. I believe most parents do the best they can raising their children. No parent wants to instill feelings of inferiority in a child. But their lack of knowledge about parenting and their own overriding psychological needs may lead them to repeat the same mistakes their own parents made.

As children we inherit our parents' shame. At some level I knew that my father's arrogance and bluster covered profound feelings of inadequacy and that my mother's excessive meekness and humility reflected deep-seated insecurities. Shame is contagious, and children are easily infected by it.

How we feel about ourselves as adults is determined in large part by our childhood experiences. If we are to grow up with a strong sense of self-worth and the ability to form healthy relationships, our parents must be able to satisfy our essential needs:

- To feel connected to those important to us
- To feel that we matter as unique individuals
- To develop competence
- To trust in ourselves and others[1]

The Need for Connection

Our most important need is a loving relationship with someone in our early years, someone who is emotionally present and accessible, someone who is tuned in to us. But what if this person, usually Mother, is distracted by her own unmet needs and concerns? What if she isn't emotionally available? She may be worried about Daddy's love affairs, she may drink too much, she may be overworked. She may be basically insecure, depressed, or anxious.

A child whose mother is preoccupied with her own problems may not feel that she is deeply loved and wanted. Instead she learns that she is a nuisance, that her needs and feelings aren't important, and—worst of all—that she is bad to have them.

Because our need to relate is so great, we may, like Tracy, give up vital parts of ourselves in order to preserve that crucial connection.

Each time a thread breaks in the tie that connects us, we conclude at a deep nonverbal level that our own inadequacy is to blame. Each time our needs and emotions are ignored, we assume it's because they are shameful.

Of course it's inevitable that the loving connection between parent and child will break down from time to time, causing momentary shame. The important question is: Is it part of a pattern? Children learn to feel defective only when this loss of connection is prolonged or occurs repeatedly. Or, as we saw with Tracy, when a parent fails to repair the broken connection.

Of all negative parental behaviors, physical and sexual abuse are the most damaging to a child. But harsh words, neglect, family secrecy, or rejection can also cut us off from the people we depend on and love, leaving us isolated and ashamed. A child is more likely to blame herself for having done something "bad" to deserve Daddy's rage than to accept the frightening fact that the man she depends on to protect her can't be trusted.

What about fathers? Usually fathers are not physically or emotionally available to provide the necessary close attachment in our early years. Instead, by the very fact of his lesser availability, Father emerges as a somewhat distant though exciting figure. Or if there is closeness with Father, it too often becomes corrupted by a girl's awareness that she is too important to him or that she must take care of him.

These old patterns of parenting are slowly changing, however. Some families now realize that fathers as well as mothers can play a vital role in the early years. By sharing in the care of his children, a nurturing yet not engulfing father adds immeasurably to their security and growing sense of self. Fathers also have an important role to play in helping their daughters to feel competent and secure in the knowledge that their competence doesn't threaten their important relationships.[2] And a father's ability to be comfortable with his daughter's emerging sexuality is crucial to her healthy development.

The Need to Matter

In order to build self-esteem, we need to be treated with respect and honored for our uniqueness. Every child needs to know she is wanted and loved for who she is—that she matters. This doesn't sound like a lot to ask, but it turns out to be more than many parents are capable of giving. We may start our life not being fully wanted. Or we may learn later that we have been discriminated against simply because of our gender.

"I've just bought my daughter her first car," Tracy told me at one of our sessions. "What a special joy that is for me. In my family the boys received new cars for graduation from high school, while the girls only received watches. My parents thought boys were more important. They were encouraged to go to college, while we were encouraged to go to nursing school."

When a child feels unwanted and rejected, she blames herself, believing she is fundamentally lacking. As one client put it, "I always had the feeling I was a nuisance rather than a pleasure. I felt as though they were stuck with me."

"THEY WERE JUST TOO BUSY"

We know we matter when our parents spend time with us and give us quality attention, when they listen to us and are interested in what we are doing, when they come to our special events.

Tracy recalls the times her parents didn't bother to come to her swim meets, even the championships. "I didn't seem to be very important to them in their overall lives. They were awfully busy, but you'd think they could have made more effort. My dad didn't even come to my high school graduation. Mother explained that he had to work, so I guess I don't really blame him."

Tracy was twisting her ring.

I asked if his boss wouldn't let him off.

"Oh, he's his own boss. He owns a grocery store." The ring seemed to become even more fascinating. Tracy's eyes filled up as she told me how all these years she had believed the family myth about Father being too busy. "It hurts a lot. At the time I didn't feel bad that he didn't show up. I guess I'd already given up wanting attention from him. But now I can feel this big lump in my throat."

"There's a lot of yearning for your dad."

Tracy nodded silently, feeling her pain for the first time.

"Look at Me, Ma"

Part of our need for attention includes wanting to be admired—a need that continues throughout our lifetime. Showing ourselves off for the praise and admiration of others is not only healthy but necessary to developing a sense of our worth. Yet many women secretly despise themselves for these normal longings.

Picture a baby pulling herself up into a standing position for the first time. She gets halfway up and looks over to Mother for a smile of approval or words of encouragement. When she finally stands, albeit on shaky legs, she looks again, triumphant in the knowledge that she has performed an amazing feat. She crows proudly as her delight is mirrored by the smile on Mother's face. This healthy narcissism is reinforced when parents reflect back to the child her "wonderfulness."

But what happens to the child's belief in her inherent "wonderfulness" when time and again she is ignored or even shamed for showing off her accomplishments? As a client of mine puts it, "There wasn't much to feel special about. And when there was, I was told, 'Don't get too big for your britches.' "

I am convinced that the need to be special lies at the root of many women's infidelities. The initial period of infatuation, the shared secrets, and the intensity fill a deep need.

"I Don't Count, and It's My Own Fault"

Another way we learn we are important is when we see that our feelings matter to our parents, and they allow or even encourage us to express them. They even accept our hurt and anger as legitimate. They take us *seriously*.

Tracy had no one to share her hurt feelings with because her mom was protecting her unavailable dad: "You must understand. He has to work, dear." When he wasn't at the store, he was home hidden behind a newspaper.

When our parents can't acknowledge or won't listen to our feelings, the consequences are profound. When her mother repeatedly didn't respond to Tracy's hurts, Tracy learned that her feelings and who she is have no impact on the important people in her life.[3] Tracy battled a depression that was based partly on her sense of not mattering to anyone and partly on the shame that accompanied this belief.

When our opinions and ideas are taken seriously, we learn that we make a difference to others. When our parents not only permit disagreements but respect them as evidence of our growing independence and thinking ability, we learn to value ourselves.

In families where children are valued as unique, individuality is recognized and encouraged. Rhonda may not be domestic, but she understands the inner workings of her car, and her parents don't compare her to her sister, who loves to cook and sew.

We know we matter when our parents convey a belief that we can be trusted to have good intentions. "I know you didn't mean to spill your milk. Let's clean it up." As opposed to "You just did that to get attention."

Ideally as children we need to feel confident that when we act in less than perfect ways, we are still loved. When love is conditional and withdrawn every time we fail to measure up to our parents' expectations, we come to feel we are defective at the core of our being.

The Need for Competence

If we are to grow up with self-love instead of self-doubt, we need to experience ourselves as powerful. Yet the idea of having power makes most women uncomfortable, because our notions of power are based on patriarchal ideas about male authority and privilege—in other words, power over someone.

I am speaking here of a different kind of power: the power to have and make choices, the power to have an impact on people and situations, the power to be in charge of one's own life, the power to be successful in our relationships. This kind of power means both being able to act in our own best interests and being caring and empathic in our relationships.

A girl's unfolding development can be viewed as a journey from powerlessness to empowerment. Consider her transformation from a passive, almost helpless baby to a competent young woman, standing on the threshold of adulthood.

COMPETENCE: A MIXED BAG

Just as she is enjoying her emerging self-reliance, however, she runs smack into what Harvard professor Carol Gilligan calls "the wall of western culture."[4] She discovers that girls have fewer opportunities to develop the kind of competence most valued by society. Sports offer boys a ready-made opportunity for public demonstration of their competence, while cheerleaders and pom-pom girls get to exhibit only their cuteness.

Our schools are badly shortchanging girls. They tend to channel girls into sex-stereotyped occupations, away from careers in math and science. (Do they reflect society's view that it is more important for boys than for girls to compete and excel in these "masculine" subjects?)

Parents contribute to this inequality of opportunity by emphasizing certain skills as more appropriate for girls and by not encouraging higher education for girls as enthusiastically as they do for boys. Many of us are familiar with the parental refrain "What do *you* want to go to college for, unless it's to meet a man?" The message is: "You don't deserve an education."

When girls struggle with math and science, they tend to blame themselves, while boys tend to blame the materials or the subject. *Even though girls are as competent in school work, they exhibit less confidence and lower self-esteem.*[5]

They get the idea their competence threatens their connections with boys. "Don't let them know you're as smart as they are. No one likes a brainy girl." No wonder girls often attribute their successes to luck rather than effort or skill![6] In the process they hide their competence from themselves.

Do girls allow themselves to be competent but not to enjoy the knowledge of their competence in order to maintain their ties with other people—ties that depend on girls keeping their secondary place? *(I'll do well, but I won't let myself know I do well or act like I do well. That way you can't reject me.)* A girl's development is partly a process of determining which areas she can be competent in or excel in without losing the love and approval of her parents, friends, and boyfriends.

While boys are concerned with making their way in the world, girls are more concerned with forming and maintaining a network of relationships. As Jean Baker Miller puts it, the self is seen "in relationship," rather than standing alone, facing the world. Yet often a girl's competence at relationships doesn't add to her sense of power in the world, because her skills in this area aren't highly valued by society.

A girl's sense of her power—what little she has in her own small world—comes in large part from having good relationships with her friends and family. She knows that she can have an impact on the important people in her life, that her ideas, opinions, and feelings count to those closest to her. Others seek her advice, and when they need a sympathetic ear, hers is available. She gets satisfaction from empowering those around her, supporting them in their growth. If this ability to affect the lives of others is missing, she will experience a profound sense of powerlessness, along with a sense of not mattering to those most important to her.

An essential part of being powerful and competent (rather than shame-bound) is the ability to function as my own person. I need to be able to see myself as separate from those closest to me. I need to have clear boundaries, to know where I end and you begin. I am close to you, but I am not you. I am different. I am me. Yet, in my separateness, I want to be able to remain connected to you. Even though I can often feel what you are feeling, I don't get confused about whose feelings are whose. For example, when you're depressed, I can appreciate your down mood, even remember when I felt the same way, but I don't crawl in the hole with you and get depressed myself.

"BE LIKE ME"

Part of being a person in our own right is allowing ourselves to be different from those closest to us without feeling ashamed. Many of us raised in troubled families were taught that to be different was unacceptable. We were scorned for thinking for ourselves, for having different interests, temperaments, talents. "Be like me," was the powerful message we often heard growing up.

When I was thirty, I had the opportunity to be in a small workshop with the late Virginia Satir, a powerful, compassionate, and brilliant family therapist. At one point, when it was my turn to "work," I discovered that I was caught between wanting to be my own person and believing I should be like the people in my family.

Virginia told me to stand in the middle of the group and pick people to be my father, mother, sister, and brother. She instructed these "stand-ins" to grab hold of me and chant, "Be like me," while I was to look each one in the eye and say, "Let go." There I was, with my "family" pulling on my arms and shoulders, and even though this was only make-believe, I felt almost powerless. When it was time to tell my mother, "Let go," I froze. I saw in her eyes her terror that she would die if I let go of her. Her eyes pleaded with me, *Don't let go, I need you to hang on.* Gripped by a paralyzing combination of feelings, I confronted both shame at wanting to be separate and shame at not being able to let go. I was also terrified of what would happen to my mother if I did let go of her.

I shook and sobbed, until I finally took a deep breath, looked her in the eye, and spoke the fateful words, "Let go." And she did. From that moment on the bonds loosened, and I was free to *be like me*. I could both be me and be like my family in many ways, but *I was now in charge of the choice.*

OUR NEED FOR MODELS

Although we need to be able to be different and separate from our parents, being like them while we're growing up serves an important purpose. We learn how to function in the world by watching the behavior of our parents and others—siblings, grandparents, friends—who figure significantly in our lives. Through a process called modeling we take on their ways of being and acting.

What Do Normal People Do?

But what if our parents were unable to guide us in appropriate ways to be because they themselves were ill equipped to handle the stresses of life? What if they simply avoided dealing with difficult situations?

Shame-prone women feel shamefully uncertain about what is normal or appropriate behavior. Such *underlearning* comes from lack of experience and from poor role models, from continually being told we are incompetent, and from being forced into roles far beyond our abilities as children. Who can't remember the wounding shame that comes from being criticized for the way we did things *without being shown the right way*? Or the panic of being asked to do something we had no idea how to do?

Here are some signs of the underlearning common in dysfunctional families, taken from *A Time to Heal*, by psychologist Timmon Cermak:

- Constantly guessing at what "normal" is.
- Wondering what you "ought" to be feeling in different situations.
- Excessive fear of the unknown.
- Overreliance on watching other people to see how you should be acting.
- Feeling at a loss when you get married or when your first child is born.
- Believing that others usually know what they're doing.
- Always deferring to others.
- Feeling as though you are pulling the wool over people's eyes.
- Making "big deals" about things other people do easily.
- Neglecting such things as daily chores and financial records out of ignorance.
- Frequently being surprised by learning there are simple ways to accomplish things you do in convoluted ways.[7]

Assuming everyone else knows what's normal, we don't dare admit that we are only "passing" as adults. My clients frequently ask me, "Is it normal to . . .?" or "Do most people . . .?" Our search for rules is doomed to frustration until we realize that *there is no one "right" way.*

Ironically our hesitancy to reveal our worst fears keeps us from the one thing that would ease them: sharing our concerns with others and learning (a) that they feel the same way; or (b) that there is more than one way to do things; or (c) that we know much more than we realize about navigating in our world. And if there are gaps in our knowledge, it helps to remember that it's not because *we* are inadequate but because our *experience* is insufficient. It's never too late to learn.

Our parents teach by example how to cope with stress. "When my mother was upset, she poured herself a drink," Donna says. Rather than drink, eat, rage, take pills, or stay in bed all day, we can call a friend, see a therapist, or have a family problem-solving session.

Now that women are claiming more power, we often face problems unknown to our mothers, so we can't turn to them for guidance.

"I don't know whom to look to as an example of a woman who can balance taking care of others with taking care of herself," Tracy says. "What I see instead is my mother. She's devoted her life to making others happy. Sometimes she's so selfless, I feel guilty. God, I'd love to believe my needs and wants are as important as anybody else's, but I'm afraid of going too far. I'd hate to be seen as selfish."

The Need to Trust and Be Trusted

In order to grow into women with strong self-worth, we must develop the capacity to trust others and the capacity to trust ourselves.

When our parents don't answer our needs, we lose trust that others will be there for us when we need them. When they are unpredictable in their responses—when they slap us for behavior that was acceptable or even funny the day before—we begin to see the world as an unsafe place. When our expectations are exposed as wrong, we feel profoundly ashamed.

"If Nothing's Wrong, How Come I Feel So Bad?"

In order to learn to trust other people, we need to know that our reality matches theirs. Family secrets such as alcoholism, suicide, or mental illness are certain to inspire in us a sense of deep shame. Mom's binge-eating or Dad's nighttime visits to his daughter's room are never spoken of.

Children usually receive confusing double messages: *Nothing's wrong, and besides it's a secret.* Events that are never acknowledged in the family make us feel crazy because, though we sense something is wrong, we don't know what. And we blame ourselves.

Julie was shattered when, at age eleven, her supposedly "happy" parents got a divorce. She never understood why her father walked out one day and never returned. Not only did she blame herself, but she became unable to trust her own perceptions, a problem that continues to plague her to this day. *When you can't rely on the general accuracy of your own perceptions about what is happening around you, you are robbed of one of the basic tools for dealing effectively with your life.*

Today Julie ping-pongs back and forth between suspecting her lover, Rebecca, of being unfaithful and closing her eyes to Rebecca's obvious deceit.

"Shame attacks me coming and going. First I'm ashamed for being suspicious when I check up on her and don't trust her alibis, and then I feel like a fool when I do trust her and later discover that she's put one over on me."

We need to be treated as trustworthy. When parents, for reasons of their own, don't allow children to have their own experience, they interfere with the development of inner trust. How many times were we told, "You don't want that," or "You're not thirsty," or "Don't be sad." Instead of learning to trust our inner states, we become ashamed of having them—and may even lose awareness of their existence. Instead *we allow others to define our experience for us.*

Once we have built a foundation of trust in others' consistency, emotional availability, and honesty, we can begin the long process of learning to trust ourselves.

What does it mean to trust myself? It means I trust the soundness, the significance, the legitimacy of my feelings, perceptions, and judgments. When I sense I'm not being told the truth about something, I trust myself enough to raise questions. When I feel a wave of sadness or anger, I let myself feel it. If my body tells me I'm hungry or tired, I trust it is signaling me to take care of myself.

Feeling connected, knowing we matter, feeling competent, and being able to trust ourselves and others make up the four basic building blocks that must be securely in place if we are to develop a strong sense of self-worth and the capacity to relate to others in healthy ways.

When these needs aren't met, we conclude that there is something wrong with us.

How Parents Shame Their Children

Perhaps the most insidious, invasive way parents unknowingly shame their children is by using them in subtle ways for their own purposes. Siblings and grandparents, too, may use children to replenish their own depleted self-esteem, to cover defectiveness, or to calm fears of inadequacy. Even though they may not openly shame a girl, or neglect or abuse her, she will find being treated as an object a deeply shaming experience.

Encouraged to make up for her father's deficiencies or to live out her mother's unfulfilled dreams, a girl may become a narcissistic extension of her parents. With no life of her own, she lives for her mother or father as they live through her. Mother, who may be unhappy or lonely, identifies with her daughter, making her a receptacle to be filled with all of Mother's hopes and fears.

Terry, twenty years old, complained that her mother, Ruth, would go into Terry's closet while she was away at college and help herself to Terry's clothes. Ruth never failed to let people know that her talented daughter had designed and made the smashing outfits she was wearing. Terry was furious.

"I feel like I don't even count. Wearing my clothes without my permission—how could she! I'm so embarrassed to have her showing off my stuff, like she was using me for her own glory. Don't my feelings matter?"

Ruth's behavior illustrates how fuzzy the boundaries can get between mother and daughter, to the point where Terry's property and Terry's talent become her mother's to take over and draw glory from. Ruth has made Terry an extension of herself. Having never been acknowledged for her own talent—she dropped out of art school to marry Terry's father—she found a way to use Terry to fulfill her own needs for attention and approval. Was Ruth aware of all this? Probably not. Motives like these are usually deeply buried.

The pressure to excel, to perform, to parade one's talents for others' admiration can be humiliating, as Terry can attest. We see, at one level, that we are being used; we know that it's far too important to our parents that we shine. Some of us are spurred on, while others give up in discouragement. Either way the message is the same: *Who we are is not good enough.*

Roles Children Play

When a child is used as a pawn in an unhappy marriage, she is drawn into the marital relationship, taking on various inappropriate roles. Often the child becomes a confidante, listening to one parent complain about the other. This puts the child in the potentially shaming and impossible position of having to choose between the two most important people in her life. We need a healthy relationship with both parents; to abandon one in order to please the other costs us dearly.

Daddy's Wife.   Children in troubled families are often cast in the role of substitute spouse. When a father turns to his daughter to meet his unfulfilled emotional needs, this is emotional incest. His inappropriate emotional investment binds her to him in unhealthy ways, leaving her with a troubling legacy when it comes time to establish adult intimate relationships.

Sexual abuse is the most damaging and humiliating transgression against a child. Even though there may be no actual sexual activity, there can be inappropriate touching, which is deeply confusing and shaming to a girl. When a father uses his daughter for his own need, violating her physically and emotionally, he impairs her ability to trust others and her ability to trust her own inner states. We'll go more deeply into this most devastating of all shame-wounds in Chapter Ten.

Surrogate Parent.   Another way parents instill shame is by encouraging a child to act as a parent to her parent—in effect stealing her childhood. Because we depend so greatly on our parents, we will do anything we can to take care of them, to shore them up, to deny their weakness, even to help them maintain the illusion that they are the strong ones, still able to take care of us.

Daughters in dysfunctional families (where parents are alcoholic, workaholic, chronically ill, or just too troubled to adequately meet the needs of their children) have special hardships. Because girls are taught to be caretakers, they are more likely than boys to assume the job of parenting the parent or caring for the family, both emotionally and physically. When Mother is too drunk, depressed, or distracted by an affair, usually it's the daughter who performs her mother's jobs, doing the cooking, cleaning, grocery shopping, and child care, often far beyond the level of her abilities. Boys are more able to leave, to lose themselves in sports, to express their anger more openly.

"I was great at giving advice, reassuring them, and listening to their troubles," Melanie says. "You could count on me to find just the right thing to cheer up Mom or make Dad's day. Mother struck a deal with me. How I got close to her was to help her carry the worry load." Such caretaking becomes second nature to the girl who has reversed roles with her parent.

Called upon to give up her self in the interest of keeping the family from falling apart, she finds that her own needs go unmet and she develops a deep sense of shame for having needs in the first place.

Of course neither sons nor daughters are spared the damage of growing up in a disturbed family. And certainly a son can adopt these caretaking roles as well. But because a daughter is socialized to shoulder the feminine burden of trying to meet everyone's needs, her attempts to do an impossible job leave her with a deep sense of insufficiency and an underlying core of shame.

Scapegoat.   Some children respond to family unhappiness by "acting out": getting into trouble, earning poor grades, being sickly—anything to draw the parents' attention away from their own pain and unhappiness. By openly inviting shame, such children protect their parents from feeling their own deep sense of inadequacy.

These and other inappropriate roles interfere with our ability to express ourselves authentically in our families and in the outside world. We become stuck in these once-adaptive, now-maladaptive ways of being, with a crippling sense of shame about not being good enough to just be ourselves.

How Parents Abuse Kids

One of the most effective yet damaging ways to get children to behave is to shame them openly, by criticizing, labeling, commanding, and comparing. When things go wrong, some parents are more interested in finding someone to blame than in doing something to improve the situation. Teasing, belittling, and sarcasm are guaranteed to inflict a wounding sense of shame on their victims.

Because we define ourselves through the eyes of others, when our all-knowing, all-powerful parents tell us we are stupid, lazy, thoughtless, mean, and hateful, we believe them. What may be just as devastating is the look of disgust or the tone of voice that tells us we are beneath contempt.

Deidre's mother would threaten to go off into the woods and not come back if Deidre didn't behave. Sometimes when Mother was upset, she wouldn't talk to Deidre for several days. At those times Deidre felt unlovable and worthless.

Verbal abuse like this destroys the dignity of a child and is often profoundly shaming. Physical abuse—beatings, face slapping, pushing, and yanking by the arm—is more extreme and is certain to produce an excruciating sense of shame.

Observing other family members being verbally or physically abused and being helpless to stop it can be profoundly humiliating. Whenever we witness another's debasement, we are likely to take on the other person's shame as our own.

Is Forgiveness Possible?

At a certain point we need to look at the possibility of forgiving our imperfect parents or at least viewing them with some compassion. I'm not suggesting that we deny our years of hurt or ignore our anger, but before we judge our parents too harshly, we need to recognize that they did the best they could given the parenting they had. It may be that they were too shame-based and needy to adequately meet our needs. Gaining a degree of compassion for their limitations may help us to get some perspective on our own.

Mothers are often unfairly blamed for the psychological problems of their children. It's all too easy to criticize a mother for being narcissistic, unavailable, enmeshing, intrusive, or overprotective without appreciating her personal and cultural circumstances.[8] Her shortcomings come partly from her position in a society that has given her limited choices and has generally devalued her for being a woman. They may also come from having been raised by parents who used, abused, or neglected her.

And what about fathers? Hasn't their absence often played a part in the confusions and insecurities of their children? Because society saddled them with the burden of being the sole support for their families, many of our fathers worked long hours away from home. And because *they* weren't raised to focus on relationships, when they came home, they were often uninvolved. Or their own debilitating shame may have led them to be physically or verbally abusive.

What Family Shaming Costs Us

The tragedy of most unhappy families is that through growing up in them we learned to give up our own truths, our own experience. Having been abandoned in a basic way by those most important to us, we in turn abandoned ourselves. In order to maintain essential ties with our parents, we broke the most important connection of all—the connection with ourselves. We took on the blame, distorted or sacrificed our reality, took care of our parents, gave up our needs and wants, and deadened our feelings. We decided at an early age that we were unlovable and that the world was a dangerous place. Although we pass ourselves off as adults, we let that three-year-old inside us run our lives.

There comes a time when we must take responsibility for our own lives and stop putting the blame on our parents. By remaining victims of our childhood we continue to disempower ourselves, just as our parents disempowered us.

We need to let go of searching for love and approval from our parents and others and to work instead on nurturing and accepting ourselves. We need to parent that little girl inside us and give her what she missed growing up: unconditional love, empathy, respect, and the knowledge that she is special.

She deserves it.

PART TWO

———||||||||||———

Locking
Shame
in Place

CHAPTER FIVE

How Shame Shapes Our Identity

The dilemma of defining a self is a particularly complex one for women. Because we are a subordinate group, our "true nature" and "appropriate place" have forever been defined by the wishes and fears of men. How, then, do we approach the task of carving out a clear and authentic self from the myriad of mixed messages and injunctions that surround us from the cradle to the grave?
—HARRIET GOLDHOR LERNER

"Sometimes I don't know who I am," said Audrey, a dark-eyed, bubbly, thirty-one-year-old legal secretary. "I know I'm Ted's wife, and Jessie's mom. But that doesn't tell me who *I* am. I guess that's why I got into counseling. I sometimes wonder if there's anybody really in here."

Audrey's difficulty in claiming an identity for herself is echoed by most women I know, ranging from those who devote their lives to their families to single, highly successful professionals. The only identity Audrey does profess is negative: "I'm not good enough. There's something wrong with me."

When we believe this about ourselves, we are affirming a shame-based identity. Even an unclear and underdeveloped sense of self may give rise to profound shame.

The Roots of Our Shame-Based Identity

Why is a clear, positive sense of ourselves so difficult to achieve? We have just seen how not having our basic psychological needs met while we were growing up can make us feel defective and insecure. We've also seen that to be a woman in our culture is to be born into an identity rooted in shame.

By adulthood most shame-prone women haven't established a solid identity for themselves. To be confused about your needs and wants, to feel as though you don't have a center, to be uncertain whether you matter to others—all these can contribute to an identity that leaves you feeling deeply inadequate or even lost.

I've heard it expressed in many ways, but perhaps the most poignant are "I feel like I don't exist" and "I don't feel real." When we are so cut off from a sense of ourselves, we feel like observers watching our own lives play out.

These feelings of emptiness are usually accompanied by feelings of self-hate. *I'm not a good person. I'm selfish. Inside I'm bad, if they only knew.* And if we look good on the outside, we tell ourselves, *I've got them fooled. I'm really a phony.*

"Who Am I?"

This is perhaps the most important question we can ask ourselves. Before reading any farther, put down this book and ask yourself, *Who am I?*

Most likely you answered by saying you were a woman, followed by your relationship connections. Women tend to define themselves in terms of other people, rather than in terms of their work, interests, or activities. We say, "I'm a mother, I'm a wife." Almost invariably we next describe qualities that also have to do with relating: "I'm warm, friendly. I care about people."

Men, on the other hand, usually describe themselves not in terms of their relationships but in terms of their occupations and accomplishments.[1]

What exactly do we mean by *identity*? The core of our identity is fashioned by what we believe in, how others see us, what we are valued for, and what we know about ourselves. Though it includes and expands with the choices we make and the priorities we set for ourselves, it basically remains unchanged throughout our lives.

According to Erik Erikson, a psychoanalyst well known for his theories about identity, an increasing sense of identity brings with it a feeling of "being at home in one's body, a sense of 'knowing where one is going.' " We don't acquire or maintain this sense of self "once and for all," but we become more skilled at maintaining or restoring it as we mature, Erikson believes.[2] A shame-prone woman's sense of identity is not so easily maintained.

A Round Peg in a Square Hole

For years psychologists have maintained that the goal of individual development is to become separate or autonomous. In fact they view autonomy as one of the hallmarks of maturity. But women don't conform to these essentially male perspectives on the human psyche. Since psychologists have generally used male experience as a norm for *all* experience, women end up misunderstood and misrepresented.

Even Freud had problems understanding women and fitting them into his theories. Since he viewed women as passive and receptive creatures whose reproductive functions are (or should be) the focus of their lives, it is no wonder he was never able to come up with an answer to his famous question "What do women want?"

Erikson, in writing about the seven stages of man, also failed to do justice to identity development in women. His theories about human development, based on studies of males, were really about male development. When women didn't fit his theories, he made them the exception. Echoing Freud's "anatomy is destiny," Erikson wrote in later years that woman's inner space (meaning her womb) is based on her unique biology, and determines her more caring, nurturing, and compassionate adaptation to life. So far there is no evidence to support the notion that our reproductive organs determine our behavior!

Erikson considered development of autonomy—rather than development of interpersonal skills—the appropriate measure of adulthood. He said that "man" forms his identity before he becomes committed to a woman. Later he acknowledged that women are different, finding identity and maturity when they leave the care of their parents and commit to a man "and to the care to be given to his and her offspring."[3] (I wonder what happens to a single woman?) I believe Erikson eventually got on the right track but the wrong train. Women *do* use their relationships to define themselves, but not just in the sense Erikson and society generally believe. Besides being someone's wife or mother, we women rely on most of our relationships (including friends and children) to deepen our knowledge of ourselves. Even though Erikson came to realize a woman wasn't "man," he never amended his original model to include his later observations about the differing pattern of female development.[4]

Realizing that these attempts at fitting females into the model of normal male development were inappropriate and demeaning to women, some scholars have begun to take the matter into their own hands by studying the lives of actual women.[5]

Dr. Jean Baker Miller points out that psychologists rarely address our commitment as women to fostering other people's emotional and intellectual development and to empowering others—a much more complex activity than that conveyed by such terms as "mothering" or "caretaking."[6] Miller believes that a woman's sense of self depends more on her ability to form and maintain relationships than on her ability to be a separate individual. I welcome Miller's validation of the importance of our relationship skills, but I think she tends to underemphasize the equally important ability to be assertive, to be able to make autonomous decisions in our own best interest, to have the capacity occasionally to put our own needs and wants ahead of others.

Traditionally the cornerstone of a woman's identity has been her role as caretaker. Yet when taking care of others becomes more important than taking care of ourselves, our identity rests on shaky underpinnings. If keeping our attachments takes precedence over expressing ourselves authentically, we end up not knowing who we are because we become who others want us to be.

Achieving a healthy identity calls for finding a balance between being an authentic person in our own right and remaining connected to those we most care about—no easy task.

As Audrey carries out her duties as family caretaker, she has little sense of self. "My life is my husband's life," she tells me. "My life revolves around his needs, his decisions, his plans. When he wants something and I want something different, it's very hard for me to put my needs first. Especially if it's something big."

"Like what?" I ask.

"Well, I've always wanted to go back east and visit my sister, but when I bring it up, he complains about my being gone so long. And I'm not sure he could manage without me." She laughs hollowly. "What would he eat?"

Having someone else be the central focus of our lives precludes the possibility of discovering what our own needs are, what independent decisions we are capable of making, what our plans for ourselves might look like.

It disempowers us.

Shaping the Self:
How Women's Process Differs from Men's

How did Audrey get to the point of defining herself in terms of her husband and his needs? In order to understand how we end up developing an identity that is weak and shame-based, we need to go back to our earliest years. A sense of self begins in infancy when we first realize we are separate from Mother.

At this point boys and girls take different routes in carving an identity. A girl discovers who she is through her relationships. A boy, however, more often defines who he is through his activities and accomplishments.

Are we actually born different? Nancy Chodorow, a social psychologist at the University of California, Berkeley, suggests that these basic differences come more from our early experiences than from biological differences. Because the family is structured so that the basic caregiver—usually the mother—is the same sex as her daughter and a different sex from her son, and because Mother is the one with whom both children originally identify, there are far-reaching consequences.[7]

Girls never have to abandon their primary identity figure in order to establish their gender identity, but boys must eventually switch from mother to father, around age three. Because they don't have to switch identity figures, girls never separate and individuate as fully as boys do, and they are more likely to achieve an unbroken sense of relatedness and enjoy a longer period of rich contact with Mother.

As a result a girl's identity forms in ways that lead to quite different patterns of looking at herself and her relationships. In our society's view of women "different" usually means "wrong," so many girls and women conclude there is something basically wrong with them.

In taking somewhat differing paths to establish identity, boys usually learn to value and define themselves more in terms of being autonomous or "different" (and usually "better than"), while girls value and define themselves more in terms of being connected or "similar" (and often "less than"). In order for boys to successfully break from Mother, they need to define themselves as "not her," suppressing both the intensity of their need for closeness and their emotions.

Reflecting the cultural bias shaped by men before him, a little boy comes to see the feminine need for love as weakness, furthering the myth of the inferior, childlike female. In this process a boy loses touch with his feminine side and eventually comes to devalue women in general—although not necessarily consciously.

A girl, on the other hand, stays identified with Mother as she expands the central aspect of her identity: her relationship skills and interests. Yet this identity doesn't allow for as much self-esteem as a boy's in a culture that doesn't value such "feminine" characteristics.

How Confident Girls Become Insecure Teenagers

Somewhere between the ages of eight and eleven our sense of self solidifies. We know who we are and what we want.[8]

Audrey recalls the joy of those years, in spite of family arguments at home: "I was now old enough to venture out into the world, away from my backyard. I got to play soccer as aggressively as I wanted. My friends and I formed secret clubs. We climbed trees and skinned our knees. We'd jump rope, play hopscotch, and collect stickers."

Girls at this age commonly feel secure in who they are. They are outspoken, trust their ability to know and see, and in general have a sense of themselves as persons in their own right. This is a time when girls are able to balance the two crucial aspects of their identity development. They enjoy their own competence and their ability to be fully themselves without worrying that these strengths may threaten their connections to others.

By the time she reaches adolescence, however, this self-possessed girl of eleven turns into an insecure young woman.[9] Her ability to attract boys (basically her reproductive role) becomes paramount in her social identity.

Audrey received a strong message from her parents, school, and society about acceptable behavior: "Don't use all your powers. Being powerful is wrong and shameful for a woman." Feeling intense pressure to accommodate others, Audrey put her own needs and talents in the background.

Audrey burns with shame as she recalls a painful lesson she learned about society's double standard for expression of power. "When I was ten, I often saw boys pummeling each other on the playground, earning admiration from both male and female on-lookers. But when I beat up a boy who started a fight with me, I was shunned by my friends, boys and girls alike. My pride at being strong turned into shame for not walking away—like a girl was supposed to do."

The conflict around being competent and powerful deepens as a young woman's relationships become more central in her life. By adolescence girls come to value themselves and other girls according to their attractiveness to boys. A girl comes to believe that her own talents and abilities count for little except as they serve in the quest for Mr. Right. She fears a strong self will scare off or even disgust others, especially boys, so she opts for maintaining these threatened interpersonal ties at the expense of full self-expression. She does this by putting others first, a pattern she has observed in her mother and most other women in our culture.

"When I was eleven, I could be sure about how I saw things," Audrey says. "I felt confident of my abilities. But later, when I started dating, I gave up so much of myself to keep my boyfriends. I'd go to the movies they'd want to see, I'd have sex even when I didn't particularly want to. I could never ask for what I wanted. And in school I didn't dare look too smart for fear I'd scare off the boys. Worst of all, I stopped trusting myself." Like so many girls and women, Audrey's need for a relationship with a man took precedence over her need to be her own person.

Studies by Harvard professor Carol Gilligan confirm Audrey's experience. She and her associates found that clear-thinking and courageous preadolescents often turn into apologetic teenagers who censor themselves. During adolescence girls learn that it's no longer safe to be outspoken about what they see and know. In fact, because they lose the ability to trust themselves to know what they know, they learn "to think in ways that differ from what they really think."[10]

This about-face society demands of girls when they reach reproductive age is, in a sense, comparable to the about-face little boys are forced into at age three when, in losing the primary connection with Mommy, they lose connection with their inner emotional world. For girls it's the primary connection with their competence that they're expected to renounce if they're to keep their connections with boys. They relinquish a self that has already been actualized, while boys relinquish a self that is yet to be developed. Isn't this a sort of genocide of the spirit for most of the world's population?

The experience of Barbra Streisand is a case in point. Although the movie *The Prince of Tides*, which she so ably directed, earned seven nominations by the Academy of Motion Picture Arts and Sciences, Streisand herself was passed over as a best-director nominee. In speculating that there might be some resistance to women as directors, Streisand says, "We're still fighting it. It's as if a man were allowed to have passion and commitment to his work, but a woman is allowed that feeling for a man, but not for her work."[11]

Not surprisingly, research shows that around age eleven girls' self-esteem begins to drop below that of boys, while depression rates rise. Eating disorders testify to girls' deep insecurities about their self-worth and their obsession with their body image. The adolescent girl either begins to feel there is something wrong with her or is confirmed in what she has already learned in her family about her defectiveness.

Another confusing change affects a girl's sense of self when she reaches adolescence. The father she knew how to please often turns into a growling or distant critic who doesn't like her short skirts, long red fingernails, and outfits that show cleavage. He, too, now relates to her in terms of her reproductive role, giving her mixed messages. Her taste in boys leaves him amused, disgusted, or angry. No longer affectionate—or awkwardly so—he moves away to protect himself from his own response to her emerging sexuality.

Today Audrey weeps over the loss of her father's attention. She recalls his hiking and telling her stories until puberty set in. "I could never understand what I did to drive him so far away. I sensed somehow that it had to do with my becoming a woman, and I felt bad. In fact I used to beat on my bumpy breasts so they wouldn't grow. I didn't want to grow up. Growing up meant giving up being Daddy's special princess."

I suspect that being emotionally abandoned by her father contributed to Audrey's finally saying good-bye to the feisty little girl who felt she had a solid place in the world and saying hello to the insecure, accommodating young woman who replaced her.

Another aspect of our eleven-year-old selves we say good-bye to as teenage girls is our natural competitiveness.

Consider Melinda, a bright and attractive teenager who came to see me because she was depressed. "I used to play hard against the boys in games and sports," she told me. "And in school . . . man, I always shot my hand up to answer the teachers' questions. Then one day I remembered what Mom said about boys not liking smart girls, so I kept quiet. I thought it wasn't feminine to compete, and besides they might not like me if I did better than them."

As teenage girls become absorbed with themselves and anxious about proving their attractiveness, the competition shifts from competing *with* boys to competing *for* boys.

Finding Our Moorings

Facing the necessity to separate (physically if not emotionally) from our parents, most of us find ways to anchor ourselves in the real world through creating families of our own or solidifying an identity through our careers.[12]

Many women have so little sense of self in our male-dominated culture that they look exclusively to marriage and children to provide them with an identity. They treat their husbands and children as extensions of themselves, gleaning satisfaction from their successes and shame from their failures. This sometimes puts enormous pressure on family members to perform for Mom's sake.

The challenge of motherhood leaves many women feeling inadequate. We don't have innate knowledge about how to be a mother. Many women feel incompetent, but they feel too ashamed to admit it. We take on this enormous responsibility with no training, and when we fail to live up to cultural ideals, we feel guilty and ashamed. ("When I yell at the kids, when I put my needs first, when I don't feel loving—sometimes I don't even like them—I feel horrible. I had no idea how hard being a mother would be.") Talking honestly with other mothers helps to allay persistent feelings of shame and guilt.

When our children have problems (in school, with friends, jobs, marriages), we heap shame on ourselves as we join society in blaming the mother. Father gets off the hook because he hasn't been that available. Isn't that part of the problem? At any rate we need to be gentle with ourselves and not hold our children's failings as evidence of our defectiveness as mothers. Talking honestly with other mothers helps to allay persistent feelings of shame and guilt.

The Second Shift

As a result of the women's liberation movement and economic pressures (among other factors), women have expanded their definition of themselves to include their role in the world of work, although this role usually remains secondary to that of wife and mother.

Those of us who work outside the home and are no longer full-time homemakers struggle with a dual identity as we try to find a place for ourselves in a changing social structure. While we embrace the freedom won by the women's movement, we begin to question what exactly it is that we *have* won.

These changes are clearly a mixed blessing. Instead of getting away from all that housework, we find that we have added the demands of a second job to the ever-present first job. Most women with shame-related issues—and maybe all women—feel they must meet the requirements of both home and outside job with total ease and competence. And when we can't, we're left with feelings of deep inadequacy.

When people around her (and society in general) fail to appreciate the modern woman's capacity to manage as well as she does, she is robbed of the validation that should come from her agility in juggling two jobs. We'll look more closely in the next chapter at women's struggles as they discover that having it all may mean having to do it all.

Women who are full-time homemakers (and who have the economic means to make that choice freely) are not only taken for granted by family and society, they risk being disparaged. We must be careful not to add further shame to women who find identity and fulfillment as homemakers.

Our ability to forge a strong identity does not seem to hinge on the particular choices we make but rather on how we achieve them. I differ with psychologist Ruthellen Josselson, who, in her book *Finding Herself,* claims that work doesn't play an important role in providing identity for most women. She maintains that relationships rather than work are central to the identities of most of the thirty-four women she interviewed in her study. Furthermore for most, "work identity is tangential."[13] She asserts that she has "worked with many highly successful professional women who spend two years in intensive therapy and scarcely mention their work."[14]

This has not been my experience. While relationships *are* central for the women I know, work comprises a vital aspect of their lives. I believe that homemaking or a career can provide a solid sense of self for the modern woman. (However, a woman who gives her career a higher priority will be judged harshly in our culture.)

Society tends to view a woman's earnings as supplemental to her husband's income, yet women's work outside the home is in most cases economically essential. Many depend on their jobs to keep themselves and their families above the poverty line. In two-parent families black women contribute 50 percent of the income, Hispanic women 40 percent, and white women 35 percent.[15]

Society's continuing to treat women's careers outside the home as frivolous is a deep social injustice, in addition to being psychologically damaging. It's interesting how hard the old attitudes die. When others don't take us seriously, we find it difficult to take ourselves seriously.

I run into a longtime male friend I haven't seen in six months. "Are you still counseling?" he asks. What if I were to ask him, "Are you still a professor?" I don't. Yet I've been a therapist for as long as he's been teaching at the local university.

When people ask what I do, and they discover I'm a therapist, more than half of them ask if I work out of my home. They seem to have difficulty accepting the fact that I'm firmly anchored in the world of work.

And in truth women's commitment to their careers *is* often more tenuous—partly because we haven't historically been the major breadwinners and partly because we have conflicting demands on our time and energy.

Besides, we're supposed to be "fulfilled" as wives and mothers; our satisfaction isn't supposed to come from outside jobs. Yet there are many women for whom earnings aren't an economic necessity who aren't content to stay home and who do feel better about themselves when they go to work.

I've seen many unhappy, depressed, or anxious women "snap out of it" when they get a job. They enjoy the contact with other adults and they like having their time structured. Even though the pay may be poor, they like having their own money because it increases their freedom and power. A woman who earns her own paycheck is no longer shamed by needing to ask her husband for money, and she has more say than usual in how it is spent.

"I Learn Who I Am Through My Connection with You"

Although outside work may give a woman good feelings about herself, it rarely replaces her relationships as the primary source of her identity.

Sometimes when we lose a relationship, we feel we've lost our entire sense of self. To have our identity defined *by* others or *for* others is in itself demeaning. When we exist only through someone else, our sense of self is grounded externally rather than internally—a shaky proposition indeed.

And we blame ourselves when our relationships fail, not only because we feel unworthy of love but because our identity hinges on our ability to form and maintain connections to others. A failed relationship means we have failed in our job.

Am I saying men don't feel shame over the loss of a loved one? Of course they do. Men suffer greatly over failed relationships, but the very core of their *identity* is not shaken the way it would be if they had career failures or lost their sexual prowess.

Ashamed of Not Feeling Grown Up

To be an adult and still not know "what you want to be when you grow up"—or not even to feel grown up because you're lacking the self-confidence and experience to navigate your way in the world—can be perplexing and profoundly humiliating.

Most women look at marriage as ushering in adulthood, yet we also know in our hearts that we haven't achieved complete independence—not the way a man seems to. For one thing as grown women most of us either remain connected to our mother or we reconnect to her after the turmoil of adolescence.[16] Even though there may be conflict and disappointment in this relationship, it continues to be extremely important. We don't need to be ashamed of our interdependency.

Although most of us hope that marriage will finally make us feel grown up, Emily Hancock points out the irony that a woman's rite of passage to adulthood lies in securing a lifelong attachment—hardly the act of independence that we equate with being an adult.[17] Finding a man to take care of us while at the same time keeping closely connected to our mother doesn't exactly meet society's standard of maturity. Our awareness that we depend on our husbands for support—both emotional and economic—keeps us from feeling fully grown up. We forget that men are also dependent on women for physical and emotional support.

It's no surprise that we feel we've never arrived as full-fledged adults. Again we find adulthood and womanhood to be a contradiction in terms.

Can a Woman Be Both Adult and Feminine?

That mental-health workers view adult women as immature was borne out by the classic Broverman study, mentioned in Chapter Three, in which healthy women were defined by practicing clinicians as more emotional, less independent, and more childlike than either healthy men or healthy adults.[18]

These investigators highlight the double standard for women by concluding, "If women adopt the behaviors specified as desirable for adults, they risk censure for their failure to be appropriately feminine; but if they adopt the behaviors that are designated as feminine, they are necessarily deficient with respect to the general standards for adult behavior."[19] In other words *it is nearly impossible to be both a healthy adult and a healthy woman.*

Until we can expand our concept of *adult* to include women's special strengths (such as ability to relate to others and emotionality), women will continue to feel that they fall drastically short of society's standards of maturity.[20] And until we expand our definition of appropriate *feminine* behavior to include "masculine traits" such as being assertive, intelligent, or independent, women will continue to hold back their power.

Loss of Identity

Changes in our life circumstances can bring painful loss of identity and accompanying shame. A move to a new community, a new job, divorce, the birth of a child, an empty nest, old age, widowhood—all challenge our sense of who we are. Loss of an identity we count on can be more disturbing than the difficult process of building identity.[21]

Most of these identity-altering circumstances occur around a change in our role as caretakers. There are some women who are undone by the emptiness and loss of identity when their children move out. In studying severely depressed middle-aged women, psychologist Pauline Bart found that the woman who accepted the traditional role of housewife was more likely to be severely depressed when her children left home, even if she worked outside the home.[22]

In spite of the unsettling loss of identity the empty nest brings, mid-life women welcome the freedom to begin exploring themselves, even to put themselves first.

But not without feelings of shame. We aren't supposed to focus on ourselves. And we aren't supposed to feel so good when the kids finally leave home.

The habit of shame dies hard.

As women we need to recognize our competence at work, our ability to maintain our numerous relationships, and our skill at running a household. If we are to claim a more powerful identity, we must give ourselves permission to "own" our considerable strengths.

We are seeking to redefine ourselves in ways that allow us to take care of ourselves as well as others. Our challenge is to find a balance between the need to be connected to those important to us and the need to express our individuality fully in whatever sphere is appropriate. Although it will take serious work on ourselves, eventually we can be both powerful *and* related. Having to buck generations of conditioning requires courage and patience. In the next chapter we look at our most pressing if not perplexing shame-related issues as we attempt to fashion an identity for ourselves in a topsy-turvy world.

CHAPTER SIX

Shame-Related Issues for Women

It all goes back, of course, to Adam and Eve—a story which shows, among other things, that if you make a woman out of a man, you are bound to get into trouble. In the life cycle, as in the Garden of Eden, the woman has been the deviant.
—CAROL GILLIGAN

There is a complex interplay between our shame and our core issues. Our level of shame shapes how effectively we face these issues, and how well we cope influences how we feel about ourselves. In order to clarify this complicated role of shame in our lives, we will explore the following shame-related issues:

- Dependency/autonomy
- Fear of failure/fear of success
- Giving/receiving
- Boundaries/walls
- Having it all/doing it all
- The mother-daughter connection

Is Dependence So Bad?

Historically speaking, women have looked to men to take care of their emotional and economic needs. We also have depended on men for their knowledge of the outside world, due to our lack of experience (and our lack of opportunity to practice). In reality there are two worlds. When a man is in "his" world, he is strong, independent, self-sufficient.

When he comes home and closes the door behind him, he seems to lose much of his ability to take care of himself. (Not that he can't, he just hasn't been required to.) In truth it is he and the children who depend on his wife, yet she gets to wear the "dependent" label.

Passivity and dependence, although they are expected of women in our society, almost always create unconscious shame, because we are a society that worships individualism. But is *dependence* really a dirty word? I think not. Needing human contact, wanting love and approval, needing to nurture and be nurtured are all part of being human.

Can dependence be a problem? Of course. When we are dependent on others to make our decisions for us, to think for us, to reassure us constantly of our self-worth, then we have turned dependence into something excessive. If we are unable to provide these functions for ourselves most of the time, we are in psychological trouble. When we make ourselves "less than" the person we depend on, we're driven by feelings of inadequacy and shame about ourselves. *But mutual dependence between equals can be a healthy and normal part of a caring relationship, and we needn't feel ashamed of it.*

On the other hand the capacity to act autonomously is also crucial to our self-esteem.

Autonomy: A Crucial Issue for Women

Autonomy has traditionally been defined as the capacity to separate from others, to act independently. In the past, psychologists have revered autonomy, holding it as the ideal measure of emotional maturity and the highest goal of development. Women rarely "measured up." More recently some psychologists have been challenging the appropriateness of this goal, especially for women, suggesting that the ability to sustain interdependent intimate relationships is a higher mark of maturity than the achievement of independence.

I prefer to think of autonomy as the capacity to act on behalf of our own best interests, with a compassionate consideration of the effect our actions have on those around us, but without letting their needs dictate our choices. Seen in this light, autonomy is, I believe, a worthy goal.

In this sense autonomy does not mean we abandon all concern for the needs of others. There will be times when I agree to do something for someone or give up something as a "gift." But I keep my own autonomy when I act out of compassion rather than out of a need to prop up the relationship or protect the other person inappropriately or at my own expense.

To act in our own best interests is not easy for women who struggle with shame. Not trusting that we are lovable, we give up ourselves in order to preserve our ties with others. Sometimes our choices are based on our belief that other people can't handle our *no*. We see them as fragile or incompetent, unable to bear disappointment. We act against our own best interests because we don't want to "hurt" them.

One way we give up our autonomy is by allowing others' opinions to carry more weight than our own inner knowing or by not letting ourselves know what we know. This way we can want what the other person wants without our own wishes getting in the way. *Not to know is safer, but costlier.* We pay the price in alienation from our true self and in the shame that inevitably follows. If I know what I want and assert it authentically, I risk conflict—an outcome that I fear might destroy the relationship.

Alice was in the throes of a familiar dilemma: whether to please herself or please someone she cares about. "My sister Sandra's ex-fiancé is graduating fifty miles away, and Sandra really wants me to go with her. There was a time when I was somewhat close to him, but I don't feel connected now. Besides, I was hoping to attend a concert that evening featuring my favorite Mozart sonata. What should I do?" When she told Sandra she wasn't going, her sister didn't make it easy.

"I thought you cared about Richard," Sandra said.

"I'm not close to him now," Alice told her, already beginning to feel guilty.

"But he doesn't have any family. We're his only family."

Alice got herself off the hook by saying she would think about it.

At her next session she and I explored how she might respond.

"Maybe I should go," she said. "I could keep Sandra company, and Richard would feel so good knowing I cared enough to come. But I don't want to miss the concert. Maybe I can do both."

Isn't this the way we make ourselves crazy, trying to meet everyone's needs while trying not to ignore our own?

"You know, Chris," she went on, "I know what I want to do, it's just so hard to tell Sandra. I can't bear to disappoint her. Maybe I'm being selfish."

"In making this decision, it seems important to put her needs ahead of yours. Is that right?" I asked.

She sat up straight and looked me in the eye. "No. I don't want to give up the concert. And Sandra can handle being disappointed. And I can handle Sandra's being disappointed. I'm going to the concert."

For years Alice hadn't allowed herself to know what she wanted. But she was learning. This time she knew from the start what her own feelings were—even in the face of her sister's need. She simply needed to give herself permission to honor them.

Our initial moves toward autonomy need not be dramatic. We can begin by making small decisions without consulting our mate, such as purchasing something for ourselves, rearranging the living-room furniture, or—like Alice—saying no when we feel like it.

The Fear-of-Failure Trap

Fear of failure is another crucial shame-related issue. Shame-prone women typically are at once afraid to fail and afraid to succeed, although these fears may be outside our awareness. Instead we simply feel that we're not good enough. The prospect of losing the love and approval of people we admire can lend heightened significance to our failures and our successes.

Fear of failure usually occurs in two main arenas: accomplishment and interpersonal relationships. Although everyone hates to fail, research shows that girls and women tend to be more affected by this universal dread. We often approach tasks expecting to fail, and when we do well, we have trouble giving ourselves credit for our abilities. We simply aren't as well grounded in our self-worth as boys and men are, so we're more prone to shame.[1]

Fear of failing in our relationships may be our worst fear and often holds us back from getting involved. When we allow the failure of a relationship to convince us of our inherent unlovability, we open ourselves up to the wounds of shame. Loving someone who doesn't return our love is a devastating experience, leaving us feeling that *something is terribly lacking within us.* In Chapters Eleven and Twelve we will explore this subject in greater depth.

One way we protect ourselves is by not trying very hard: this way we have an excuse if we don't succeed. It's more comfortable to say "I didn't put out much effort" than to face the shame of not measuring up. Or we may persuade ourselves that we didn't want whatever it was in the first place. Or we procrastinate so that we can tell ourselves we just didn't have enough time.

Indecisiveness can also be a disguise for fear of failure—fear of making the wrong decision.

Consider Tara, thirty-five, married and mother of three, who tells me she can't decide whether to be promoted to supervisor. She doesn't want the additional responsibility a promotion demands. Lacking the confidence to perform well, she is comfortable with the familiar. "I just can't quite picture myself having authority over others. What if they won't like me now that I'm their boss? What if I make bad decisions? They might not respect me." Eventually she accepted the promotion, discovered that she could do the job and do it well, and allowed herself to enjoy her capabilities as a manager. Who knows how many others, skilled yet scared, are hiding in positions beneath their abilities because they are afraid to fail?

The Fear-of-Success Trap

Fear of failure isn't the only shame-related fear that holds women back. Some women are ruled by their (mostly unconscious) fears of success. Why would anyone be afraid of success? For one thing, we're afraid we can't maintain it. *I didn't deserve it,* we tell ourselves. *Maybe I was lucky,* or *I fooled them just this once.* A shame-prone woman rarely lets herself know that the reason she succeeded was that she actually deserved it. It's not uncommon for talented and successful women to be plagued with fears of being exposed as impostors. Although men have similar fears, my guess is that women are more prone to them because they don't feel as entitled as men do to positions of influence or status.

There are other, perhaps more central, reasons women avoid success. Women, because of their place in society, face conflicts few men ever have to contend with. Along with our deep need to be in relationship, we also have a strong desire for the sense of accomplishment that productive work can bring us. Yet there are times and situations when these two needs are in direct opposition, *when we fear that success will threaten our relationships.*

Psychologist Matina Horner concluded that a high proportion of women were motivated to avoid success because of fears about the consequences of their achievement, especially in competitive situations. She found that women who inhibit their tendencies to be successful do so because they believe they will lose friends or reduce their eligibility as a date or marriage partner, and will be left isolated, lonely, or unhappy as a result of their success. Loss of femininity is another powerful deterrent to being competitive, successful achievers, says Horner. These fears are based on deeply ingrained notions acquired early in life about what is appropriate sex-role behavior for females. Attitudes of the men important to us regarding what's appropriate for women can exert a powerful influence on whether we avoid or seek success, Horner maintains.[2]

When Emily, age thirty-one, came to see me, she was in the throes of an almost paralyzing conflict. She was a graduate student, halfway toward earning her Ph.D. Recently remarried, she was undertaking one of life's greatest challenges: blending together two families. Her new husband had young children who lived with them. Emily had a child of her own to add to the ménage. With her energies split between family and career, she wondered whether she should continue with her Ph.D. We also had spent a good deal of time working on her fear of failing, especially her fear of flunking her orals. "I'm terrified," Emily said. "I just know I'll freeze up and not be able to talk at all."

One day Emily sank down on my couch and looked at me for a long moment. "I've decided to give up my degree," she said finally.

I could tell she was struggling to stay composed. I sat quietly, waiting to hear how she had arrived at this decision.

"Last night my husband told me something that kind of changes things, I guess. We had a long talk about my getting my Ph.D. and he told me . . . he told me that he felt threatened to have a wife with a higher degree than him. We're both in the same field, you know."

When I asked how this was for her, she said, "It's really not that important anyway. It isn't something I've longed to have. I'll be fine without it. I've got my master's. That'll be enough."

I could see that Emily was rapidly sinking into denial of her feelings of loss and anger. That she had given up a part of herself as a way of dealing with her fear of failure *and* her relationship conflict didn't surprise me—although it saddened me. It echoed the solutions chosen by many women today.

Afraid to Fail Yet Afraid to Succeed

Emily's story is complicated by many factors. She provides a good example of the crippling effects of both fear of failure and fear of success in women. First of all, that she was influenced by her fear of failure cannot be disputed. She was a victim of her own inaccurate self-appraisal: She didn't think she had the ability to pass the oral exams.

Yet it wasn't simply fear of failure that led Emily to give up her doctoral studies. It was her *fear of success* that struck the fatal blow to her ambitions. For one thing, Emily's decision reflects that of many women who choose not to take on a demanding educational challenge or career because it threatens to take away time and energy from their strong commitment to rearing children. Yet Emily's inability to claim her powers stemmed in larger part from her need to preserve her relationship, which she felt was threatened by her accomplishment.

Emily chose to put her husband's needs ahead of her own, a predictable choice, given her years of training by her parents and society. Perhaps if she had been 100 percent confident of her ability to succeed, she might have been willing to chance destabilizing her relationship. But her fear of failure tipped the scales.

Ashamed of Having Too Much

There are more subtle aspects of the fear-of-success syndrome that we must not ignore. Our deep-seated reluctance to surpass family members is an important concern that keeps us from expressing and enjoying our full powers.[3]

Besides taking care of her husband, Emily also took care of her *own* discomfort. She had learned long ago that when she earned something special, she had to be careful that her younger sister wasn't hurt. She had come to believe early on that her own gain was someone else's loss. So when her husband said he felt threatened by her degree, it fit right into her belief that her success could damage another.

I see many variations on this pattern.

Gail, a forty-year-old dynamo, was raised in a family where parental attention and approval were scarce commodities. She and her three sisters competed for the meager scraps that were doled out, but because Gail was a gifted singer, she garnered far more than her share of the "goodies." Although she went on to be an accomplished performer, she was unable to enjoy her success.

"After every performance, when I read the reviews and know that I've done a good job, I get depressed. I used to think it was just the normal letdown after all that work and excitement. But now I'm not sure."

Why would Gail want to feel bad about her success?

It turned out Gail was not only uncomfortable but actually *ashamed* of her accomplishments. In fact she was careful not to talk much about her work when she was around her mother and sisters.

"I feel like my success is at their expense. I must be a greedy person to have hogged all that limelight. And when I look at my sisters' lives, I'm ashamed to have so much more." She started crying.

"What did you do that was so wrong?" I asked.

"I stood out. I got something for me. I tried so hard to blend in, but I got better grades; even now I've done better. *I have too much.* I'm forty, have my own home, a successful career, a husband. That's a lot compared to my sisters."

When we grow up in a family where love is limited or where

nurturing is in short supply, it's like sitting down to the table where there isn't enough food to go around. If we are one of the "lucky" ones who got more (for whatever reasons, ranging from birth order to gender, pleasing personality, disabilities, illness, or life circumstances of the parents), we often suffer from guilt and shame. Haunted by fear of others' envy, we hold ourselves back from having success or pleasure in our lives. We're ashamed of our disloyalty in abandoning those we leave behind in order to have a life of our own.

"Givers Shouldn't Be Takers"

Striking a balance between giving and getting is difficult for all women, but especially shame-prone women. We women have little trouble giving. We send flowers and cards; we give of our time to help friends and co-workers; we praise others for their accomplishments. When someone needs a good listener, we're ready to lend an ear. But when we need help from others, many of us become very uncomfortable. Why is it so hard to switch roles?

First, we learned as little girls that it was important to please others if we wanted to keep our ties to them. Women ridden with pathological shame don't trust that they can keep their closest relationships without giving up themselves.

Second, we aren't accustomed to acknowledging our own needs. When we focus exclusively on the needs of others, we may have trouble even *knowing* what we need. When others sense a need in us and try to fill it, we tend either to deny it or to feel ashamed of it because we believe we're not supposed to have needs (we're supposed to take care of others' needs).

And if we begin to allow ourselves to feel our need, we risk feeling overwhelmed. Better not to open that Pandora's box of insatiable need deep inside us. *Close the lid quickly and focus on someone else's need,* we tell ourselves.

Sally, a wife, mother and full-time nurse, had given away so much of herself, there wasn't enough left for her to know who she was. For years she "did for" everyone—her extended family, her friends, her community.

"I'll drop whatever I'm doing if I get a call from my sixteen-year-old niece that she needs a ride home from school. If a friend gives a party, I bust my buns to help her with the food and the cleanup. They know they can count on me, 'good old Sal.' Well, old Sal is gonna be making some changes by and by."

Like Sally many of us are starting to question our role as caretakers. Not that we would ever make relating successfully to others a low priority. But we need to draw a line between taking care of others' needs in healthy ways and giving compulsively. Although we value our ability to care for others, we must challenge time-worn notions that women should always put their own needs last. We need to realize that giving has for too long meant giving up ourselves in order to keep others happy.

We are also learning that excessive caretaking can be controlling. When we manage other people's lives, we prevent them from experiencing the consequences of their actions. We're discovering that being responsible for others' happiness is not only an impossible job, it does not serve them.

Realizations like the above thrust us into a dilemma: How do we balance our newfound permission to take care of ourselves with our familiar and valued need to give to those we love? Where are our boundaries?

Walls Are Not Boundaries, Boundaries Are Not Walls

"Last week I slept with a guy I don't know very well," Phyllis said. "I feel so yucky that I did that. In fact I feel sick to my stomach just thinking about it. And he turned out to be such a jerk. I had no boundaries with him. And now when I run into him, I act like I don't recognize him."

The major function of boundaries is to establish limits of contact, thus protecting us from the intrusion of someone who threatens us. Family therapists Merle Fossom and Marilyn Mason use a wonderful zipper metaphor to describe how such boundaries can work. People with unclear boundaries have their zippers on the outside, allowing people "to unzip them at any time, taking them over. . . . The boundary intrusions take many forms, from subtle and not-so-subtle mindreading to parent-child incest."[4]

On the other hand, those of us with clear boundaries have our zippers inside, allowing us to regulate our own barriers, preserving our self-respect and integrity. Fossum and Mason work in therapy to shift the zipper from the outside to the inside. Inside zippers help us to draw a line that says, *This is where I take a stand. You may go no farther*, or *That's as far as I go. I have a limit to what I will give or do for you.*

When we can't zip up, walk away, or say no, we feel victimized and ashamed. We don't have a clear sense of what is safe and what is dangerous. We build walls to protect ourselves from being hurt or shamed. While they serve to keep people out, walls can also lock us in when we automatically hide behind them to stay safe. Because we built them to defend ourselves against childhood intrusions, they often have little to do with our present situation and can even keep us from knowing what our present boundaries are.

Boundaries differ from walls in that they are permeable and flexible.[5] A boundary is based on a process of checking in with ourselves from moment to moment about how much and what kind of contact we want. A wall, on the other hand, is rigidly in place and is rarely responsive to our inner or outer environment. A wall prevents contact, and without contact there can be little growth.

Boundaries allow for the possibility of empathy, which is a wonderful thing. But women's highly developed capacity for empathy (being able to feel the feelings of others) can get us in trouble—we tend to feel others' feelings and needs as if they were our own and may even be confused as to who's feeling what. For instance, when someone close to us is sad or depressed, it's often hard to maintain our own good mood rather than sinking into theirs. And because we feel others' disappointment so keenly, it may be hard for us to say no when we need to.

A woman with shame-related issues has even more trouble maintaining healthy boundaries. She may have walls instead—or she may have boundaries that are too weak. Either extreme signals that her boundaries were violated when she was a child, through enmeshment, neglect, or intrusion. Having had little or no say in the kind or amount of contact adults made with her, she never learned she had a right to set her own boundaries. She may have no idea what her feelings, needs, and wants are, and this confusion makes her an easy target for takeover or intrusion. She may even *invite* people in against her own best interests. And most likely she is afraid that the act of setting boundaries and limits will threaten her connection to those most important to her.

Phyllis went beyond her boundaries in going to bed with someone she didn't feel comfortable with, experiencing deep shame about having "no boundaries." And now when she runs into this man, she puts up a wall to protect herself. But she is learning. In the same session she tells me, "Even though my boyfriend is pressuring me to let him move in, I told him I'm not ready and I don't want to be rushed. It was hard, because I know things would be easier for *him* if I did what he wanted. I have a wall up, I guess."

No, this time she has a boundary.

It took courage for Phyllis not to accede to her boyfriend's demand. "I was afraid he might walk out the door and I'd never see him again." Fortunately she had enough inner strength to take that risk. And he didn't leave.

Although she regrets going beyond her sexual limits, she has gained valuable experience in setting boundaries. *Only by going beyond our boundaries do we learn what is comfortable and uncomfortable, what works and what doesn't.* We must ask ourselves, *How will I feel later if I tell this person something intimate about myself? If I lend my favorite sweater? If I give in to his demand to do things his way?* Experience is still the best teacher.

When Phyllis felt a stronger sense of self, her ability to honor her own boundaries improved, and so did her self-esteem. Strengthening our boundaries affirms that we are both capable and worth taking care of.

Do We Have It All, or Are We Doing It All?

Judy, a thirty-three-year-old homemaker, was referred to me by her doctor because she was having chest and neck pains. Having given up her career as a legal secretary when she became a mother three years ago, she was finding her life as a full-time homemaker increasingly boring and lonely. She wanted to get out of the house, have a paycheck of her own, enjoy the social stimulation of other adults. "I can only go so long conversing with a three-year-old before I start to feel my brain shrinking," she said. "Besides, society doesn't put much value on being a wife and mother. When I go back to work, I'll feel better about myself." Having a paycheck buys more than just groceries.

Whether forced by economic circumstances, governed by fears

of being "just a housewife," or motivated by desires to fulfill herself in a challenging job in the "real world," a woman who works outside the home only adds to her already taxing caretaking duties. When Judy returned to her job, she found she had unwittingly traded in free time and loneliness for added hassles and an increased workload. The dirty dishes and hungry family members await her when she returns home as she marshals her flagging energies for her second job. In trying to do it all, she suffers deep pangs of inadequacy because she can't do it all perfectly.

"At home I'm overworked and taken for granted, and at work I'm underpaid and I still end up taking care of everybody," Judy complains. "And something always seems to get neglected—the kids, my marriage, the house and yard, my work, or of course myself. I'm juggling too many balls. I'm constantly afraid I'll drop one."

The ball we most fear dropping is labeled Motherhood. "Because I'm so darn committed to being there for my kids," Judy says, "I feel really inadequate because I'm not living up to my idea of what it is to be a good mother. I'm always looking for signs that my kids might be having problems, and when they do, I blame myself for failing them." Failure as a mother is perhaps our deepest source of pain and guilty shame.

According to sociologist Arlie Hoschchild, in her aptly titled book *The Second Shift*, the women's revolution has stalled because women's lives have changed, yet men's attitudes have not kept pace either at the office or at home. Most of the women I know report that their husbands are unlikely to share fully the tasks at home, and many complain bitterly about the inequity of their situation. "I come home from my job and begin my second job. He comes home and is basically done," says one woman. "Husbands empty the garbage and they think they're sharing the load," says another. Hoschchild found that only 20 percent of husbands of working wives help at home. She figures that in any given year the typical working woman with a family puts in a full month more of work than her husband does. This uneven balance of power confirms our deep-seated belief that we are less worthy than men. Even in couples committed to sharing the load, the woman still ends up doing a major portion of the work.

"I oversee the running of the household and the care of the children," Diana says. "And on weekends he's free to come and

SHAME-RELATED ISSUES FOR WOMEN   III

go while I stay with the kids or ask him to 'baby-sit' while I go out. It makes me feel like a second-class citizen. I'm angry. Besides, I envy his freedom. I wish I had a wife."

Diana tries to stuff her anger and wonders why she yells at the children so much and is not interested in sex. Wonderwoman couldn't hold a candle to her. I don't know of any woman who doesn't feel there is something wrong with her when she finds she can't do it all.

I don't have a ready solution to the dilemma of being overextended, but one obvious way to ease the difficulty would be to ask for help. So why don't we? We don't want to risk his anger, for one thing. For another, the belief that we are supposed to be caretakers is so deeply ingrained that we try to handle everything ourselves, no matter how overextended we are. And no matter how easily some of us could afford to hire outside help, this belief keeps us from using part of our paycheck to pay for help with cleaning, cooking, and other tasks that don't require our special emotional skills. Does a woman stay overburdened because she and her husband feel (probably unconsciously) that she should have to suffer for her "selfishness" in making a career for herself? As one husband put it when his wife asked for help, "It wasn't *my* idea for you to go to work."

Another factor is operating here: Having him take on household chores demeans him in our eyes. Sensing that women's work is more lowly than men's, we feel confused and guilty watching him bend over the sink to scrape garbage off the dishes. And it's hard to shake off the deeply held belief that his time is more valuable than ours; so instead of asking him to stop for stamps, we add it to our ever-growing, never-completed "to-do" list.

It also helps to let go of trying to be perfect. Ask yourself, *Does my family really need me to fix this complicated recipe tonight when I'm tired and short on time? Will missing the kids' Saturday soccer game for once and taking time for myself really hurt anybody?*

Even though our ability to take care of others is central to our self-concept, we need to trust that we *are* caring—and recognize that having needs of our own and putting them first from time to time is not selfish.

Shame and Our Mothers

Of the many shame-related issues for women, one of the most central is our relationships with our mothers. Of course our relationships with our fathers can also be fraught with shame. We look to them for many things, including validation of us as females. And a little girl looks to her father to provide excitement—a change of pace from the more routine contact she has with Mother. He acknowledges her growing competence, and his opinion matters a great deal to her. If Dad is too distant, too critical, or too enmeshed, a girl comes to believe that something is wrong with her.

While a woman's relationship with her mother has many of these same pitfalls, there are added complications that arise out of her identification with Mother as a female and her often closer attachment to Mother—an attachment that gives rise to conflicts and confusion around separating and being her own person.

Because we usually observe Mother being treated as "less than" Father, we find ourselves identifying with a female who is disempowered both at home and in the "real" world.

In spite of—or is it because of?—their importance to us, we encounter a wide range of problems with our mothers. And we usually end up blaming ourselves as much as we blame them for the distressing aspects of our relationship.

Is it healthy to want to grow closer to our mothers? Shouldn't we strive for independence? After all, we are adults now. There is a bias among many therapists who consider any degree of attachment to Mother to be unhealthy, reflecting the general attitude that women are too dependent or passive.[6] Is it too much to suggest that men (still smarting on some level from their loss of Mommy at age three) resent women's ability to remain attached to Mother and draw nurturance from the relationship when such a relationship for the men is taboo? Some women believe that separation from Mother signifies the end of childhood and the proof of maturity, and consequently they feel defective when they haven't become completely independent.

I personally feel that those who denigrate our need for this important relationship are mistaken. A balance between connection and autonomy seems to me the most appropriate goal, for connection with others helps us grow, and the ability to connect deeply with others *is* a mark of a mature person.

Can we be too attached to our mothers? Of course. Sometimes the connection can be too intense or the boundaries between mothers and daughters too muddy, making it impossible for us to claim our own power and identity. If our mothers discourage our attempts to separate, we feel shame and guilt. We worry that Mother will feel abandoned.

Many mothers can be invasive, deeply enmeshing themselves in their daughters' lives. We find a classic example of such a mother-daughter relationship in *The Glass Menagerie* by Tennessee Williams. Amanda, an intensely lonely woman, manipulates her son into bringing home to dinner a young man who might be a prospective suitor for her daughter, Laura, who is crippled as much by her debilitating shame as by her physical deformity. Amanda rides right over Laura's feelings of panic and pushes ahead with the plans. It becomes clear that the "gentleman caller" is invited more for Amanda than for Laura. And when Laura fails to win him, her mother's scorn is scalding.

It's important to understand that Amanda's attack on Laura comes from her own deep well of shame. Her overinvolvement with Laura serves as a distraction from the painful awareness of her own emotionally crippled self. Just as Laura's courtship becomes her mother's, so does Laura's rejection become Amanda's. Shaming Laura serves to cover up her own unbearable humiliation.

Risking a Better Life

The fear of having more than Mother may also keep us from leading successful and satisfying lives. We hold ourselves back in order not to surpass (and thereby hurt) Mother.

First of all, some of us simply feel too much guilt at the prospect of going beyond our mothers. We're afraid that implicit in our success (in career or relationships) is criticism of the poor choices Mother made for herself. We are tacitly saying, "I'm doing it differently. Your way wasn't so good."

We also fear her envy. So, to protect Mother—and to preserve our connection to her—we hold ourselves back from having full and happy lives.

The closest way to connect with people is to be like them. It's the loyal thing to do. If Mother had a hard life, I can still be like her if I don't have more than she does—or at least not much more. If I don't allow myself success in *all* areas of my life, I can still keep the bond by having some suffering to share with her.

Leslie, a woman in her fifties who seemingly had it all, managed always to have something troubling her. In her attempts to keep herself from having too much, she was like an accountant with a balance sheet. If her relationship was at a point of closeness and joy, she would worry that she was on the brink of failure in her work. If work and her relationship were going well, she would dwell on the fact that her children hadn't turned out as well as other people's. She could never let her credit balance get too high. Psychiatrist Arthur Modell refers to this process as an "unconscious bookkeeping system."[7] Having something to feel ashamed of allowed her to keep a tie with her mother, who had much less than Leslie.

While this conflict is by no means reserved for women, the pattern of women's lives today differs—often dramatically—from their mothers' in ways men's lives don't differ from their fathers'. Often we see Mother as disempowered and unfulfilled, so when we surpass her (as today's woman often does), we grapple with guilt and shame.

As women we have much more freedom today to enter the professional world, to travel independently, to seek therapy—in short to have more than our mothers. We are more assertive than our mothers, think more for ourselves, and think more *of* ourselves. We are closer than our mothers ever were to having it all, and we needn't feel ashamed for having more.

Resolving Our Anger at Mom

Although a thorough exploration of anger at our mothers goes beyond the scope of this book, anger can be a shame-related issue. Our anger covers our shame at seeing Mother's lack of power and the disrespect she receives from Father and from the world. We are angry about her unhealthy ways of keeping us involved with her, ways that arouse feelings of guilt and shame for not paying enough attention to her, for not giving enough.

We feel shame for being angry at someone who seems so powerless, and shame for the inevitable mixed feelings of being both an adult needing to be separate and a little girl longing for protection, understanding, and love. We are angry at her for reminding us of our need and our inadequacy.

When we can get past the anger to the longing, the hurt, and the shame, healing of the relationship becomes possible.

Although I believe that we must honor our anger and hurt, I think in most cases we can gain enough empathy for our mothers and what they are dealing with in their lives to create a relationship that is mutually caring and empowering. Compassion often comes with understanding the kind of mothering they had.

Eventually we grow to appreciate our mothers' strengths. Although I saw my mother as very nurturing of others, I'd also seen her as weak, under the thumb of my father. I felt her shame, and that made me angry at her, although I didn't dare express it. It wasn't until I was well into adulthood that I appreciated her many strengths. I was able to see how she took care of herself through deep and satisfying friendships that she maintained throughout her lifetime. I grew to appreciate her contribution to her community in creating a mental-health volunteer organization. I recognized that her abiding interest in psychology influenced me to become a therapist. I saw her enormous courage in attending Al-Anon meetings in the days when a twelve-step program sounded more like a new dance than a self-help group.

As we struggle to deal with the myriad shame-related issues confronting us today, we need to be gentle with ourselves. These are knotty problems, and there is no easy way to untie them. Shame-prone women, who are especially hard on themselves, have an inner critic who shames and undermines them when they fail to measure up to stringent internal and external standards. In the next chapter we look at how this self-shamer operates and ways we can deal effectively with it.

CHAPTER SEVEN

Standing Up
to the Inner Shamer

Jane, top in sales for her office, awakens to the alarm clock and gives herself a few extra minutes in bed before getting ready for work. If we were to tune in to the conversation going on in her head, we might hear something like this:

Get up. You're so lazy to lie here in bed! Why can't you be like other people who just leap up ready to greet the day? What's wrong with you?

But I'm tired. I'll just lie here a few more minutes.

No! You should be up and about. Look how much you could get done if you got right up instead of lying here. Besides, you'll be late. And you'd better jog this morning. You're getting entirely too fat. Who would look at you twice?

Later, while jogging, instead of praising herself for having increased her distance to three miles, Jane tells herself, *How come you had to walk twenty yards at the end?* As she drives to work, the battle continues to rage inside her: *Slow down. You don't want another ticket. How could you have gotten two speeding tickets in less than two years?* With one hand she opens her purse, whisks out her makeup, and gives a quick glance in the rearview mirror. *You look terrible. My God, is that a zit? Yuck. You should stop eating so much junk food. You're such a pig. No wonder you're still single. Who would want you?*

Stopping at the red light, she wonders if the man in the next car saw her driving and putting on mascara. *Bet he thinks you're vain. And a reckless driver, to boot. You know, you're really stupid to drive and put on makeup at the same time.* Then her thoughts turn to work. *You'll never get everything done today. And that report. . . . They said it was good, but you were just lucky. You won't be able to fool them again.* Then she remembers she left her checkbook sitting on the kitchen table. *You dummy. How could you do a stupid thing like that?*

Her mind wanders to her mother. *You really should call her. You've been neglecting her lately.* She sighs deeply. *How can you be so self-centered?*

Our relationship with ourselves is the most important relationship we'll ever have. Would we ever talk to our best friend in the brutal way we talk to ourselves? Our Inner Shamer rarely gives us respite from its yammering. If we were to record all the times we speak harshly to ourselves in the course of an ordinary day, we would be shocked.

This ruthless inner critic, the most insidious and effective way we have of shaming ourselves, is a major cause of psychological suffering. Put in place years ago, it continues the shaming that began in our childhood. As we shall see later, the Inner Shamer takes on many roles, including those of Protector, Faultfinder, Punisher, Motivator, and Underminer. Unrelenting in its attack on our self-esteem, it confirms the fact that there is something inherently wrong with us—that we are worthless and disgusting. It demands perfection. It persecutes us mercilessly, making us our own worst enemy.

The cost of this critical inner voice is high. It affects all aspects of our existence. It keeps us from being fully ourselves and undermines our relationships. *In effect it runs us.*

Why Women Are Experts at Self-shaming

Women in general have a more active inner critic because we carry a greater burden of shame. Not only do we rebuke ourselves for not performing well or accomplishing enough (an arena crucial to a man's self-concept), we also berate ourselves for failing in our relationships (an arena more central to a woman's self-esteem). Because relationships are our main concern, we are never at peace. When we fail, we tell ourselves that we are unlovable. When we don't live up to the role of the perfect caretaker, we are quick to scold ourselves for being thoughtless or, worse, selfish. Yet when we give too much, we castigate ourselves for "having failed to take care of ourselves," for being "codependent." Our self-reproaches get us coming and going.

We continually find occasions to scold ourselves for not being more assertive, for not speaking up for ourselves—abilities underdeveloped in women in our culture. But when we do stand up for ourselves, we reprimand ourselves for being bitchy. We're trapped in shame either way.

In addition our second-class status in a society that worships youth and beauty creates fertile ground for the germination of shame over our physical imperfections.

How Self-Shaming Works

Our Inner Shamer has its own distinct language, relying heavily on *should, never,* and *don't.* Cracking a whip over us, it never lets up on its accusations and demands.

One way it brutalizes us is by comparing us to everyone else. *Why can't you be more like so and so? You'll never be as good a mother and wife as she is. She's more organized, has a better job, is prettier, neater, smarter, nicer.* This is a game we have no hope of winning, because our Inner Shamer doesn't even care whether its nasty comparisons are true. It simply assumes everyone else is better.

It also makes contradictory demands. Jane's Critic, while carping at her for still being single, also warns her not to get too involved because she might get hurt.

With rigid standards this self-shamer operates on the assumption that if we are not perfect, we must be fatally flawed. The Inner Shamer doesn't like gray areas; it needs black and white to sustain itself. Nothing less than absolute perfection counts. One flaw erases all the good in us—as if adding a little black paint to a gallon of white paint could turn it completely black.[1]

Another person doesn't even have to be present for us to feel exposed and shamed. Why? Because our Inner Shamer serves as stand-in, shaming us in situations that remind us of similar painful experiences stored in our memory bank.

An example from my own life: I was parallel-parking in a tight space one day and got stuck, my car jammed between the curb and the car in front. I was annoyed with myself, but when I noticed a man sitting on a nearby stoop watching me, my cheeks flushed, and I wanted to fall into a hole and disappear. I was certain the onlooker was silently laughing at my ineptness as I confirmed his already low opinion of women drivers. In a minute I extricated myself from my parking bind and moved on to a larger parking space. But I hadn't extricated myself from my shame bind, as I was to find out later.

A month passed before I parallel-parked again. As I successfully and skillfully completed the maneuver, I felt the heat rising in my cheeks, even though there was no one watching me this time. I no longer needed a critical observer to trigger shame; I had become my own shaming critic. No matter how well I parallel-parked, embarrassment was automatic.

A Familiar Voice

If we listen carefully, we can usually recognize the voice that shames us. Most often it belongs to our parents, sometimes a sibling or grandparent. Or it comes from our culture.

I asked Jane, "Who does your critical voice sound like?"

It didn't take her long to answer, "Why, the early-morning voice is my father's—he always harassed me about sleeping late. I can hear him now. 'Get up. Don't be so lazy.' But it's my mother's voice nagging me about eating junk food." She thought for a moment. "And I can hear that authoritative male voice behind the Clearasil commercial taunting me about my acne."

This merciless self-shamer takes up residence in our minds when we swallow our parents' (and later society's) attitudes and values, making them our own. Taught to believe in the greater wisdom of our parents, we take on whatever they pronounce as the truth. When they tell us we're stupid, bad, ugly, selfish, careless, or lazy, we believe it. When we fail to measure up to our parents' expectations, we become deeply ashamed of who we are.

Are we aware of our shame and self-hate? Usually not, according to the late eminent psychoanalyst Karen Horney.[2] She maintains that we usually experience self-contempt only when we are in distress. When the distress subsides, so do the feelings of self-hate. Because these feelings are quickly forgotten, we remain aware only of being depressed, irritable, and momentarily down on ourselves and miss the full impact of our self-loathing.[3]

Doing to Ourselves What Was Done to Us

How do we learn to talk to ourselves in such a shaming way? We learn to treat ourselves the way our parents treated us. Whether they shamed us blatantly or subtly, their criticism turns into our criticism of ourselves. We become experts at finding fault and are unforgiving when we make mistakes.

I remember frequently being in the middle of an animated conversation with my dad, only to have him interrupt me to correct my grammar. As a college professor he was a stickler for perfect English. Not only was I frustrated by his disrupting my conversation, I was ashamed to be caught speaking incorrectly. And I was humiliated that my father seemed to care more about proper form than he did about me.

In spite of vowing I would never do that to *my* children, I am chagrined (even ashamed!) to catch myself doing the same thing. Because deep down, embedded in my belief system, is the message *Daddy's right, I mustn't allow grammatical errors to stand uncorrected.*

My children are not the only victims of my "shamer." I never let my own grammatical mistakes slip by without a moment of anxiety. *Did anyone catch that? Better correct it fast.*

Labeling children teaches them to call themselves names. When a two-year-old asks her parent, "What's that?" her parent tells her, "That's a chair." So when this same all-knowing parent says, "You're clumsy" or "You're a bad girl," the child accepts that as *the truth.* To label a child is to instill in her a belief that she *is* what she is labeled. We are stuck with these inaccurate perceptions for the rest of our lives.

While labeling constricts and limits people, it also may foster intense competition between siblings: "She's our little troublemaker," or "She's the quiet one in the family."

Comparing, a more subtle form of shaming, goes hand in hand

with labeling of children: "Why can't you be more helpful like your sister?"

Margo, the woman in Chapter One whose husband left her for her best friend, had been told repeatedly that she was the "pretty one" and her sister, Nancy, was the "smart one." Margo concluded that she was stupid. "Though I did well in college, I didn't apply to graduate school because I wasn't the 'smart one' in the family." There is little doubt that this contributed to her panic about surviving on her own after her husband left. Her message to herself was *Why can't I be like Nancy? I'm stupid, and stupid people can't make it by themselves.*

On the other hand her sister, Nancy, recently confessed to Margo how ashamed she had felt when Margo occasionally would beat her on a test, because their father loved to tease and ridicule her. Today when she fails to do her best, her father's voice taunts her: *Ha, ha. Gotcha—I knew you couldn't keep it up.*

Shame-based women chronically compare themselves to other people and rarely measure up. Occasionally the comparison will be favorable and for the moment shore up their foundering ego, but such relief is soon replaced by more familiar feelings of defectiveness.

Preserving the Ties That Bind

Sometimes when we blame and attack ourselves, we do so for a kind of self-protection, to preserve our ties to those who are important to us. When we were young, we depended on our parents for our survival, so their criticism of us seemed life-threatening. We decided (unconsciously) that the best way to survive would be to join in their attack on us. When we join them in their criticisms, warnings, and worries, we are rewarded by a sense of belonging and closeness.

Understanding this process is crucial to understanding why shame becomes embedded in our concept of who we are. *It's not them, it's me. I'm just no good,* we unconsciously decide, keeping our parents on the pedestal we deem necessary to our survival.

Also at work here is the sense (again at an unconscious level) that our parents need us to see them as perfect. We shore them up when we absorb the shame.

As adults we call on our Inner Shamer to keep us connected not only to our parents but also to others whose love or approval we depend on. The Inner Shamer keeps unacceptable wants and feelings at bay by invalidating them. Needing to keep our parents' love and approval, we end up disowning these vital aspects of ourselves. When we have needs—to be held, comforted, listened to, admired, loved—we join what Roquelle Lerner calls the "committee in our head,"[4] which tells us we're childish, weak, and needy. We shame ourselves with *Don't be a crybaby.* Or, *What have you got to cry about?* If we get angry, we may accuse ourselves of being cruel or out of control. When we are aware of wanting something, we tell ourselves, *You're asking for too much,* or, worse, *You have no right to ask in the first place.*

The Inner Shamer colludes with our frightened little girl inside to keep us from being fully and authentically ourselves.

Finding Fault with Ourselves

We become our own worst enemy. The degrading eye of the Inner Shamer spares nothing as our body, our intelligence, and our character become easy targets.

If we leave our husband to cope with the kids while we go out to dinner with friends, we berate ourselves with *You're being selfish.* Yet we also come down on ourselves for being too giving: *How come you didn't say no when she asked to borrow your new jacket? Don't be weak. Stand up for yourself.*

We're painfully aware of every flaw in our personal appearance. We scold ourselves for being too fat, too ugly, having too many zits, and in later years for being too gray, too wrinkled, too flabby.

We accuse ourselves of being a fraud. Because we have had to keep most of ourself hidden, we present a facade to the world, appearing aloof, confident, unflappable, while inside we may be quaking. Or we sense that our interest in people isn't quite as genuine as we put on, that our nice act is phony.

In addition to our personal flaws and weaknesses, our motives are fair game to the critic I call the Faultfinder. *(Maybe I didn't really want to ease Karen's burden by picking up her kids at day care. Maybe I just wanted her to like me.* Or, *That time I was frank with Kay about her bad*

*breath, did I really have her best interests at heart, or was I just trying to be
superior?)*

Horney says, "Our motivations rarely are pure gold; they are
usually alloyed with one of several metals less noble than what is
visible."[5] Shame-bound women have difficulty accepting any motives that are not pure gold because they think, *If it's not pure gold,
it must be totally contaminated.*

We are full of self-recrimination when we make mistakes.
What's so bad about making a mistake? "I learned that mistakes
are bad," Jane says, "because my father never admitted he made
a mistake—although he made plenty. Instead he always found
someone to blame. And Mother was terribly careful to avoid
making mistakes. It's like I'm a bad person for making a mistake."

Our Faultfinder has an unfailing memory for our mistakes and
failures. Days, months, or even years later we may "reshame"
ourselves, as we obsess over something we said or did that we
deeply regretted.

Our Faultfinder has no sense of fairness. It accuses us of being
negligent when circumstances occur that we couldn't have pre-
vented. A woman whose sister committed suicide has never for-
given herself for not being home the night her sister called for
help. "I should have been home. *I should have known.*"

Criticizing ourselves before anyone else has a chance prepares
us psychologically so that we won't be caught off guard by criticism from others.

People raised in troubled families almost always experience
deep, often unconscious anger—an anger that feels dangerous.
To avoid hurting or angering people important to us, we either
deny or try to divert our anger, to prevent it from reaching others.
When we turn anger inward, converting it into self-criticism, we
offend only ourselves.

We need to realize that having flaws, acting from impure motives, or making mistakes does not confirm our worthlessness. Not
being perfect doesn't mean we are bad and wrong. It just means
we're human.

The Shamer as Taskmaster

When our Inner Shamer goads us, it spurs us on to do better. Jane's gets her going and keeps her from being late to work and getting fired. But the Taskmaster can be harsh in its prodding. To whip us into shape, it calls us cruel names, such as "Lazy" and "Stupid."

Now, is it really necessary to motivate ourselves in such a derogatory fashion? Absolutely not. But shame-prone women don't know that. They think they need to abuse themselves to get anything accomplished. *They treat themselves the way they were treated.*

Believing there is only one right way to do things, only one correct solution to a situation, we castigate ourselves when we don't meet these impossible standards.

Why Punishment Feels Good

When we have done something wrong, verbally beating ourselves up actually makes us feel better. A form of atonement for our misdeeds, it eases our guilt and shame and brings us back into our internal parent's good graces. We also gain confidence through aligning ourselves with the strong punishing parent inside us.

As I've said before, sometimes we need to punish ourselves for having more than others or to pay our dues for being a separate person in our own right. Many successful women hold on to being defective partly because they feel guilty, believing their success was at someone else's expense. I may say to myself, *What I have takes away from my mother.* But I can assuage this guilt by shaming myself: *Look how defective you are. You're not really any better than anyone else. In fact you're worse.*

Enough? It's pretty sickening to listen to, yet listen we do, as we allow the Inner Shamer's trickery to cheat us out of living life to the fullest.

How the Inner Shamer Undermines Our Self-confidence

Caught in the Underminer's vicious grip, we continually belittle and compare ourselves to others, falling drastically short. The Underminer keeps us from taking ourselves seriously, as it discounts what we feel, what we want, or what we know about ourselves: *Come on, don't be so sensitive,* or, *It's selfish to ask for that.* It may keep us from trusting in our abilities as it invalidates us at every turn: *You'll never pass that exam.* Or it belittles our capacity to think for ourselves: *Who do you think you are? You think you're such an expert on relationships, child raising, politics.*

The wife and mother who skillfully balances demands of job and home discredits herself by thinking, *I should be doing more,* or, *This should be easy. Why do I have to make things so hard?* Another woman, praised for her success at leading a difficult meeting, may say, "But I ran overtime and I talked too fast."

We often project our voices of self-contempt onto others "out there," rather than recognizing them as stemming from our own shaming feelings about ourselves. We may be convinced that others really don't care for us, that their friendliness is suspect. Perhaps they want something from us or are just being nice when they include us in their plans. We're sure they're silently criticizing us.

Deep down we know that we haven't fooled people with our pleasing facade and believe our every action betrays our unworthiness. For instance not offering to be on the cleanup committee because we are eager to get home can cause us anxiety over being seen as selfish.

At a deeper level we can't believe anyone would love us, so we miss or sabotage opportunities to be intimate with others. If we can't love ourselves, how can we expect someone else to love us?

The Inner Shamer as Pleasure Stealer

The self-shaming process robs us of joy. It warns us not to get too excited. When we start to enjoy the applause after delivering a successful talk, the Pleasure Stealer cautions us, *Don't get a swelled head. Pride goeth before a fall.* Or it tells us, *That wasn't bad, but you could do better.* Or it forces a gourmet cook, after serving a dinner that earned raves, to focus on the one thing that went wrong: The rolls were overdone.

We find the Pleasure Stealer at work when we tell ourselves it's unfeminine to be loud or aggressive during sex. Or when we want a new outfit and say to ourselves, *You don't deserve it.* Or, even though we're exhausted at the end of the day, we don't let ourselves rest until everyone else is taken care of.

This relentless inner voice tells us, *You don't have a right to enjoy your life.* Whenever we start having too much fun or too many good things happen to us, we expect the boom to fall.

The High Cost of Listening to the Inner Shamer

The self-shaming process inhibits us to the point where we end up leading half lives. It spares nothing, limiting us in our work, hobbies, relationships, and personal growth. By instilling doubts and devaluing our abilities, it keeps us from pursuing our interests or taking on challenges. We turn down promotions, don't ask for a raise, don't write that book, don't pursue a degree, license, or credential. Our fear of making the wrong decision or of doing something less than perfectly makes us miss important deadlines or fail to complete projects.

Listening to the Inner Shamer leaves us chronically fatigued, anxious, or depressed. And when the critical voices get too abusive, we sometimes silence them with our addiction of choice: alcohol, drugs, food, work, or love affairs.

Perhaps the greatest price we pay is in alienation from ourselves. In the process we lose vitality, spontaneity, and authenticity. Because it's so important to earn approval and avoid criticism, we often lose touch with our legitimate needs and wants. We come to want only what we believe we "should" want, or we become paralyzed with indecision, torn between what we want to do and what we think we "should" do. We also numb our feelings, robbing ourselves of a crucial source of aliveness in our lives and our relationships. When we relate to ourselves in a critical, uncaring, cruel fashion, we are unable to feel love or compassion for the hurting little girl inside.

The Inner Shamer sabotages our efforts to have healthy relationships. Because we can't care about ourselves, we find it difficult to accept that others care about us. We may project the Inner Shamer outward, turning its verbal abuse on others. Or we may become too passive, taking abuse or settling for much less than we deserve. We may take on others' criticism because it matches our own critical voice. We may avoid getting involved because we listen to our inner voice cautioning us not to get hurt, rejected, or swallowed up.

Some of us end up lonely, abused, and unfulfilled. How does the Inner Critic succeed in exacting this outrageous price?

The Tyranny of the Should

The inner voice dominates us like a malevolent dictator, with one of the most powerful verbal weapons in its arsenal: *You should.* Do any of these sound familiar?

- You shouldn't get angry, hurt, or disappointed.
- Never make mistakes.
- You shouldn't be too pushy—it's not feminine.
- You shouldn't need a relationship.
- Don't be so sensitive. You're too emotional.
- Never hurt another's feelings or cause pain.

The Inner Shamer doesn't care whether we are capable of carrying out its unreasonable demands. Nor does it care whether circumstances permit us to act on its dictates. It whips us into line regardless, creating what Horney calls the tyranny of the *should.*[6]

Aside from the general command to be perfect, the most popular *should* for women is, *Always put the other's needs first.* So ingrained is this dictate that we find it difficult to consider our own best interests. As one of my clients put it, "I'm last on my list."

Another common rule is, *You should always be understanding and helpful.*[7] Who hasn't caught herself automatically offering solutions, taking on others' problems as though they were her own? Am I saying we shouldn't be helpful? Of course not. But this process is so automatic, I point it out so that we can gain some freedom within it. If we choose to get involved, fine. But there are times when we don't have the time, energy, or inclination to help people with their unresolved dilemmas, yet we still feel pulled to do so. Often the other person isn't even asking us for help. We're especially fond of jumping in with our partners and children, often robbing them of the opportunity to find solutions to their own problems. And of course when the problem is serious, such as alcoholism or other addictions, our efforts may actually be counterproductive.

I can't cover here all the myriad *should*s that rule us, but each of us has her own exacting list, shaped by the expectations she grew up with and the solutions she devised to cope with her feelings of worthlessness. Take a moment to write down your own list of *should*s. You might include your relationships, chores, work, community activities, money and finances, self-care, sex, eating, behavior, thoughts, feelings, and wants.[8]

Silencing the Inner Shamer

Even though the internal critic is deeply entrenched, we can destroy its ability to undermine and attack us. It may be like the dull roar of traffic in the background—so familiar that we're hardly aware of it. Therefore our first step in disarming the Critic is to increase our awareness of its pernicious presence as it accuses, blames, warns, and undermines us.

Next we must ask ourselves who the voice belongs to and put a face on it; it may be a parent, grandparent, sibling, teacher, or friend.

Ginny, the nurse with panic attacks whom we met in Chapter Two, discovered that her most debilitating critical voice belongs to her mother, Helen.

"When I went to my supervisor with some criticisms and suggestions about improving a situation at work, I could hear Helen scolding me for even *thinking* that my opinion was worth anything," Ginny tells me. "*What makes you so smart, Miss Know-It-All? Who asked you, anyway?* I just say to her, *Okay, Helen, that's enough.* I'm getting good at catching her."

The ability to say "That's Helen speaking" frees Ginny to explore whether she really wants to pay attention to the internal Helen's scornful insults or to counter them with more supportive, self-affirming messages to herself.

After we recognize and label the voice of the Critic, we need to unmask its purpose in our lives. Ginny discovered that listening to her mother's voice kept them connected. For instance, although she could afford it, she seldom bought anything for herself. By not spending money on herself, she wards off her mother's possible envy. She also appeases Mom by staying loyal to her teachings: *Give to others, not to yourself.*

Usually the Critic does more harm than good, but occasionally it's on our side, in spite of its rough tactics. It's useful to ask ourselves what difficulty the Critic might be helping to resolve, then dealing with the uncovered problem more directly and effectively—perhaps even negotiating for a compromise. When Jane realized her self-shamer was trying to motivate her into taking care of her well-being, she took a serious look at her diet. She "agreed" to eat healthy foods during the week and eat junk food only on the weekends. She discovered that, after taking back the power, she no longer needed the Critic to whip herself to follow through. She also gained compassion for her own slipups and refused to submit to the Critic's attempts to punish her.

Empowering Our Own Inner Voice

After recognizing, labeling, and unmasking its purpose, we need to talk back actively to our inner critical voice. We must replace it with a positive, self-affirming voice. Look over your list of *shoulds* and claim only those that empower you.

Ginny can tell her internal "Helen" she doesn't need her criticism anymore. She can say, "Mom, I have a right to my own life. I can no longer take care of you by holding myself back. My success doesn't have to be hurtful to you. I can be different from you, even have more, and still stay connected. I am a valuable and deserving person, and so are you."

Sometimes it helps to ask ourselves, *What would I say to my best friend in this situation?*

Wouldn't it be wonderful if we had a nurturing voice inside us as we go about our day? What if Jane, the salesperson at the beginning of the chapter, could tell herself, *Good job! You ran three miles?* What if she could look in her rearview mirror and say, *You look great, Jane, old girl?* And what if she let in the praise of her co-workers with *Good job, Jane. I knew you could do it?*

When we make a mistake, we need to be gentle with ourselves. Instead of saying, *You dummy. How could you do that?* and obsessing about it for days (or even years), we can tell ourselves, *I have a lot on my mind right now,* or *I didn't have enough experience,* or *I did the best I could under the circumstances.* Mistakes are often a necessary part of growing because they show us what we need to work on.

Though we can never entirely tune out the Inner Shamer, we can turn down the volume on its pernicious chatter, while turning up the volume on our self-affirming inner thoughts. We need to counter the internalized critical voice with an empathic inner voice. One reason therapy works is that we learn to treat ourselves with empathy by taking inside us our therapist's accepting voice.

The following list may help you stand up to your Inner Shamer:

Shoulds	*Rights*
I shouldn't feel angry, hurt, or sad.	I have the right to my feelings.
I should always be logical and consistent.	I have the right to change my mind.
I shouldn't ask for anything.	I have the right to ask for what I want.
I should take care of others at all times. I should be able to solve everyone's problems.	I have the right not to be responsible for other people's behavior, feelings, or problems.
It's selfish to put my needs ahead of the needs of others.	I have the right to take care of my own best interests.
I shouldn't impose on people.	I have the right to ask for help or emotional support.
I should always be accommodating.	I have the right to say no.
I should always be aware of the needs of others.	I have the right not to have to anticipate the needs of others.
I should take other people's advice.	I have the right to think for myself.
I shouldn't make mistakes.	I have the right to make mistakes. I *never* have to be perfect.
I shouldn't be too happy or have too much.	I have the right to a life of my own, the right to feel good about myself, and the right to be happy.

Take another look at your list and replace your *should*s with a statement of rights that are appropriate for you. And buy yourself a plaque, like the one I saw that says I WILL NOT SHOULD ON MYSELF TODAY.

Above all, we need to quiet the inner voice that originates in early family messages and is reinforced by society's dictates, and listen instead to the emerging authentic inner voice that comes from being deeply in tune with ourselves, trusting our feelings and wants. Before we can meet that difficult challenge, we need to understand the powerful forces that keep us from giving ourselves permission to be fully who we are.

The Silent Suppressor

> Women have been so encouraged to concentrate on the
> emotions and reactions of others that they have been
> diverted from examining and expressing their own emo-
> tions. . . . [Furthermore] women are made to feel that
> to think and act for themselves will jeopardize their
> relationships.
> —JEAN BAKER MILLER

Perhaps the deadliest role of shame is its position as gate-keeper of our inner life, keeping guard against the emergence of "unacceptable" parts of ourselves. As women we learn to link shame with certain vital areas of our being and thereby lose access to experiencing our deepest feelings, needs, wants, and dreams. Shame stops us from thinking and acting for ourselves.

How Shame Destroys Access to Feelings

Our male-dominated society assigns little value to the ability to be in touch with our emotions. Emotions are generally seen as a hindrance to the process of self-understanding and meaningful activity. We fear being overpowered by our feelings, losing control, looking foolish. Although some emotions are considered more appropriate for one sex than for the other, both men and women learned as children to feel ashamed of their fear, hurt, sadness, pride, anger—sometimes even their excitement and joy. Rather than seeing our feelings as a source of passion and aliveness, we consider them to be at best a disruption or a nuisance, at worst shameful evidence of weakness or deficiency.

Even though little girls learn, early on, to ignore their own feelings, they are encouraged to pay attention to the feelings of others, to become caretakers. Being highly attuned to the emotional states of others is a skill little valued by our culture, yet it is crucial to fostering intimate connections in relationships.

The price we women pay for this interpersonal sensitivity is that we often lose our ability to pay attention to what's going on inside ourselves.

Learning Not to Feel

When we were babies, we expressed ourselves freely and robustly. If we felt like crying, we wailed until we felt like stopping. If we were angry, we screwed up our faces and yelled until we were beet red. If we were happy, everyone knew it. Where did all that natural expression go?

We learned that our feelings weren't acceptable by the way our parents responded to them. At an early age we learned—either by direct punishment or by indirect inhibition—that our parents could not tolerate our feelings. There were threats: "I'll give you something to cry about if you don't stop." There was humiliation: "Don't be such a crybaby." There was denial: "Don't feel sad. After all, you've got so much to be thankful for." Boys were given even less permission to cry than girls, taunted with "Only sissies cry." *Sissy*, or *sis*, for short, used to be a common word for sister. Boys were shamed by accusations of being like a girl!

By discounting our feelings, our parents unintentionally taught us not only that feelings were bad, but that *we* were bad to have feelings. Because we became ashamed of them, we not only lost the ability to express them, many of us lost the ability even to feel them. *To have one's feelings discounted time and time again is to have one's self discounted.*

Lynn, a delicate-featured woman in her early forties, part-time journalist, wife, and mother of three, began therapy because she felt emotionally numb—except for recent sudden bursts of confusing anger directed toward her husband.

"Keep control of your emotions. Don't let your emotions control you," her mother had often admonished her. And she does just that. She keeps her feelings so stifled that others rarely see them. In our therapy sessions they remain hidden not only from me—a possible shaming onlooker—but from Lynn herself. In nine months of intense therapy only twice did she have tears in her eyes.

Lynn learned as a little girl that her feelings were taboo. When she was two, she got angry at her daddy. He spanked her so hard, she wouldn't go near him for two weeks. Her anger went underground and, except for one time, didn't resurface again until she was in her early forties.

"When I was eight, I cried when my best friend moved far away, but my mother said, 'Cheer up, you'll make a new friend soon. Have a cookie now and stop that crying.' Instead of being encouraged to talk about my sad feelings, I was taught how to stuff them. And when I didn't feel better, I thought there was something wrong with me."

As adult women we continue to feel ashamed of our feelings, especially our hurt or anger. As Lynn puts it, "It never ceases to amaze me how relieved I feel when I tell a friend how so-and-so hurt my feelings or made me angry and my friend says, 'I'd feel hurt too' or 'I'd be angry too.' Maybe I'm not flawed. I always used to think normal people wouldn't be hurt or angry over something so petty. I used to think I was just too sensitive."

As women we have an additional burden: Society demeans us for being "ruled by our emotions." So when we *are* able to listen to our feelings, we risk criticism and shame for not having the male ability to be "rational about things."

Anger: Taboo for Women

Anger and shame interact in a complex fashion. In this chapter we will explore the ways our shame blocks expression of anger. In Chapter Ten we will look at anger as a response to feelings of shame. In the first case we are ashamed of being angry. In the second we are angry about being ashamed.

Is shame at the root of all anger? Probably not. For instance fear can fuel anger. But it's a more common component than we realize. While maladaptive shame compels us to lash out destructively, healthy shame motivates us to stand up for our rights or our dignity, to insist on fair treatment, to right social wrongs. Or it signals us that too often we are putting others' interests ahead of our own. Anger has value. It mobilizes us to act.

Anger is a complicated emotion, especially for women. While men tend to become angry when they feel ashamed for being helpless or when they suffer a loss of power previously enjoyed, women tend to become angry when they are chronically disempowered in all the ways we've discussed or when their attempts at relating are thwarted.

Women are far more suppressed than men in their expression of anger. Society witnesses and applauds open male anger (or its product, male aggression) in the movies, on television, and in contact sports such as prizefights, wrestling, and football. Anger in men is often a sign of power. But anger in women is considered unfeminine at best and bitchy at worst. Women aren't rewarded for their anger; they are chastised for it. Girls are socialized to be "nice," to be ashamed of their anger. Consequently women have few acceptable outlets for anger.

In a family that tolerates children expressing their feelings, writes Alice Miller, "I can be angry and no one will die or get a headache because of it."[1] Our power to hurt or destroy with our anger can be frightening.

Our greatest fear is that our anger will hurt those we care about and drive them away. Or we may have expressed our anger at our parents, seen them enraged or crushed by it, and felt ashamed.

Let's return to Lynn, who was nineteen when she finally got angry again. "I got mad at my mother for harassing me about going longer than three minutes on an important long-distance phone call. I stamped my foot and shrieked, 'Leave me alone!' Mother left the room abruptly. When I got off the phone, I found her on the back porch sobbing about what a bad mother she was. I ended up comforting her. I felt so guilty and ashamed, it was *another* twenty years before I allowed myself to get angry again." It was then that Lynn's fury came out in the unexpected bursts that frightened her enough to make her start therapy.

Another closely related factor that makes expressing our anger so shame-laden is its contradiction of all we've been taught about our *responsibility* to take care of others. The tendency to put others' welfare ahead of our own is deeply ingrained in us. If we believe our anger is damaging, it follows that we would choose not to hurt those we are supposed to be caring for.

Shame also stops us from expressing anger because we believe it's not normal to be angry. Since our anger is rarely validated, we come to believe that something is wrong with us, that we have "no right" and "no cause" to be angry.

The Powder Keg of Suppressed Anger

Jean Baker Miller writes about the spiraling effect of women's anger. Because even small amounts of anger feel dangerous to a woman, she stifles its expression. This leads to frustration and inaction, which in turn leads to helplessness and loss of self-worth, which creates more anger. The buildup of anger begins to feel overwhelming. "She begins to feel 'full of anger,' which then surely seems irrational and unwarranted."[2]

It was the sudden appearance of angry eruptions that frightened Lynn into seeking therapy. As Miller points out, when anger is finally released, it seems exaggerated, often accompanied by yelling or screaming, earning women the label "hysterical." Most women express their anger, if at all, by crying or nagging. Either way we are ineffective. Since we have no other place to go with our anger except to turn it against ourselves, it becomes expressed instead through physical or psychological "symptoms." Lynn had suffered from moderate depression for years. Other women have panic attacks, headaches, or eating or drinking problems, to name a few.

We end up disempowered: We don't get our needs met, we don't stand up for our self-respect and defend our dignity. Sometimes we become martyrs with barely disguised hostility seeping out at our seams. Thus the price we pay for swallowing our anger is high.

Lynn began to recognize that she had a right to her anger— that it was not abnormal, given the circumstances of her life. She had many reasons to be angry. "My entire life has been devoted to taking care of everyone else. My needs don't count. Now when I finally act on these needs by going back to college, don't you think my husband could muster up a little support?" Perhaps a deeper source of Lynn's anger lay in the realization that since childhood she had lost touch with vital parts of herself.

Eventually she was able to find healthy, constructive ways of expressing her anger. For instance she learned to tell her husband, "When you don't support my dreams, I feel angry because I think you don't care about me," rather than striking back with "You're incapable of caring about anyone but yourself." When she expressed the hurt and fear underneath her anger, her husband was eventually able to express his caring and his fear that she no longer cared about *him* because she wanted to stop being a full-time homemaker.

Anger, if expressed in a nonblaming way, with the intention to resolve a problem, can create rather than destroy connection. We need to remember we are not *bad and wrong* to be angry. Having the capacity to be angry in no way cancels our capacity to care for others. Expressing our anger responsibly increases our chances of being heard and bringing about desired change.[3]

"Feeling Sad? Shame on You!"

Sadness is a necessary part of grieving and letting go, yet we often feel overwhelmed by our pain or ashamed of it. We associate weeping with being weak or childish. Most of my clients feel ashamed when they cry. They apologize, hide their faces, or try to erase any visible sign of weeping by a hasty mop-up job with the tissue. Some women's tears are so bound up with shame that they are kept out of awareness. Other women weep and don't know why. I had a client who, for no apparent reason, wept for an entire session tears collected and stored from years of hurt and loss.

Lynn believed her tears were bad. "I feel childish. And sometimes I feel manipulative, like I'm trying to get you to feel sorry for me. And sometimes I feel too weak and needy. I'm ashamed when I feel like that. I learned at an early age to swallow my tears and put on a happy face."

The few times she cried, she would apologize for "breaking down"—a shame-laden expression if I ever heard one. Lynn's sadness when she was eight and her friend moved away made her mother feel inadequate, so she couldn't be with Lynn's unhappiness without trying to make it better in the only ways she knew. When our own children express feelings that were forbidden to us as children, we feel we must stamp them out. It would have been more helpful if her mother could have let Lynn cry, telling her she understood how hard it is to have a friend move away. *When our feelings are validated, we are validated.*

Sometimes there is profound pain and sadness for all the years of not being allowed to be who you are. To grieve for the lost self is an essential part of the healing process. You can't heal what you can't feel.

"I Feel Hurt. What Did I Do Wrong?"

Hurt feelings are especially difficult for women who have problems with shame. We think having these feelings means there is something wrong with us.

First, we believe we brought the hurt upon ourselves. Often as children, when we asked for a sympathetic ear, we were told, "Well, what did you do first?" *Our hurt somehow becomes our own fault.*

Raised to be caretakers, women are often expected to be understanding, not hurt. There is little room for feeling the hurt. And we want to protect those we are close to (parents, friends, spouses) from their guilt and shame for hurting us. Many shame-ridden women grew up in homes where there was a chronically ill or alcoholic parent. They either were told or simply figured out that they couldn't go to their parent with upsetting feelings. Lynn says, "When my dad didn't go to my championship playoffs, I couldn't tell him how hurt and angry I was. I was too afraid he'd have another heart attack."

We feel bad and wrong for being "too sensitive." It's hard to trust that we have a right to our feelings. If we have been bruised, rather than numbing our hurt feelings or dismissing them as unimportant or exaggerated, we must begin to take them seriously. Learning to express our hurt is a necessary step in healing our shame. Rather than blaming ("You are cruel and arrogant"), it's better to say what you are feeling ("It hurts when you dismiss my ideas"). Generally shame lies beneath hurt feelings.

Excitement Can Be Dangerous

Generally it is not possible to suppress just one emotion; the mind doesn't operate that way. We can't numb ourselves selectively, as a dentist does with Novocain shot into a particular area of our mouth. Instead we give our emotions a general anesthetic and censor not only our "negative" emotions but also our pride, joy, and excitement.

Marta enjoyed a flurry of dates with several attractive men and worried that her co-workers would judge her for being too much of a "gadabout." When we did some reality-checking, Marta discovered that she actually feared they'd be jealous.

"It's hard to have something others want." Even her excitement worried her. "It's unhealthy to be that excited, isn't it? I feel like a teenager. And when I told my mother how much fun I was having, all she said was, 'Aren't you afraid you'll get too tired?' "

Marta learned to suppress her excitement and enthusiasm. One day she told me she worried about being "out of control." As we explored what this meant, she became quite animated with a lot of gesturing, setting her black hair swinging. "This is me—being out of control."

This is out of control? When I asked her if this was a familiar feeling, she burst into tears. She remembered giggling as a child with her sisters and being told, "Get control of yourselves. You're giving me ulcers." *She came to believe her enthusiasm was damaging to others.*

The suppression or denial of our feelings costs us in aliveness, joy, vitality, creativity, intimacy—in short it steals the passion from our lives. And it limits our ability to truly know and fully be ourselves.

"Pride Goeth Before a Fall"

Having more than others, being competitive, or experiencing pleasure in one's competency can often be a source of shame.

When she was given a plum assignment for her newspaper, Lynn worried that her colleagues would resent her. This triggered memories of worrying about others' envy as a teenager.

"I was a good writer in high school—the best in my class. I won an essay contest."

I ask her what's it like to tell me about this.

"It feels like I'm bragging," she says. "I guess I felt I was being a little superior."

Is that bad?

"I'm probably not really that good at writing." She picks at a loose thread on the arm of the chair. "I guess I'm confused."

Suspecting there was a reason she needed to get confused just then, I ask her what just happened.

"I got scared you'd think I was getting too big for my britches. That you'd say, 'What does *she* really know?' You're probably thinking, *So you were the best . . . but it was only thirty kids, and why is it so important to bring it up twenty-five years later? Big deal.*" By shaming herself she cuts herself down before I can, an old pattern now used to protect her connection with me. Why would she pull the rug out from under herself now?

"It got dangerous. My mom would say to get off my high horse."

I ask why a mother might want to cut her daughter down like that.

"Competition" is the fast reply.

Lynn goes on to confess her worry that, as a stand-in for her mother, I might envy her talent, feel threatened, and shame her. So she avoids competition with me and my possible withdrawal or anger while maintaining her connection to me by shaming herself, a familiar pattern of cutting herself down before her mother could.

Competitive feelings are natural and nothing to be ashamed of. Because I was taught as a little girl that to be loving and giving was the highest ideal, I never acknowledged my own competitiveness, in spite of my secret relish for winning at games and being right. Instead I felt ashamed of my competitive thoughts and behavior whenever they managed to slip my guard. It wasn't until I was in my late twenties that I could admit to feeling competitive with my sister—no easy thing, because it didn't fit my picture of being a good girl. Good girls just weren't competitive.

It's a relief to know competitive feelings are normal, and that *they don't make us any less capable of being generous givers.*

Learning Not to Have Wants and Needs

Most women who struggle with shame have difficulty taking care of their own needs and wants. Raised to be caretakers, they feel they are supposed to give to others, meet others' needs. Indulging their own needs and wants would be selfish. Thus, giving to oneself or allowing oneself to be given to are often alien experiences. In some women's eyes having needs means being dependent—something to be avoided.

"Me Last!"

"I've got to stop putting everybody else's needs and wants ahead of mine," Lynn says. "Except I don't even know what mine are, I've been so busy figuring everybody else's out. If I do know what I want, I don't let myself ask for it or have it. When I come home after a long, hard day at the office, I'd give anything to be able to soak in a bubble bath first thing."

I ask what would be so bad about doing that.

"That would be selfish. I'd be neglecting everybody."

This dilemma, familiar to most modern women, has a powerful impact on women's lives. It keeps women from taking care of themselves, from going after what they want in life, from having lives that nurture and fulfill them. As we begin to claim an identity for ourselves, we have more freedom to answer the crucial question, What do I really want? But first we need to ask it. Allowing ourselves to know what we want is key to understanding who we are.

It is in our families that we first learn to deprecate our needs and wants. As youngsters we learn to be ashamed, believing that something is wrong with us for having needs. When parents actively shame us for having needs or respond inconsistently (sometimes with comfort, sometimes with neglect or scolding), we learn:

- I'm not going to get my needs met because I'm not lovable.
- Because I can't count on getting my needs met, the world is an *unpredictable* place. I'm not safe.

- I am *stupid* for expecting someone to be there for me. I am defective.
- I shouldn't be needy in the first place. I am acting like a baby. I am *bad*.

Why We Learn Not to Need and Want

After enough shaming experiences we eventually learn to swallow our pain, suppress our needs, and even deny their existence. Sometimes we do this to protect our parents (and eventually others) because we assume they can't handle our needs and wants—or because we sense their deep well of unmet need. Instead of tuning in to our own needs, we become overly attuned to theirs.

They may be coping with chronic illness or alcoholism, they may be distracted by worries, or they may be already stretched too thin. As little girls, we learn that our needs can threaten the stability of the family.

Consider Mary Catherine, a thirty-seven-year-old bookkeeper, who was raised in a Catholic family with seven sisters and brothers.

"I knew how overburdened my mother was. It seemed like the whole family was a house of cards, precariously balanced. If I interjected my need, I knew my parents couldn't handle any more and the house would tumble down. I was too busy taking care of their wants. I couldn't afford to have my own. I even felt ashamed for the times I did get my needs met—as if I was taking away from somebody else." She sighed. *"I guess there just wasn't enough to go around."*

Another compelling reason to ignore or deny our needs is our commitment to take care of our parents' self-esteem or protect them from shame. We hide or deny our need because we sense that they see our need as criticism of them: If we need something, they will feel they somehow failed to anticipate or provide for our need.[4] Mothers are especially vulnerable to feelings of inadequacy stemming from the belief that *their job is to anticipate and meet all needs*.

How We Stop Ourselves
from Fulfilling Our Needs and Wants

When, as girls growing up, we are faced with the possibility of not having our basic needs met, we develop certain strategies to protect ourselves from pain and humiliation.

WE BECOME NUMB

First we lose touch with ourselves. We learn not to *know* what we want. "I often take my daughters shopping, but I almost never buy anything for myself," Mary Catherine said. "I've just never wanted anything for me. I can hear my mother telling me I'm selfish. You see, she only bought one good dress a year."

When I asked what's it like not to want anything for yourself, tears welled up in her eyes as she allowed herself for the first time to experience her pain from years of never wanting.

When we get in touch with our wanting, we tap a deep well of pain and loss that comes from facing all we needed and didn't get. Mary Catherine would often refer to this session as a milestone in her therapy, when she learned her wants are important.

RAGGEDY ANN AND ME

Many "good girls" don't allow themselves to want. They try not to be selfish, they don't want to put any burden on others, and they believe their needs and wants don't matter. I was one of those girls.

One day, when I was six and my sister was eight, my mother brought home a beautiful handmade Raggedy Ann and Raggedy Andy. We both had loved the stories about the little girl with the red heart that said "I love you." Mother had us whisper in her ear which one we wanted. When it was my turn, knowing my sister wanted Raggedy Ann, I murmured "Raggedy Andy." For years I pretended to myself and others that I loved my Raggedy Andy.

Later in therapy as a young woman I told the story of how I didn't choose Raggedy Ann. I was astonished to find myself weeping, releasing tears that had been locked up for twenty years. I wept for the loss of Raggedy Ann, and even more for the loss of the little girl who had had to give up herself to keep peace in her family. Not being able to be who you are and want what you want is a source of great suffering.

I had plenty of reasons for choosing Raggedy Andy. Knowing it would be too hard on Mother if my sister and I chose the same doll, I took care of Mother. Also I feared my sister's anger and envy if I won. I didn't feel brave enough to have something for myself at her expense! For all these reasons it just wasn't safe. The way I resolved my dilemma was to accommodate and not want at all. It's significant that I couldn't let myself choose the doll I wanted, but even more crucial was my inability to let *myself* know for more than a moment that I wanted her. I not only fooled them, I fooled myself.

Raggedy Ann has become a symbol to me of my reclaimed self. After I told my husband this story, and wept in the telling, he gave me a Raggedy Ann for my next birthday. I now have a small collection—the newest one, three feet tall, graces a small rocker in my bedroom. She happily reminds me that it's okay to know what I want and it's okay to give to myself. It's now safe to be me.

Ashamed to Ask for What We Need

Not knowing what we want can be an effective way of taking care of our pain and longing. Another way we protect ourselves is by shaming ourselves when we do know what we want. We call in the Inner Critic, who tells us we're selfish and spoiled, that there is something wrong with us for wanting or needing something. That way we curb our wanting for a while.

"I want to be acknowledged for a good job at work, but I never ask for it," Lynn told me. "Needing appreciation from my boss doesn't seem quite normal." Eventually she felt strong enough to actually invite appreciation. Now, when her boss says he likes her report, she's learned it's okay to say, "Thanks. What did you like about it?"

Many shame-based women are ashamed of their need for attention, and I was no exception. One day I ran into a friend who had just had a cast removed from her broken arm. "You must feel great," I said. "Yes," she replied, "but I miss all the attention." I was awed that she could openly admit what was for me a carefully guarded secret. It dawned on me that many people love attention and that I was probably normal after all. I also realized that perhaps I had a greater need than some because I hadn't had enough attention as a child. When our childhood needs go unmet, they leave a gaping hole in our adult life.

Children from dysfunctional families—accustomed to years of needing and not getting—often believe they are greedy and feel ashamed. "Greedy" feelings are kept locked up in one of the darker dungeons of our imprisoned self.

Another way to curb our wants is to decide that what we need or want is not really that important. Compared with others' wants, our own seem trivial. Also it is not uncommon for women to feel so ashamed or guilty for having their wants fulfilled that *they don't allow themselves to fully enjoy what they have.* Or they find other ways to "punish" themselves.

Or we buy "disappointment insurance." As Mary Catherine says, "I never let myself want too much because I'm afraid it won't happen." We associate deep feelings of wanting something with ultimate disappointment and humiliation, so we "decide" it's better not to want.

All the strategies I've described above serve to protect us from pain by warding off disappointment and shame or by preserving our connections to others. But because the cost is high, sooner or later many of us decide to make some changes. As we grow in defining ourselves, we come to realize that our needs and wants are vitally important. Yet discoveries like these thrust us into a dilemma: What do we do about balancing our newfound permission to take care of ourselves with our need to stay connected to those we love? Like Mary Catherine, whenever we put our own needs first, we feel selfish. Yet if we bow down to the needs of others—putting their needs first—we are told we are being "codependent."

With either choice, women assume the burden of shame. We are convinced that to consider our own best interests proves we aren't really the loving, caring women we were raised to be. We need to remember that it is possible both to be caring *and* to reserve the choice to make *our* wants as important as another's. As we grow stronger in knowing and loving ourselves, we learn that it's permissible to consider our own best interests, and sometimes that means putting ourselves first.

Feeling Ashamed of Our Way of Thinking

When women's ways of thinking and knowing differ from stereotypical male models, they are often subject to ridicule. To ward off such treatment, women tend to avoid thinking for themselves. *Yet being different doesn't mean being wrong.*

Women are supposed to feel complimented to be told they "think like a man." To think like a woman implies being inconsistent, indecisive, and ignorant of the facts. Women tend to think laterally, taking into consideration adjacent bits of information about people, concerning themselves with the impact of their decisions on those around them. They also prefer to take time to discuss what they are thinking and feeling with those closest to them. And they are more inclined to collaborate on projects, again reaching out sideways for support, ideas, and consensus.

Because we have been invalidated for these ways of thinking and being, we too often keep quiet and hold back our opinions on weighty matters. Yet communications expert Deborah Tannen, in her important book *You Just Don't Understand: Women and Men in Conversation,* suggests that it's not insecurity or lack of competence that holds women back from speaking out, but rather lack of experience coupled with a desire not to threaten connection to others by standing out, knowing too much, or holding themselves above others.[5] One important way women maintain connection, Tannen says, is by being careful to keep the relationship on equal terms and to avoid taking a superior position—the opposite of men's style of interaction.[6] I suggest that what keeps women silent is *both* our insecurity *and* our need to keep relationships "symmetrical" (Tannen's word).

Afraid to Think for Ourselves

Clearly women's failure to think for themselves often comes from old patterns of putting their major focus on maintaining connections and avoiding shame. It's not that they lack the capacity; they either choose not to use it or don't trust it. And so they usually defer to men when it comes to major decisions. Even the myriad daily decisions women pass off to men suggest that not thinking for themselves has become a habit ("What shall we have for dinner—pork chops or chicken?" "What movie shall we see?").

Sometimes we ask for unnecessary advice, information, and help in order to make the other person feel important, strong, and knowledgeable.

We need to balance our healthy ability to be concerned about the needs and wants of others with our need to be individuals in our own right. It takes becoming conscious of how often we *routinely* opt out, back down, negate, or step aside, then asking ourselves, *What is my payoff, and is it worth it to discredit what I really think and know?*

We numb our feelings, neglect our needs, learn not to have wants, inhibit our ability to think for ourselves, and give up having a life of our own in order to stay connected. We lose vitality and creativity when we lose access to these crucial areas, and end up living unfulfilled lives.

If we consistently avoid angering and upsetting others by not asserting our needs and wants and by not acting in our own best interests, we cripple ourselves and diminish the quality of our lives.

It is time to risk fuller self-expression in spite of fears of jeopardizing our relationships. Just as we women are growing, men are growing too. We can begin to cast aside outdated and inappropriate "rules" about the necessity of denying or suppressing ourselves in the name of maintaining connections, and reclaim our right to feel, want, think, and have.

PART THREE

DEFENDING
AGAINST
SHAME

CHAPTER NINE

Meet the Impostor

*All of the good/bad, strong/weak/ridiculous Janus faces
must be seen, if I am to have any time to live with my
mask off. And should I wear my mask too long, when I
take it off and try to discard it, I may find that I have
thrown my face away with it.*
　　　　　　　　—SHELDON B. KOPP

"I'm not the person people think I am," says Marcy, a recently separated owner of a bookkeeping business and mother of three. "The person I present to the world is cheerful, gets along just fine, likes her life—a good worker. But inside I feel like I've got everybody fooled. I feel like an impostor. I act one way with my employees, another with my friend, and another with my family. Will the real me please stand up?

"People at work tell me I'm organized. If they could see my closet! Everybody says how well I'm managing, with working and being a single mother. But I'm not doing either job well enough. I cut corners a lot, and sometimes I panic about having to do it all. I feel like a twelve-year-old in adult clothing. I just go about my daily life pretending I'm a grownup, hoping no one will find me out." Marcy blushed. "If they only knew how selfish I am, how little I know . . . how lonely I feel. I only have one good friend.

I don't feel comfortable with people. I'm afraid if people get to know me, they'll decide they don't like me."

I ask what makes her think that.

"Well, I know some women who are pretty and real skinny. They have similar jobs; they're single and like to go dancing. They even call me, but I make up some excuse even when I could get a sitter. I picture them talking about me behind my back: 'Marcy could stand to lose a few pounds.' "

Marcy's words are echoed by many of my clients at one time or another—women who, to protect themselves against shame, have developed a way of being in the world based on a "false self." This facade hides their unclaimed and neglected natural self, which they perceive as inadequate, damaged, or childish.[1]

As adults many of us have lost touch completely with our ability to be authentic. Chronic shame prevents us from revealing who we really are. We are like voluntary prisoners, exchanging our freedom for protection against the onslaughts of the real or imagined world.

Feeling Like a Fake

Marcy wears a mask of confidence and happiness. Yet underneath her mask we find an unsure, often troubled woman who, *in spite of her proven competence,* doesn't believe in herself. Instead she believes she is pulling the wool over people's eyes. For instance, after starting a new relationship she says, "I'm afraid that when he gets to know me better, he won't like me anymore. Besides, if he thinks I'm attractive, he must be a loser." About her career she says, "My son recently said to me, 'I can't believe you ran your own business for five years yet you can't even get your videotapes back on time.' I defend myself, but inside I'm thinking, *He doesn't know that I'm really a fake and that my success was all luck.*"

We think we're the only one who feels so inadequate, uncomfortable, anxious, and ashamed. We believe other people don't have self-doubts, that their successes come easily, their relationships are untroubled, their children are without problems.

We explain our accomplishment by factors other than competence: "I didn't really deserve that award or job." "I was simply in the right place at the right time." "I was promoted because of my looks." "They made a mistake." "I conned them." Any reason will do, except the real one: "I am a capable, worthwhile person."

I spent many years feeling like a fraud. For example I believed I got into one of the best women's colleges because my mother had gone there, not because I deserved it. I was certain they had a policy of always accepting daughters of alumnae. Getting an F on my first English paper confirmed my unworthiness. Throughout my college career I carried with me a sense of not belonging with all those women who seemed so much smarter than I was. This, in spite of maintaining a B average my junior and senior years. (Of course my Inner Shamer told me I should have all A's.) And when I was asked to apply for and was granted a graduate fellowship, I told myself it was only because my professor liked me.

One reason we feel like an imposter is our tendency to think in either/or terms: "Either I'm perfect or I'm completely flawed." "If I'm not a good ———, then obviously I'm a bad ———." In my case, if I wasn't among the very top students, I was no good at all. There is no place for just being human: some good, some bad, some ordinary. We're sure others judge us the same way. If we fail to measure up 100 percent, they are sure to dismiss us as practically worthless. And if we *are* successful, we feel we don't deserve it.

Alex, a successful attorney, worries that at some point she will be exposed as a phony, as someone who has managed thus far to fool everybody. She is haunted by Lincoln's words: "You can fool all of the people some of the time, and you can fool some of the people all of the time, but you can't fool all of the people all of the time." Passing yourself off as someone you believe you are not inspires shame and anxiety at the profoundest of levels.

Driven by a perfectionism that is taking its toll on her health, she overprepares and doesn't delegate tasks as often as she could. Concerns about high blood pressure brought her to my office.

Although Alex very much wants to succeed, even to be special, she finds it difficult to accept her success. When colleagues praise her, she finds ways to discount their compliments. "I had to work long hours on that brief." (As though success for other people came easily without hard work.) Or she will say, "It was luck. The judge likes me." (As though skill had nothing to do with it.) Or "I'll never be able to do it again. I had a lot of help from my paralegal." (As though the ability to make good use of help diminishes her accomplishment.)

When she does let herself enjoy moments of success, she may

dampen her joy with the thought *I'm just doing what my parents expected. I'm not special.*

"I wanted to be a lawyer like my dad," she tells me. "He was one of the top attorneys in town. I got into law school because of my father's stellar reputation. But I'll never be as good as he is." (Notice Alex's either/or thinking: *Either I'm as prominent as my dad or I'm nothing.*) Because she was raised in the shadow of her father, she never gained confidence in her own exceptional abilities.

"My father expected me to do well in everything I undertook," Alex says. "When I got an A or the lead in the school play, he took it for granted. Even when I got into law school, I never had the sense that he was pleased. My mother was just the opposite. She praised me all the time, probably to make up for Daddy's criticism. 'You can do anything you want. You're wonderful.' If I came in third in the prize speaking contest, it was 'Those judges were unfair. I thought you were the best.' I couldn't figure out why I was so lacking in confidence. After all, I could do no wrong in her eyes. Then it finally dawned on me that *I didn't believe her.* I saw that she needed me to be as perfect as Daddy did. I think as a kid I somehow knew that if she found out I wasn't as wonderful as she thought, she might stop loving me—so I had to hide who I really was. While she *saw* all the mistakes, she *never* pointed them out. I got the message loud and clear from both: 'Be perfect. We don't want to see mistakes.' Who could live up to that?"

Why a False Self Is Necessary

When basic needs are adequately met, a child remains in touch with her feelings and wants and is able to express them without fear of upsetting her parents. She knows she will be loved no matter what. Not so for the child who has learned that her authentic emotions and wishes don't count for much and only burden or annoy her parents. This child learns to survive by disowning her unacceptable parts and constructing a self that doesn't alienate those she loves. She is robbed of the opportunity to experience her feelings and misses out on a crucial aspect of self-development: *she fails to learn to be herself.* Instead she masters the ability to be the way another wants her to be, losing herself in the process. She learns she is most lovable when she is not being herself. Unfortunately the love she earns doesn't give her much comfort because she believes it is based on pretending to be someone she knows deep down she isn't.

Alice Miller writes about the painful discovery as an adult that our parents' love was in fact conditional. "What would have happened if I had appeared before you, bad, ugly, angry, jealous, lazy, dirty, smelly? Where would your love have been then? And I was all these things as well. Does this mean that it was not really me whom you loved, but only what I pretended to be? The well-behaved . . . and convenient child, who in fact was never a child at all?"[2]

The most important relationship we have is the one with ourselves. When this vital connection is broken, there is shame, acknowledged or unacknowledged. I have devised the following tables to clarify the notion of the false self.

The abandonment of the self is so gradual and insidious that, sadly, many people don't realize just how out of touch they are with themselves. They live with the fragile fantasy that this imposter represents who they really are, in spite of an underlying sense that they are inadequate. For years I clung to the belief that I was a wonderful mother and thought I loved (almost) every aspect of motherhood. I knew it was important to my parents to see me that way. I also subscribed to the either/or school of thought: Either I was a perfect mother or I was unfit.

My facade began to crack only when I became embroiled in intense power struggles with my willful daughter. "Imagine," my internal critic would say, "an adult who lets a six-year-old defeat her!" By the time we made it to the car most mornings, I would be close to tears of frustration and shame for being such an inadequate mother. I finally had to face the fact that I was trying so hard to be the perfect mother (who never got angry, never made mistakes) that I wasn't being "me" with her. Giving myself permission to be human freed me to be more spontaneous with my daughter and to set limits (even if I wasn't sure they were exactly right).

As I started to shed my false self, I began to see some of the ways I was an imperfect mother: I was impatient, I was distracted, I was critical. I had immense expectations for my children and hoped their glorious successes would redeem me from my feelings of inherent defectiveness. Once I was able to admit I wasn't an ideal mother, that I resented my kids at times and thought motherhood

AUTHENTIC SELF
(outside matches inside)

On the Outside We:	On the Inside We:
• Can own competence	• Feel competent yet can accept mistakes
• Are fully human: Acknowledge mistakes Express feelings	• Have access to vital inner child
	• Acknowledge feelings: sadness, anger, hurt, happiness, fear, confusion, healthy shame
• Act in our own best interests with concern for others	• Know our own mind
• Are spontaneous	• Are aware of being inauthentic from time to time, yet feel fully human

FALSE SELF
(outside doesn't match inside)

On the Outside We Act:	On the Inside We Feel:
• Competent	• Incompetent
• Together	• Defective
• Mature	• Childish
	• Like a fraud
	• Numb to our pain

wasn't all it was cracked up to be, my relationship with my daughter improved. I began the long process of learning to love the mother I was. (I'm still working on it, with three grown kids.) A mother who has to be perfect can't be human.

Being inauthentic consumes a lot of psychic energy. Until I was able to admit these feelings, I needed to hide my shameful imperfections (and my children's) because I believed they would reveal my *total* inadequacy.

As I gained compassion for myself and began talking with other mothers, I realized I wasn't alone in my feelings. I discovered that being a mother is not easy for most women. By telling the truth I lifted a load of guilt and shame. I began to let myself be who I was, a mother who struggled just like every other mother to be the best she could while coping with inevitable shortcomings and sometimes difficult circumstances.

The Cost of Concealing Our True Self

Emptiness. Denying our deepest self creates many problems. One of the most common is the feeling of emptiness that comes from not knowing what we think and feel, from being dependent on others to tell us who we are. We lose access to our inner self and feel hollow inside.

When we allow others to define us, we're never sure who we are.

"It's like there's nothing there," Marcy said. "Like I'm empty." There was a long pause as she pulled her sweater together over her ample breasts. "I've never said that before," she said finally.

I asked her how it felt to say that.

"Terrible. I have always defined myself through my reflection in the eyes of others. But since each person sees me differently, I never know who I really am. I guess there's no 'me' inside at all. Maybe that's why I'm so uncomfortable with people. I'm afraid they'll see there's nothing there."

Sometimes those of us who feel empty and false describe ourselves as "not being real." To fill up the terrifying emptiness, we drink, take drugs, overeat, have affairs, or get ourselves into unhealthy relationships. What reinforces these destructive attempts to dull pain is their ability to temporarily shore up our false self and provide heady, if brief, feelings of being lovable and wonderful.

Self-loathing. The pain of self-loathing is another curse for those who have abandoned their natural selves. The real self is considered unworthy and defective. These parts are relegated to the unconscious but, as Gershen Kaufman puts it, "Always, there are faint murmurings of it that can be painfully felt. Any degree of conscious awareness of what has been intentionally cast adrift brings on the most acute inner pain."[3]

The loss of self also creates anger or depression, which are usually disturbing and deeply puzzling to us because we have no understanding of their source. The gift of therapy is the opportunity to reconnect with lost parts of ourselves.

Needing to be forever on guard. People with a need to maintain a facade live with the constant fear of being exposed as impostors. A nagging sense of being transparent adds to the anguish. "I feel like I have to be constantly on guard to make sure I don't inadvertently reveal who I really am," Marcy says. "In fact half the time I think they've already found me out and are just putting up with me."

The fear of being exposed as a charlatan keeps many women from taking promotions or applying for jobs they mistakenly feel are going to reveal their inadequacies. It also robs them of intimacy in relationships because they're afraid of becoming vulnerable and being seen as stupid, empty, or selfish.

Missing out on the joy of success. Many of us, like Alex, believe we don't deserve our achievements, professional or personal. "If people only knew what a selfish, mean person I really am, they'd never have made me 'Citizen of the Year,'" one woman says. Somehow we have the idea that we have to be flawless before we deserve recognition for our accomplishments. Our job performance has to be perfect, our relationship has to be perfect, before we can allow ourselves to take pleasure in it. Because we don't feel we deserve our success, we tell ourselves, *I may have my success, but at least I won't let myself enjoy it much.*

Hanging on to feelings of being a fraud, denying our accomplishment, or killing our pleasure in our success serves to ward off possible envy or rejection from people important to us, especially parents or siblings we've surpassed in salary, education, successful relationships, or generally happy lives.

The lack of permission from society for women to excel, to

enjoy positions of power and authority, makes successful women especially vulnerable to feeling like impostors. We don't feel we belong among the movers and shakers. And the fact that we often don't earn equal pay for equal work (even in positions of high rank and influence) reinforces our view of ourselves as less competent than men.

Feeling like an impostor is one way to disown our ambition. *(I got here by luck, not because I wanted it badly enough to work for it.)* Lack of trust in ourselves is another reason we find it difficult to claim our competence. We believe that our success was a fluke, and we are plagued by self-doubt about our ability to sustain our level of performance.

Lack of access to inner resources. Because we are unable to claim our intelligence and our competence, we often achieve far less than we are capable of. Whether we stop ourselves for fear of success or for fear of failure, in the end we resist challenging ourselves to be as creative and accomplished as we can be.

After years of suppressing and abandoning such fundamental aspects of our selves as our feelings, wants and needs, competence, sexuality, and capacity to think for ourselves, we end up not only alienated from ourselves but disempowered. When we don't know what we think or feel about things, we limit our ability to make choices that are in our own best interests.

What Happens to Disowned Parts?

When we suppress and eventually disown our shameful and dangerous feelings, we convert them into more acceptable forms.

At the beginning of one of our sessions Alex sank down in her chair and said, "I feel terrible. I had dinner with my parents last night and ended up getting angry at my mother. While we were getting dinner ready, Mother began complaining that I never called. She does this all the time. The truth is I call her every week. I was angry. I think it's the first time I ever stood up to her. I said, 'Stop. I'm not going to do this with you, Mother. Now, what kind of dressing would you like on the salad?' "

I asked what happened then.

"Mother daubed at her eyes—and stopped speaking to me for

the rest of the evening. I felt like a terrible daughter. I really hurt her feelings—she's sensitive, you know. I probably shouldn't have stood up to her like that."

Is it more comfortable to feel ashamed than angry? Sometimes we talk ourselves out of a legitimate feeling and substitute another. Alex's mother may also have been ashamed of her anger, but turning it into hurt by becoming a martyr.

When we are unaware of our particular needs, such as the need to be held and loved or the need to matter, we convert these needs into something more acceptable or attainable. For instance we turn to sex in order to feel good about ourselves even though it may not be sex we want, but rather comfort or warm contact.[4] Ann Landers discovered in her now famous survey that the majority of women convert their need to be held into the need for sex.

Women with eating disorders are the first to admit it isn't hunger that drives them to eat. It's the impostor who says, "I'm horny" or "I'm starved" when underneath we are crying out for love and attention.

When we disown our creativity and competence, we are vulnerable to living our lives through others, riding on our husbands' coattails, or experiencing the thrill of creativity or achievement through our children. I can say, "I'm not a competent professional, but my husband is." When my daughter makes a soccer goal and is cheered by parents and teammates, the little girl inside me who is starving for acknowledgment gets fed.

Reclaiming Our Lost Selves

When we begin healing our shame, we often discover that we have misjudged other people's feelings about us. During her therapy Marcy became friendly with one of the women who she was sure didn't like her. She was surprised to discover that *the other woman had felt just as intimidated by her*. In the end they became such close friends, they decided to rent a house together.

In order to begin recognizing the impostor's handiwork, we need to ask ourselves the following:

- Are we overly concerned about how others see us?
- Do we worry about what we "should" be thinking or feeling?

- Do we find ourselves having delayed responses to situations (such as feeling anger or tears an hour or even days later)?
- Are we different with different people?
- Are we settling for jobs for which we are overqualified because we feel unentitled to higher positions?
- Are we unable to enjoy our successes? Do we dismiss praise?

If we answer yes to any of these questions, we can assume the impostor has probably been at work.

To maintain a facade while feeling like a fraud is to experience the deepest kind of pain. To be alienated from ourselves is to be our own worst enemy because *our relationship to ourselves is the most important one we'll ever have.*

When we hide behind a mask, we end up depriving ourselves— as well as others—of the experience of knowing our natural selves. We need to take off the mask and tell ourselves, *I deserve this job, this relationship, these friends. I have a right to my feelings, my opinions, my thoughts, my competence, and my success. I am lovable just as I am.*

It's never too late to get acquainted with that special person we abandoned years ago.

Protecting
Against the Pain

"I was raised in a caring family," Joanie tells me, "although my mother did take her anger out on me once in a while."

I ask how.

"She hit me sometimes."

With what?

"A hairbrush, her hand, sticks, a hanger." Now choked with tears, she can barely talk. "One day the school principal saw the welts on my legs and warned my mother never to beat me again. She didn't do it as often after that."

I ask Joanie what sense she made of the beatings.

"Since I never knew what I did wrong, I just figured I was a rotten kid for her to get *that* mad at me."

Eventually Joanie went to live with her aunt. Maintaining the illusion that her childhood was happy was a way of adapting to an unbearable situation. And her memories of the good times reinforced her denial. Although she had never forgotten the bad memories, for years she had been numb to the pain, experiencing little of her shame, anger, terror, and despair as a child. This was how she survived emotionally.

Only in the presence of a caring listener, *only when she learned to treat herself compassionately*, did these feelings become bearable enough to surface. Eventually she was able to embrace the wounded little girl inside her, acknowledge her pain, work through her anger, and even create a new and better relationship with her mother.

The Power of Denial

To deny or limit our awareness of underlying shame is to become numb to our pain. For most of us, chronic shame remains mostly unfelt and unacknowledged, except for painful eruptions or moments we call embarrassment, self-consciousness, or insecurity.

Denial may take the form of being oblivious to the inequities around us at home, on the job, or in society at large—situations that might threaten to trigger shame. We can be dismissed, criticized, put down, yet hardly notice. Or we fail to grasp that our mate is alcoholic, workaholic, addicted to drugs, unfaithful.

Many women use food, drugs, alcohol, overwork, excessive exercise, or affairs to help them deny the pain of their perceived defectiveness.

Even depression can help us deny our deep-seated feelings of shame. Miserable as depression is, it may be preferable to our unowned feelings of underlying shame, inadequacy, powerlessness, and lack of connection to others. Women are particularly vulnerable to depression, partly because it is a more socially acceptable defense against shame than being angry.

As a therapist I find that working with depressed clients to help them gently and slowly uncover their shame—and the underlying reasons for it—is crucial to their healing process.

Shame as a Defense

Sometimes our shame leads us to adopt certain other defensive maneuvers, as we shall see later in this chapter. Yet there are times when we enlist shame to protect ourselves. Although this may seem counterproductive, we sometimes shame ourselves as a defense against delving into deeper levels of shame, anger, or grief—especially grief over loss of self. Sometimes we use shame to cover up unacceptable assertiveness and competitiveness. It can also help us maintain our ties to people important to us.

Remember Ginny, the woman in Chapter One who had anxiety attacks that kept her home from work? An exceptionally bright and competent licensed vocational nurse, Ginny improved enough to get back to work and to tolerate being out socially.

"Can you believe, Rosa's husband gave a party for her when she got her R.N. and I actually forgot to go?" she told me. "I had it on my calendar and everything. Oh, God, I'm such a jerk."

I asked what she might be feeling if she weren't judging and shaming herself.

"Maybe I'm a little jealous that Rosa got her degree. I care about her, but it's hard to see her get her degree when . . . I guess I'm jealous."

I asked what she meant by jealous.

"Well, it doesn't feel good. Like I'm mad that she made it. It's not fair. I'm such a weirdo to be jealous."

Was shaming herself more comfortable than allowing herself to want something?

She sat silently for a long time, tears slowly filling her eyes. "You're saying I want what she has?" There was a long pause. "You mean it's okay to want?"

What's so bad about wanting?

"I can just hear my mother saying, 'You're not the only one around here, you know, young lady. Don't be greedy.' Besides, my mom always wanted to be a nurse, but she was sick all the time and had all those kids to take care of. I don't have any right to expect more than she had."

While Ginny wept quietly for the little girl who had been ashamed of her own wants and needs, I remembered how she had made her own needs secondary to everyone else's as she took on her mother's job of caring for the family. Small wonder she found it hard to let herself want something for herself.

As Ginny thought about our discussion, she realized how much she wanted to be an R.N., but with three mouths to feed she couldn't see a way to go to school and keep her job. She eventually enrolled in a demanding independent-study program and after four years of dogged work she called me with her good news. She had earned her R.N.!

Because Ginny had been ashamed in the first place of wanting something for herself, and then for wanting more than her mother had, she had never let her longing to be an R.N. come fully into awareness. Instead, when it appeared in the form of envy, she clamped a lid on it by shaming herself for the envy. Then, when we uncovered the wanting underneath the envy, she again shamed herself to avoid the double pain of admitting to bad, unacceptable longings and facing all that she had given up. Staying an L.V.N. had been an unconscious compromise to have more than Mother but not too much more.

Ginny's shame preserves the crucial connection to her mother, who in subtle ways asked her not to have more success than she did, because Mother couldn't tolerate being exposed as having made wrong decisions about her own life (such as settling for an unhappy marriage and not having a career). Out of misguided loyalty Ginny held herself back.

It's important to remember that these motives are largely unconscious for both Ginny and her mother. It's equally important to recognize that messages from our parents are often ambivalent: They also want us to be happy and successful in our lives. Sometimes shame is the price we pay for the good things in our lives.

How We Stifle Ourselves with Shame

Shame also stops us from expressing ourselves in ways that are unacceptable for women. We have trouble asking the waitress to take back our overdone steak (for fear of seeming "pushy") or talking to our boss about something he did that upset us (for fear of seeming "too sensitive"). We hold back our anger (for fear of seeming "bitchy"). Shame keeps us in line—even *behind* the line drawn to keep women from competing, asserting themselves, or being powerful. We incorporate society's shaming prohibitions and make them our own to protect ourselves from further shaming.

Shame even keeps us from *feeling* dangerous emotions, such as anger or hurt, that might threaten our connections to others. When Lynn starts to feel angry, she blushes with shame. She shames herself out of sad or hurt feelings by dismissing them as "just feeling sorry for myself."

Getting Our Act Together

As children we unconsciously created ways to protect ourselves
from our intolerable feelings of shame. Because these defenses
allowed us to survive then, we continue using them as adults, even
though they constrict and impoverish our lives. These survival
strategies influence our thoughts, feelings, and behavior. Some of
these protective masks are pleasing, others abrasive. Each hides a
frightened person.

Here are some strategies we use to feel safe in the world and
avoid shame:

- I'll tear you down and build myself up.
- I'll be a victim and avoid taking responsibility.
- I'll be superior to others.
- I'll be right and make you wrong.
- I'll be perfect—then they won't criticize me.
- I'll always be in control of myself and others.
- I'll get angry—then they'll back off.
- I'll withdraw and just observe.
- I'll be needed—then they won't leave.
- I'll rebel—who cares anyway?
- I'll be humble and please others.
- I'll be a good girl—then they'll love me.

Designed as attempts to rid the self of the anguish of shame,
these protective stances guard the boundary between self and
world, serving to keep others at a safe distance. Each has a high
cost.

As you read my characterizations of these adaptations, remember that none of us is entirely one type; we all use most of these
protections from time to time, and they overlap to a large extent.
Yet we tend to have a favorite strategy or a combination that has
served us well through the years. We may depend on one more
than another at certain stages of our lives or in dealing with
certain situations or people. Remember, too, that these adaptations aren't necessarily pathological.

The Faultfinder

She is the blamer, who has learned from her family that when things go wrong, someone has to be at fault, and it had better not be her! So today she is quick to point the finger away from herself to get off the hook. This eases the feelings of shame that stem from her deep-seated belief that if things go wrong, it's usually her fault, even when she has no idea why. If she can find something wrong with *others,* she avoids confronting her fear that something may be wrong with *her.*

When Vanessa learns she's overdrawn her account, it eases her feelings of inadequacy to blame the bank for not honoring her bounced check. "After all these years of banking with them, you'd think they'd pay it. I wasn't over that much. And the fee they charge—outrageous!" When she finds out her sixteen-year-old daughter is pregnant, Vanessa blames her ex-husband. "If only he'd given her more attention, she wouldn't have looked for it in a boy." When she discovers her lover is unfaithful, she blames him entirely, refusing to listen to any of his feelings.

Although making others wrong brings Vanessa that addictive feeling of being right, she pushes people away with her constant blaming and picking at them. The big benefit is that she doesn't have to look at her own deep feelings of inadequacy. "You're the one who should be ashamed, not me," she implies.

The Victim

This woman is also a blamer, but she is more subtle about it. Her purpose is not so much to find fault with others (to build herself up or avoid being criticized) as it is to *avoid* responsibility for her life (to gain pity and agreement from others that she is not to blame for her problems). Her strategy conceals her fear of being exposed as a failure and her deep resignation about the impossibility of things ever changing. Taking *any* responsibility for her life not working out would be the same as admitting that she is *completely* at fault, a worthless person. Resigned to being powerless, she has decided that if she can't have what she wants, she'll at least settle for enlisting others' sympathy. She also believes that she doesn't deserve a better life. She solicits advice from her friends but wears them out by responding with "Yes, but." They have no idea that her victim stance camouflages her despair and shame that stem from deep feelings of inadequacy.

She is known to create drama, chaos, and confusion as a way to distract her from her inner pain.

When her current husband leaves, she says, "It wasn't my fault that he found another woman. Men always do something to hurt me. My last two husbands were worthless too." This approach is preferable to looking at her part in her troubles—a terrifying prospect indeed.

THE STAR

Caroline exudes confidence as she elbows her way through a crowd, headed for an important board meeting. Her cool beauty and style evoke stares, which give her a moment of pleasure and interrupt her incessant stream of negative thoughts about herself: *How stupid can you get? You know you aren't well prepared for this presentation. You'll probably screw it up. You shouldn't have worn this skirt. It makes you look fat.* Suddenly her thoughts shift as her self-contempt becomes too painful. *I hope Gail won't be there. I can't stand that woman. She thinks she's so great. She gets away with murder in this office. I can't believe she actually cried at the meeting yesterday.*

Most people would be surprised to know that underneath this seemingly confident woman hides a frightened and wounded little girl who believes she is fundamentally flawed. The narcissistic woman is so insecure that she constantly acts superior in the hope of convincing herself and others of her inherent worth. She clings to what analyst Karen Horney calls a glorified image of herself.[1] A fragile version of self, it nonetheless helps keep shame at bay.

Her successes, which are many, serve only as short-lived intoxicants whose effects soon give way to depression.

Grandiose and contemptuous at times, the Star has learned that if she is better than others, she can ward off shame. She has a way of making people around her feel clumsy, not too smart, less attractive. Often what she most disdains in others are traits she has rejected in herself. For instance she may be contemptuous of a woman (or her own child) who appears dependent. By projecting the rejected "shameful" part of herself onto someone else, she manages to deny her own neediness.

Her parents failed to form a deep connection with her that

assured her she was loved. They may also have squelched her natural exhibitionism, so she craves the attention she lacked as a child. The Star demands special treatment. She hates to wait in lines, to be ignored, to be put on hold. She has to have the best seat in the restaurant, in fact the best of everything.

Arrogance helps justify the Star's existence as it covers up her shame—the shame that fuels her judgmentalness or condescension toward others. Though her arrogance armors her against injuries from the outside world, it can't really protect her from the internal pain stemming from her deep shame. Her feelings of unworthiness are easily triggered as she takes offense at or over-reacts to every possible slight.

The Star never lets herself become vulnerable enough to reveal her inner self or let someone else matter too much.

If Caroline were to find out her man had been two-timing her, she might go out and buy a smashing outfit and have an affair herself in retaliation. She reassures herself of her lovableness: *I'll find a man who is better-looking and earns more money. After all, I deserve the best, and this jerk obviously isn't worth suffering over anyway.*

THE RIGHT ONE

Stemming from all the times as children we were criticized or made to feel wrong (stupid, bad, or worthless), the need to be right dominates our thinking and behavior. When you feel like you are a mistake, you can never admit to making a mistake. When you are drowning in self-criticism, it's difficult to accept constructive criticism from others.

Most commonly we reveal our need to be right simply by insisting that we're right about our viewpoint, our knowledge, our experience. "I told you so" is a favorite expression. We continually justify, explain, or excuse our behavior. "I only said that because I was trying to help," we say. "If I hadn't been so sleepy, I'm sure I could have come up with the answer." Anything to ward off accusations of being mean, selfish, or stupid.

Needing to be right—one of the most powerful driving forces for human beings—creates a self-righteousness that can be insufferable. Needing to be right can also kill communication. Sometimes being right is more important than having intimate relationships or even being alive. One woman, when asked if she'd rather be happy or be right, replied, "Being right is what makes me happy."

When the woman who needs to be right discovers that her boyfriend has been unfaithful, she may respond with, "I knew it all along. He didn't fool me one minute. I knew I couldn't trust him the minute I laid eyes on him."

The Perfectionist

Attempting to make up for never being quite good enough, this woman goes all out to be the best, settling for nothing short of perfection. If she can be perfect, she can ward off criticism. The only problem is that she becomes her own worst critic and lives with chronic shame for never measuring up to her impossible expectations. But at least she can say she tried if anyone accuses her of being less than perfect. Her parents were probably highly critical of her and demanded perfection. ("You got a ninety-nine on your test? Why not a hundred?")

The Perfectionist may be a workaholic, losing out on life as it passes her by. She often takes on more than she can handle and rarely rests or lets down because she is terrified of being less than perfect.

Whereas the Right One needs to *be* right, the Perfectionist needs to *do* things right—her sense of self depends on it. When she makes mistakes, her self-esteem plummets. Her own worst enemy, she tends to compare herself unfavorably to others. She lacks an internal sense of how much is "good enough."[2] She is ruled by her all-or-nothing mentality: *If I'm not perfect, I'm no good at all.* Her loud and persistent Inner Critic rarely rests.

It's no surprise that the Perfectionist is almost as hard on others as she is on herself; she invariably expects too much. If others fail to meet her high standards, she criticizes them and is badly disappointed.

When human tendencies show up, such as pettiness, greed, or anger, the Perfectionist has to deny them. Any hint of the presence of "shameful" qualities becomes a threat, and she tries even harder to be their opposite as she condemns herself. "It's not easy being a perfectionist. *I try to do it perfectly, but I don't know the rules.*" She lives her life according to her external *should*s rather than in relationship to her self.

When the Perfectionist finds out her husband has taken a lover, she tries harder than ever to be perfect. She prepares gourmet meals every night, goes on a diet, and buys five books on how to keep your man happy. Her Inner Critic goes crazy: *How could you have missed the signs? All you do is think about yourself. If you thought about others some of the time, this might never have happened. You didn't work hard enough at this relationship.*

THE CONTROLLER

Trying to control everything and everyone protects this woman from her fear of being helpless. She tries to convince herself that she is in charge of her life. She also hopes to avoid getting caught in unexpected situations where she might be shamed. And if she can get others to do what she thinks they should—by telling them how to do things the "right way"—she inflates her own sense of power and knowledge. Whether people comply or resist, they resent her controlling behavior. She has trouble letting go and trusting that others are capable of running their own lives.

Kathleen, in spite of having had a complicated major surgery, was so used to being in control that she found herself unable to let go. Bandaged and groggy, she was asked how she was feeling.

"I'm okay, but I'm worried about one thing."

"What's that?" her sympathetic friend asked.

"I'm worried about Harry [her husband]."

"What's wrong with Harry?"

"Poor Harry has been sitting here all this time with nothing to do. It gets so boring for him."

Unable to let life go on without her, she created something she could be responsible for so she could focus on fixing it. This ploy also allowed her to avoid her shame around needing to be taken care of by others.

When she discovers that her husband is unfaithful, the Controller gives him the names of three therapists to call. And when she sets up the appointment, she lets the therapist know about her husband's personality problems. By controlling what she can, she avoids feeling her pain and shame. She focuses instead on what he should do to handle the problem.

THE VOLCANO

This woman may be quick to anger, venting her shame-fed fury on others, or she may suffer chronic smoldering rage that erupts only rarely, usually when she has been deeply humiliated.[3] Her anger accomplishes two major things: She manages to keep others safely at a distance, thus protecting herself against a shaming attack; and she counteracts internal feelings of defectiveness and helplessness (shame equivalents) by converting them into anger at others.

Shame-based anger gives the illusion of taking back power. Often the perceived weakness that triggers the Volcano's anger is her awareness of having needs, along with her fear that others will see her need and mock it or fail to meet it, leaving her humiliated at her own unworthiness and insignificance.[4]

Besides defending against feelings of helplessness or need, shame-based anger may cover up hurt and, beneath that, shame over being treated hurtfully by someone she cares about.

Not all anger is volcanic. Nor does all anger cover shame. But we often miss the underlying cause if we assume we know what is at the bottom of either our own or another's rage. More often than not shame is at the source.

We can predict the response of the two-timed Volcano, Vivien: She flies into a rage, packs her bags, and leaves when she learns of the infidelity of her partner, Anne. But first she dumps all Anne's clothes on the lawn after writing her a letter telling her what an unforgivable bitch she is. She also calls Anne's lover and gives her a verbal blistering. Her anger keeps her from feeling the pain. After things die down, she feels ashamed of her outburst and lack of control.

THE OBSERVER

She withdraws emotionally and/or physically, sitting on the sidelines watching the parade go by. By not participating fully in life she lessens her chances of being shamed. Though she is often in denial about her feelings of defectiveness, she may admit to strong feelings of self-consciousness and embarrassment (more acceptable forms of shame).

She reduces exposure by burying her flawed self deeply inside.

Most of us don't withdraw so obviously as the Observer does, except on occasions when retreating or being indifferent might protect us.

The Observer learned that staying emotionally uninvolved in her family worked as a child, but now she is feeling lonely and unconnected to other people. Her husband wants more affection, more conversation, more contact.

Her response to her husband's affair is to do nothing. She simply burrows deeper into her shell and carries on as if nothing had happened to upset her world. She doesn't try to talk things over. "What good would that do? There's nothing I can do to change things. If he wants to leave, that's fine." She has no close friends she can call and may not even recognize her need for support, since she manages so well to distance herself from her hurt, anger, and underlying shame.

THE ACCOMMODATOR

An obvious sex-linked protective strategy, taking care of others has become second nature to most women. If we can focus on relieving the pain of others, we don't have to feel our own. My own Accommodator came to the fore when my grown son was having problems with his ex-wife. I got in the middle, carrying messages back and forth, focusing on their needs and feelings rather than feeling the pain that came from my own guilt, shame, and sense of helplessness over their divorce. Fortunately, my women's support group helped me refocus on my own pain and let go of trying to fix theirs.

Having something "constructive" to do allows the Accommodator to ease her worries about being unlovable. If she can make herself indispensable to others, they won't leave her. She needs to please others in order to get fed, since she doesn't feed herself. "I'm so busy worrying about what other people want, I never find out what *I* want" is her common complaint. At least being needed is a solace for not having her own needs met. There's another payoff: her chronic compliance helps her to minimize conflict and ward off others' anger.

When the Accommodator finds out her husband has been cheating on her, she immediately feels his pain and wants to take care of him. Concerned that he might get overstressed, she avoids making demands on him to help with the dishes or put the kids to bed. She understands he needs time to be with his feelings. When he suggests that he move in with the other woman to try it out, she's upset but goes along with the idea and assures him he can always come back.

THE REBEL

This woman throws over the constraints of family and society and prides herself on being her own person, but inside she feels like a scared kid. Unaware of the shame that lies at the core of her being, she thinks of herself as a free spirit. But she isn't really free, because she is *reacting* rather than *responding* to her world. She resists paying taxes or wearing her seat belt because *no one's going to tell her what to do.*

Her rebellious stance keeps her from caring enough about anyone to feel any shame in the event she's rejected. So when the man she's living with gets involved with someone else, she lets him go because she knows he, too, is a free spirit. Although deep down she needs him, she is too ashamed to admit to herself or anyone else how important he is to her.

THE HUMBLE ONE

This woman doesn't deflect, deny, or convert her shame, but readily acknowledges her feelings of inherent defectiveness. Opposite of the Star, this modest person attempts to fit the stereotype that society approves for women: passive, not too smart, dependent. Self-deprecating, she puts herself down before others get the chance. She is sometimes known as a doormat or people pleaser. Above all she is uncomfortable being powerful.

"I learned to make fun of myself so that I could control what people would laugh at me for," says Heidi, who felt stupid as a girl when teased by her friends. "This way I ward off criticism by getting there first. Even if I'm not sure whether I've done anything wrong, someone else might think I have. So if I berate myself first, I'm somewhat protected from being attacked. I can say, 'I already know that.' "

Another benefit of this stance is that she gets to be right about how bad and wrong she is.

Where the Observer learned that the most protected place was *apart* from others, Heidi learned as a little girl that the safest spot was *below* others. The Humble One refuses to compete (but may still harbor strong competitive feelings). Her "incompetent" act may be so successful that she herself may not know her real capabilities.

One purpose of her self-effacing strategy is to shore up those around her so that they can feel strong in her presence. Giving up her power as a child may have helped limit angry outbursts from her irate parents. Because she doesn't let herself know her own mind, she avoids condemnation for having ideas that might differ from others'. She often acts confused, a sure way to leak power. Or she holds back her opinions and avoids talking about her successes for fear others won't like her. She's afraid that being seen as too competent might hamper her relationships. She disempowers herself by deliberately drawing attention to her goofs and inviting others to see her as scatterbrained, often in spite of evidence to the contrary. And she frequently asks others for advice, which allows them to feel important.

Compliments are a sure way to bring on a shame attack. "I get so embarrassed and self-conscious when people compliment me," she says. "I don't believe them anyway—I know I just fooled them. I never know what to do. Saying 'thanks' makes me look conceited—like I agree with them."

We are all too familiar with the joke about the person who automatically apologizes to the owner of the foot that stepped on her. But saying "I'm sorry" is no joke for the Humble One, who has an apology for every occasion.

Although Heidi never offends anyone, she suffers from loss of vitality or real connection with others because so much of her natural self is submerged.

When the Humble One finds out her partner has been having an affair, she blames herself. "I wasn't really there for him. I should have been more available for sex—less tired. It's all my fault. I should have nagged him less. I knew it was only a matter of time before he'd get bored with me." She hopes that if she takes all the responsibility and represses any anger or distress, she might keep him a little longer. She also makes unfavorable comparisons: "The other woman is probably much better for him. She's probably a lot smarter and prettier."

The Good Girl

It's difficult to distinguish this defensive adaptation from some of the others—perhaps because it's so common among the women I see. The good girl doesn't seem to stand alone, but rather appears in combination with the Perfectionist *(I'll be good by being perfect)*, the Accommodator *(I'll be good and take care of you)*, the Controller *(I'll be good and insist you be good)*, the Observer *(I'll be good and quiet)*, or the Humble One *(I'll be good by letting you be the good one)*.

The Good Girl (in any of her composites) conforms to what others expect of her. She aims to please and she denies any unacceptable feelings such as anger. Because she doesn't want to be a burden to anyone, she defers or denies her wants and needs. By being good she hopes to avoid being shamed for being the bad girl she secretly fears she is: *I do nice things in order to get other people's approval. Inside I'm not nice. I'm untrustworthy, I'm cold. I'm needy. And I'm terrified of being found out.*

Of course no woman is just one of these types. We all combine these strategies and resort to others I haven't mentioned. The point of this gallery of caricatures is to illustrate how we defend ourselves against feelings of shame and what sacrificing our authentic selves costs.

While these adaptations have enabled us to survive both troubled childhoods and shaming experiences in our larger world, they become outmoded when we become adults. Perhaps by being angry as a child I could get my family to cater to me. Perhaps my being incompetent would make my mother feel important and therefore be kinder to me. Perhaps trying to do everything just right would ward off my father's anger when I made mistakes.

But I'm no longer a child who can't survive without her parents. Now I'm an adult, with adult skills. I can find ways of taking care of myself that are less costly to me. I know I can survive anger or criticism. I can negotiate: "Let's talk it over." Or set limits: "That's enough. Back off." As an adult I can find ways of taking care of myself that are less costly. Although connection with others will always be a major pleasure for me, I no longer need to suppress who I am in order to keep another person's love. Nor do I need to depend on old strategies that deprive me of the happiness, success, and healthy relationships I long for.

We will probably never entirely let go of these familiar protections that were created to stand between us and our deep feelings of defectiveness. But as we become aware of their grip on us, we are freer to consider other more authentic and satisfying ways of being.

PART FOUR

―――――|||||||||――――

How Shame Infects Our Relationships

CHAPTER ELEVEN

How Shame Kills Intimacy

Relationships are central to the lives of most women. We yearn for an intimacy that nurtures us, fosters our growth, and adds to our vitality and happiness. Unfortunately women contending with maladaptive shame look to their relationships to provide them with feelings of self-worth they are unable to provide for themselves, and they have trouble establishing the satisfying connections they long for.

We depend on our closest affiliations to provide us with identity and feelings of self-worth, yet our ability to form healthy relationships rests on our having sufficient self-esteem, a scarce commodity for those of us who struggle with shame. In addition, tradition demands that we assume a position of inferiority to men—a role so much a part of the fabric of our society that we women simply aren't aware of how insidious and pervasive it is or how it undermines our attempts to enhance our self-worth through forming close emotional attachments.

Because we feel responsible for the success of our relationships, if there are problems, we are quick to blame ourselves. Each time an important connection fails, we feel inadequate; yet the more inadequate we feel, the less we have to bring to the next relationship.

"Tell Me Who I Am"

"I married Glen to fill up a missing part of me," says thirty-six-year-old Beth, a shy, soft-spoken music teacher, voicing what many shame-ridden women feel. "I felt empty and wanted my hollowness filled by a man. I was a nonperson. Glen was so exciting. He knew where he was going in life. He always knew just what he wanted, whether it was steak or pizza, or which movie to see—decisions that would always be so hard for me. His decisiveness was reassuring to me, because I didn't know who I was. I still don't," she adds somewhat sheepishly.

Relationships provide women with a sense of identity. Many of us, like Beth, no longer know with any certainty who we are, what we feel, what we want. Not knowing, we turn to a man for *all* the answers.

As we saw in Chapter Five, a woman tends to develop her sense of self in the context of her relationship to others, while a man tends to develop his identity according to his work or accomplishments. This isn't a problem unless we depend so heavily on our affiliations to define us that we never develop a solid sense of self. Historically a woman took on her husband's name: "I'm Mrs. *John* Smith." While men were raised to find a place for themselves in the world, women were raised to find a place by a man's side.

Being in a relationship can enhance our self-esteem by providing us with the opportunity to associate ourselves with a man's strengths and accomplishments. By marrying somebody we become somebody. Our hope is that our bad feelings about ourselves will go away if only we can connect with someone who is smarter, more powerful, richer, better-looking, or more accomplished than we are.

But there are more subtle ways we let those closest to us define us. They tell us, "You're selfish. You don't need that, you need this. You shouldn't feel that way. I expect this of you. You're so indecisive." And we believe it. Women caught in the struggle to define themselves find relief in being told who they are. I know a woman who, with her husband, had season tickets to the opera for twenty-seven years before she could admit that the opera fan in the marriage was her husband, not her. She had never even *liked* opera. She no longer attends, and she appreciates the luxury of having her Saturday nights open during opera season. Her husband continues to attend and enjoys indulging his long-standing passion for opera. Although the fabric of their marriage was stretched, it gained a healthy flexibility that allowed them both to express their individuality.

Why Opposites Attract

Besides helping to shape our identity, relationships provide us with an opportunity to experience disowned parts of ourselves. Many of us who have abandoned vital aspects of ourselves seek to be with someone who expresses these rejected parts. For instance if we have suppressed our anger, we may be drawn to someone who gets mad easily. (Men also do this; a man often finds that his partner provides the emotional juice missing in his life.) Through identifying with the other, we vicariously get to experience a wider range of feelings and experiences. For instance Beth, having suppressed her ability to think for herself, relied on Glen for his decisiveness. She feels buffered from the confusions and dangers of the "real world" by Glen's ability to navigate its treacherous waters.

Caretaking: Doing What Comes Naturally?

A relationship offers us the opportunity to solidify our identity by carrying out the job we have trained for since our early days of playing house: taking care of others. Almost all women are caretakers to some extent. Not taking on that expected role can leave us with a shaky identity.

The capacity to care for another affirms our sense of worthiness: "I am a person who is capable of caring deeply, who nurtures and supports others."[1] Yet when we consistently put the needs of others ahead of our own or take care of others out of duty rather than choice, we damage our self-esteem. In the next chapter we will look more fully at the ways we give up ourselves to take care of others.

"Prince Charming Will Make Me Happy"

Finding a mate eases many of the emotional insecurities that stem from our feelings of unworthiness. Never having learned to be secure in the knowledge that we matter, we look to a significant other to make us feel special. Not knowing who we are, we need someone to give us an identity. Feeling something is missing in us, we need someone with whom we can merge in perfect union to make us feel whole. We need someone to take care of who will also take care of us. It may seem as though our very survival depends on finding a partner. But when two shame-bound people connect in a significant relationship, they will encounter many roadblocks along the way.

Eileen was a thirty-year-old single mother who told me, "If only I could find a man, I'd be happy." She had been in therapy with me for a few months when she met Joe.

In the beginning, in order to capture each other's romantic interests, Eileen and Joe hid their less-than-perfect selves behind facades aimed to please. Each was thrilled at being mirrored by the other as wonderful, exciting, and sexy. What an irresistible balm for the ache of shame.

Eileen was sure she'd found happiness at last. Joe found her fascinating, hanging on her every word. "He's so open," she said. "We can talk about anything and everything. At last I've found someone I can connect with on a feeling level. I think I've fallen in love."

But Eileen was mistaking infatuation—a state Ambrose Bierce calls "temporary insanity curable by marriage"—for love. In this state neither sees who the other really is; both only see a reflection of what they want to see. For many of us such moments of infatuation are the only times we feel lovable or can experience loving ourselves.

Some women so need this kind of respite from their feelings of being flawed that they can't stay in a relationship once this phase passes into a more realistic form of love. Also they may be so out of touch with their own aliveness that they only feel truly alive

when they're in a state of infatuation. Some women have ex-
tramarital affairs to recapture these powerful feelings.

Because her childhood had been difficult—her mother was
critical and her father absent—Eileen was searching for the loving
parent she never had.

Since both Eileen and Joe are looking to diminish their feelings
of unworthiness and since neither is equipped to deliver for the
other, the longed-for union can only result in anger, disappointment, and increased feelings of inadequacy. Unmet expectations
and unfulfilled needs leave us feeling unloved and unworthy of
love.

Like Eileen, women dealing with shame often believe that if
only they had a relationship, they'd be able to fill up these empty
holes. But when we look for happiness "out there," when we look
for someone to save us from ourselves, we are looking in the
wrong place.

True happiness comes from an inner state of well-being, from
self-love, not from an outer state of knowing we are loved by
another. We need to be secure in the knowledge that we can take
care of and love ourselves. Ultimately we are in charge of our own
happiness.

We Bring Baggage Loaded with Shame

Let's explore what we bring with us to our relationships. First
there's our cultural baggage—the ways women are conditioned to
be: passive, dependent, self-sacrificing. Tagging along is our inner
little girl with her emotional baggage. She feels unlovable and is
needy and angry—afraid of being either taken over or abandoned. We bring our unresolved developmental issues, such as
lack of trust, fear of autonomy, and sexual insecurities. Next, as if
this bicycle-built-for-two weren't already overloaded, we bring
along our parents (who were probably shame-based), with their
distinct rules for navigating relationships.

If we could set all this baggage down and relate to our partners
as they really are, we would avoid a lot of problems. But unfortunately how we see people is colored by what we've learned in our
growing-up years about relating and what we've learned to expect
from people close to us.

Eileen's father left her and her mother when she was four, so when Joe comes home a little late, she gets angry, a defense against her anxiety around being abandoned again. Now sometimes she is able to catch herself and respond instead of reacting: "Oops. I almost forgot. He's not my father. He's Joe. My father left. Joe's here."

For a woman like Eileen it seems almost impossible to have successful relationships, given the emotional and cultural baggage she brings to them. Yet a woman's self-esteem depends on her ability to make her relationships work. Paradoxically a woman too often ends up feeling inadequate in the area most crucial to her self-worth.

From Infatuation to Disillusionment

As Eileen and Joe settle into domesticity, familiarity leads to loss of fascination. They begin to be more fully themselves, revealing their anger, their messiness, their criticism, their bossiness. Eileen is no longer Joe's highest priority. Work and other activities take up most of his time. She longs for him to talk to her more, the way he used to.

What happens to couples at this point? They try to *change* each other, a frustrating if not impossible undertaking. At the same time they revert to their old painful feelings of not being good enough. They begin to fight, distance themselves with activities, develop physical problems, drink too much, work too much, sleep too much. They are crushed at losing their perfect love and frightened that something is terribly wrong.

Eileen decides, *I married the wrong man* (blaming him), or *No one can get along with me* (blaming herself), or *This relationship isn't working, so let's end it* (blaming the relationship). Whoever she chooses to blame for her shaken marriage, her falsely propped-up self-esteem topples, and her level of shame begins to rise again.

It may be that we aren't completely aware of these feelings of self-blame, but they make it difficult for us to relate in successful ways. As psychologist Harriet Goldhor Lerner points out in her book *The Dance of Intimacy,* these feelings make us anxious, causing us to be reactive in interpersonal situations when we need to respond with a level head.[2] Drawing on our ready supply of protective strategies, we get upset, depressed, or angry. As we ricochet between self-blame and other-blame, we destroy any chance for real intimacy.

In spite of our well-meant marriage vows, we end up at times deliberately hurting each other; breaking promises; being unfaithful, critical, intolerant. We even hate each other at times. We want out.

And then we feel ashamed. *How can I be so disloyal? So uncommitted? So mean? There must be something wrong with him to have picked me,* Eileen tells herself. She is not happy to see her prince turning into a frog, but deep down she believes a frog is all she deserves.

How We Become Shamers

Eventually these shame-related feelings become part of the fabric of our marriage. Our inner shame makes us hard to live with, turning us into demanding faultfinders. If we were shamed as children for certain traits, we are quick to criticize these same qualities in our mate. For instance, if we were shamed for our natural narcissism and learned always to take a backseat, his love of telling stories will make us extremely uncomfortable, and we will accuse him of being a show-off.

Some women project onto their mates their own difficult-to-own characteristics. Eileen's mother frequently told her she was lazy, so she harps on Joe for procrastinating, even when he's not. "You're the one with the problem, not me," she tells him.

Although Eileen relies on Joe for his strength and confidence in the "real world," at home she sees his weaknesses, his human qualities. She becomes superior, for instance, openly flaunting her more highly evolved ability to be intimate. Or she demeans him by telling other people (even in front of him), "I have two children, you know—my kid and Joe." Shame-based women, as we saw in the last chapter, take back their power in ways that can be destructive to a relationship.

Where Shaming Attitudes Come From

These "hateful" attitudes stem from the inevitable disappointment that comes from failed expectations of our relationships and resentments over any imbalance of power—both interlaced with our inner shame.

FAILED EXPECTATIONS

I asked Eileen what she'd hoped for in marrying.

"I was going to find the one man in the world who was destined to be my mate," she told me. "We would be like two lost halves, roaming the earth, until we found each other and merged into one blissful whole."

What Eileen didn't mention, because it was largely unconscious, was her central expectation that Joe would be an antidote to her toxic feelings of shame. He would be the nurturing parent she never had. At last there would be someone to make her feel lovable.

Was Eileen asking for disappointment? Of course. And out of a deep disappointment in the relationship not delivering on its promise come feelings of anger and resentment.

RESENTMENT OVER INEQUITIES

Another source of our shaming attitudes is the inequality we experience in the relationship, the uneven balance of power, our lack of autonomy. Taking care of our husband's or the family's needs before our own creates resentment. We suffer from consciously or unconsciously knowing that we have not developed ourselves fully. We may even have been discouraged from doing so. It may be that we worked to put him through school but our turn never came. We didn't take a night course because he objected, didn't get a job because he wasn't supportive, or dropped therapy because he didn't approve.

Or maybe, after putting in a long day at work, our resentment builds while we put the children to bed, clean up the kitchen, gather up his dirty laundry, sort his clean socks, send his mother a birthday present, or make his lunch while he watches TV. These kinds of inequities, if left to accumulate over time, can fester into chronic bitterness or acute rage. As long as we stay in the role of server, we will suffer periods of hostility, anxiety, depression, or psychosomatic illness.

We can't really blame men. For centuries they have been boxed in by their own social roles, having to carry the burden of supporting their families. They never expected they would have to work at home too. But now that women are sharing the financial load, they are asking men to share the domestic burden. The modern woman, while carrying almost half the economic responsibility outside the home, also carries about 80 percent of the domestic responsibility.[3]

Although many couples are moving toward a satisfying degree of equality, I see many women who are angry—even outraged—at their husbands over these injustices. What do they do about it? Usually very little beyond ineffectual nagging or complaining. For many complex reasons, which we'll address in the next chapter, women continue to stay in old patterns rather than work for change.

The Impostor Marriage

I realize I haven't told a story that ends with "happily ever after" because there is no "happily ever after." Rather, there is a conspiracy in our culture to conceal this truth about marriage—a basic dishonesty that idealizes it, avoids telling us how it really is. The media play a large part in this idealization, smoothing over marital rough edges, dishing up pabulum to television viewers.

We believe we are the only couple who treat each other like this, except of course the ones we know about that end up divorcing or bickering publicly. We feel our marriage is the only one rocked by outbursts of nastiness or subtle undermining of each other. We feel terrible and isolated in our shame.

"Now that I can see that Joe isn't perfect," Eileen says, "I feel uncomfortable with—even ashamed of—my critical feelings. But I'm beginning to love Joe for who he is—a good man, but not a perfect one.

"My friends are starting to be more open in discussing their marital problems," Eileen continues. "I'm learning that my marriage is not so shameful or so different from everyone else's." Through sharing we realize that most marriages are laced with moments of deep hurt, periods of hatred, and fantasies of divorce. We also learn of ways couples resolve conflicts, create intimate moments, and work hard—and successfully—at keeping their love alive.

How Relationships Trap Us in Shame

We have looked at the many ways we turn to our relationships to help us ease the burden of shame. Rather than finding the relief we long for, we often discover that our closest involvements become an added source of pain.

Shame is inherent in every affiliation between lovers. Remember from Chapter One the notion that shame is an inborn, *automatic* response to the interruption of interest or enjoyment? As Nathanson puts it, "The more we are excited by the person who has become the object of our love, or the more we anticipate the contentment to be achieved from this relationship, so much more are we susceptible to the misery of shame."[4] This makes love a fertile ground for experiencing shame, because we never find our partner consistently matching us at exactly the same level of interest or enjoyment. Any loss of love or intimacy creates shame.

Shame is also predictable when a man and a woman connect because they stand on unequal footing, with the male almost always dominant. A factor in this imbalance, as sociologist Erving Goffman points out, is that our relationships are patterned after the parent-child model, with men serving as protectors of women (opening doors, lifting heavy loads, etc.). According to Goffman, the protector is seen as competent, capable, and deserving of respect. The protected one is seen as incompetent, incapable, deserving of indulgence—not "respected and treated like a full-fledged person." As he puts it, men are to women as adults are to children. While this situation does allow for certain privileges for women, it also brings with it distinct liabilities. Just as a child's activities, time, and territory are subject to interruption or take-over by the parent, so are a woman's subject to the man, Goffman implies.[5]

Another similarity to the parent-child relationship is the position of authority held by the man over the woman. Many women feel they need their husband's permission to do or have certain things. Occasionally I hear women say, "My husband won't let me . . ." (buy a new coat, invite over a friend he doesn't like, get a job) as if they weren't capable of making their own decisions.

Adding to the imbalance of the relationship is the role of woman as servant, taking care of the man and cleaning up the messes he makes. In doing so she puts his needs ahead of her own.

Her stance toward him is usually one of deference. Tannen points out that the man takes the role of teacher, the woman that of student. He talks, she listens and agrees. He leads, she follows. He performs, she applauds. In all these combinations women occupy a lower position, even though they may not be aware of it. I do not blame men for these imbalances. They are carrying out roles inherited from their forefathers and reinforced by the women in their lives, including their mothers, who bring up sons differently than they do daughters.

Differences: Breeding Ground for Shame

One profound and crucial difference between men and women lies in how they value their primary relationship. For most women it is their central focus, the foundation of their life. For most men, while relationship may be important, it is not the most important thing. Rather than recognizing and accepting that men and women are different, women end up feeling undervalued or un-loved when their partners don't make the relationship their high-est priority.

We could say, with the French, *Vive la différence!* but the problem is that women feel that their difference from men means there's something wrong with them.

Take, for example, women's need to be connected. Tannen says that women are fascinated with details of people's lives and prefer to connect by talking about problems—"troubles talk." Yet men don't understand. "You waste so much time gabbing on the phone," he may say. "Just like a woman." Or because he feels helpless or uncomfortable when she easily expresses feelings, he may belittle her for being "too emotional," leading her to ques-tion the soundness of her own experience. Too many times women doubt their own reality in the face of men's differing way of being in the world. (In all fairness I must add that women find ways to put men down, too, in condescending remarks such as "Boys will have their toys.")

Women usually don't want advice, they want someone to listen. When men don't listen, women conclude their feelings don't matter. It's not that men don't care, they simply don't show it in ways that women do.

These imbalances in power and difficult differences don't deter us much, however. We value relationships enough to spend considerable time and effort in finding and keeping one. And when we fail, we lose esteem not only in our own eyes but in the eyes of the world.

"Not in a Relationship? What's Your Problem?"

By adolescence any girl can tell you that her greatest value lies in being attractive to "guys." If she doesn't have a date, she's terrified that there's something wrong with her.

Am I saying that boys and men are spared the pain and shame of rejection? Absolutely not. They face it every time they get turned down for a dance or a date. *But embedded in our culture is the belief that a woman's worth hinges on being chosen by a man.* Having a relationship is living proof that at least one man finds us worthy of love.

Women who don't marry or who marry late are more likely to suffer shame than men in similar circumstances. Just look at your response to the words *spinster* and *bachelor*. One depicts an unwanted, dried-up old maid; the other, a fun-loving, available gentleman. The stigma attached to being single stems from the belief that women, unlike men, are not married because they are flawed. People assume a pecking order: at the top are single men, next widowers, then widows, followed by divorced men and women. Except for homosexuals, single women occupy the lowest status.[6] Rarely is it assumed that a woman is single because she simply chooses to be. We don't use the word *spinster* anymore, but the negative attitudes symbolized by that word still have the power to shame us.

Lydia, a bouncy twenty-six-year-old dental hygienist, came to see me because of her relationship concerns. "My mother keeps telling me that she's worried, that I'd better think about settling down. She says my biological clock is ticking away."

Would this same mother worry about her son at age twenty-six? I doubt it.

Not only do we feel badly about not having a relationship, some of us even feel shame for *wanting* a close involvement. Women who have no intimate partner yet yearn for one are ashamed of their unsatisfied longing. Afraid of being seen as too dependent, they try to hide their need. A forty-eight-year-old divorcée echoes the feelings of many women: "I feel like apologizing for wanting a man. My children are grown. I should be self-sufficient, not dependent. It's my fault for needing too much. I should be secure enough not to need the affection, the *I love you*'s."

"You Failed. Shame on You."

Because we are raised to seek the approval of others, we are especially vulnerable to shame when our relationships don't work out. When a lover or spouse ends the relationship, our self-esteem suffers a serious blow. Our loss confirms our deepest fears that we are inherently defective: *He saw what was wrong with me—I knew he would sooner or later. I was just too needy, too independent, too boring, too ugly, too smart, too stupid.*

The worst form of rejection—betrayal by a husband or lover who has an affair—plunges women into deep shame. Women whose husbands are in the public eye suffer especially intense mortification as they stand by their sides on national television, wearing strained smiles that barely hide their internal bleeding. No small part of their shame lies in the public exposure of their inadequacy: their failure to keep their man satisfied. Deeply embedded in most women's consciousness is the belief that responsibility for the success or failure of our relationships rests with us. If he leaves, we have somehow failed. We ask ourselves, *Where did I go wrong?*

Valerie, a thirty-four-year-old, highly successful, bright and beautiful woman, rakes herself over the coals and weeps bitterly after each breakup of a relationship: *Was I giving enough? Why did I pick someone so messed up? I'm running out of opportunities. All the good men are taken. There must be something wrong with me.* While everything in her life should reinforce her good feelings about herself, her self-esteem depends on her having a lover: "When I'm without one, I feel lost, fat, and ugly."

Divorce is a sign to the world that a woman has failed in what she believes is the most basic task of her life—to find a man and make him happy. Even if he is verbally or physically abusive or chronically unfaithful, she will blame herself. I know a woman with three divorces who calls herself a three-time loser.

If the divorced woman has children, she takes on added shame from those who judge her for lacking "family values." News commentator Linda Ellerbee writes of her experience, "It's especially tough when society . . . continues to tell you there's something wrong with you because you're a single mother. Instead of making you feel proud of the way you cope, proud of doing the best you can—often within a bad situation—you're made to feel, at best, that you're incomplete and, at worst, that you're a danger. *You're* to blame for much of society's ills."[7]

Shame Traps Us in Bad Relationships

A woman stays in a bad relationship for many complicated reasons, most of them rooted in shame.

"I'm miserable and I'd like to leave," says Suzanne, a thirty-nine-year-old housewife who hasn't worked since her first child was born. "But I can't muster up enough resources, either financially or emotionally, to make it on my own. But staying in this unhappy relationship is eating away at my self-confidence. I'm starting to feel like a flawed person."

Years ago a woman was economically dependent on her husband, almost like a child. For women today, economic reasons still play no small part in the need for a mate, keeping too many of us in bad relationships. Suzanne will face financial hardship when she reenters the labor force. Besides her prospects of minimal income (based on unequal pay), she can't count on her husband to support their children—less than 50 percent pay full child support. Child-care costs will take a big bite out of her paycheck. While her standard of living will probably drop (about 30 percent) if she divorces, her husband's may go up.[8] And if she has to go on welfare, she will feel added shame. The high rate of poverty among single mothers testifies to this double standard.

Suzanne also has emotional reasons for needing to stay in her unhappy relationship, stemming from total lack of confidence in her ability to survive on her own. The theme "I can't live without you," which runs through so many popular songs, reflects this shame-ridden woman's profound and disturbing belief. Suzanne was emotionally dependent, never having learned how to take care of her own psychological needs. She didn't know how to reassure herself, to give to herself, to love herself—all capacities necessary to function as a healthy, independent person.

"Besides, maybe he'll change," she says. "Some men do. I

should be able to make things work. Maybe he's not really being abusive, I'm just too sensitive. Maybe I'm too needy. Besides, I'm terrified no man will ever want me."

Growing Through a Bad Relationship

One final and often overlooked reason women stay in troubled relationships is the opportunity to grow.

Take Cheryl, a seemingly confident, articulate woman in her mid-thirties, who is living with an alcoholic. "I feel ashamed of staying with Peter. My friends tell me our relationship is too codependent. We've been together for three years, and I still love him. I've been going to Al-Anon meetings, and it's easier now to let go of rescuing him. I used to call his boss and say he was sick when he was really hung over. I'm working on shifting my focus from trying to change him to getting clearer about my own feelings. And I'm getting pretty good at setting limits with him about what's okay. I'm learning to take care of my own needs, like going out with my friends when I'm depressed."

Cheryl is learning something of enormous value, something that she may keep longer than this particular relationship: namely, how to give up trying to control another person and how to take care of herself. She is discovering a whole new way of being in a relationship while gaining a lot of valuable practice. For the first time she is beginning to develop herself as a full-fledged separate person.

"What's Wrong with Me That I Want More?"

Marla and Tom came to see me after thirteen years of marriage. It was Marla's idea to seek marriage counseling, but Tom was quite willing to be present (a typical pattern for couples initiating therapy). There was very little contact between them: she had thrown herself into raising her children, and he had become a couch potato.

"I need more intimacy with Tom," Marla said right away. "I want to spend quality time with him and to have him be more interested in my thoughts and feelings. I also want him to share more of himself with me. But Tom seems to be withdrawing further with my complaints. I feel ashamed for wanting so much from my relationship. I feel greedy, like I should be satisfied with what I've got. Tom's a good man in so many ways. I don't know. . . ."

When a woman openly expresses her need for comforting, for closeness, for hearing a man's feelings, it may trigger anxiety in him about his own hidden neediness. He may also be afraid that her neediness will take him over. He may hear her requests as demands and feel shame and helplessness at not being able to fulfill them.

For all these reasons he becomes distant, angry, or condescending. As he withdraws, she is left feeling more hungry for contact, convinced of her insatiable neediness. She may actually push him farther away by resorting to whining and complaining. Psychologist John Gottman reports that women's number-one complaint is that their husbands are too withdrawn. Is it any surprise that men's number-one complaint is that women complain too much?[9]

When I asked Tom how he saw their problems, his response was typical of men I see for marital counseling: "I don't see any problem. I think things are okay between us. I love her, but I put in a long day at work, and when I come home, all I want to do is read the paper and be left alone. I don't know why she can't understand that. Why does she have to be so unreasonable?"

Although he resisted her demands for intimate contact, he felt deep down that he was incapable of giving her what she needed, being unskilled and unpracticed at communicating on an intimate level.

As our sessions unfolded, a significant theme emerged: Marla's shame around her need for more intimacy. Sometimes she felt justified in her requests for more emotional contact, but often she would confess that maybe she was just too needy. When Tom would explode in anger at her pleas or withdraw further, his behavior confirmed her belief that she was at fault.

Shame Locks Love Out

We discovered that while Marla longed for intimacy, she was also afraid of it. There were times when Tom would move closer to her, either emotionally or physically, and she would become uncomfortable.

One evening Tom opened our session with the following: "Last night after dinner I sat down next to Marla and began telling her about some of my fears about my presentation tomorrow. And what did she do? She got up and started cleaning up the kitchen!"

I asked Marla what she thought that was about.

"I don't know," she said. "I guess I didn't want to hear about Tom's lack of confidence. It feels a little scary to me. I need him to be strong."

We say we want intimacy (and I believe we do), yet at the same time we are often uncomfortable with it. Marla discovered that she is deeply afraid of being taken over by Tom. If she lets him get too close, she feels she'll get swallowed up. This is a common and crucial concern for women: how to stay separate in the presence of strong connectedness.

Like Marla, we have compelling reasons for ambivalent feelings about intimacy, part of which is fear of exposing our vulnerable parts, lest our tender shoots get stomped on by careless boots. Our partner may treat our revelations roughly, even use them as ammunition to attack us.

Ultimately we are afraid to reveal our inherently flawed self. *It is our shame that makes us want to hide.* We are terrified of being rejected or abandoned for not being good enough. To be intimate is to be vulnerable. Simply put, we don't feel safe enough to risk intimacy.

Letting in Love

When the gift of love is offered, women who feel flawed have trouble accepting it. Marla's lack of self-love created a barrier to letting in Tom's love. She didn't believe that Tom could love someone as unworthy as her. *Until we learn to love ourselves, we can't trust the love others offer us.*

Paradoxically the very feelings of unworthiness that make us yearn for a relationship are the same feelings that can undermine or destroy it. If we have a solid enough sense of self, we don't need to depend on our relationships to define us, to protect us, to make us happy—a demand that puts our relationships in jeopardy. Instead of *taking from* we need to *bring to* our relationships vitality, joy, and authenticity.

Women with a solid inner core or women who have healed their shame are the most able to grow in their relationships.

Because they feel safe enough to become vulnerable, they use the other person to explore their deepest feelings. They are more open to receiving helpful feedback about how their behavior affects others. They are more able to use their relationships to practice new ways of being related: ways that promote greater contact with another or that allow for continuing development of self.

Women with healthy relationships experience the growth and satisfaction that come from being in a mutually empowering connection.[10] If we heal the shame that keeps us from being authentically ourselves, we free ourselves to create relationships—imperfect as they are—that fulfill both our need to be deeply connected to another and our need to be deeply connected to ourselves.

CHAPTER TWELVE

The Challenge: Being Me While I'm with You

We know ourselves as separate insofar as we live in connection with others, and . . . we experience relationship only insofar as we differentiate other from self.
—CAROL GILLIGAN

Leah, a thirty-four-year-old teacher's aide, homemaker, and mother of three, sought couples' therapy because of her conflict over whether to go back to school for a teaching credential. "I dropped out of college when Daniel and I got married so that I could put him through graduate school. Now it's time to pay some attention to my own education. But I always seem to lose ground when I discuss it with Daniel—he gets so angry. He tells me I'm being selfish. He tells me I can't do it. The kids need me at home."

Leah found herself torn between her need to take care of herself and her need to take care of her family. She wanted to find a way of being responsive to both.

"How can I be connected to my husband and my children in ways that nurture us all? I don't know what to do. I feel like I can't go on letting Daniel tell me what to do. And I can't seem to get it through his head that my wanting a life of my own doesn't mean I don't love him anymore."

Eventually Leah decided that she could not give in to Daniel's wishes. Her need to establish a career for herself was not negotiable. When she told Daniel of her decision, he warned her, "I'm against it. You'll get no help from me."

When I explored with Daniel his feelings, we discovered that underneath his bluster he was afraid—afraid that he would lose her, that she would meet someone else. As her dependency needs diminished and she began to create a separate identity for herself, his dependency needs surfaced. It helped them both to understand that his anger was a cover-up for his fear. When he was able to express his fear, he began to hear and accept Leah's need for a life of her own.

Enough time went by that he was reassured of her continued commitment to him. He began to help more with household chores such as cooking and doing dishes and took over more with the children. And when she earned her credential, he threw her a big party.

Could any woman do what Leah did? Not necessarily. Leah was strengthened by knowing that she would survive emotionally and financially should Daniel decide to leave her. And while she loved Daniel, she concluded after much soul-searching that for the sake of her own well-being she was willing to take that risk.

Leah's story illustrates the central issue facing today's woman— the struggle to resolve her seemingly opposing needs for connection and separation. This is a dilemma we've been grappling with throughout this book: How can we keep our relationship as we attempt to claim an identity for ourselves? Does having a relationship require us to give up important parts of ourselves? Can we have it all—a successful relationship and a solid, separate self?

Caught between the need to love ourselves and the need to love and be loved by others, we walk a fine line. If we step too far on one side, we are called selfish or uncaring, and we risk losing our relationship. If we step too far on the other, we are told we love too much or are codependent and we risk losing our self. Either way we are caught in the shame trap.

Deluged with self-help books telling us to take charge of our lives, we worry that we aren't independent enough, that we aren't changing fast enough, and our worry adds fuel to our shame.

Women's Need to Be Connected

To appreciate and understand the importance of our need for connection, let's look again at how we first learned about relating to others while we were growing up.[1]

First of all, regarding relationships, women have different needs and capacities than men do—and for good reasons. As girls we enjoyed a longer period of intimacy with our mothers. We patterned ourselves after Mother, whose focus was clearly on tending family relationships.

Boys, on the other hand, left the closeness with Mother to pattern themselves after Dad (or another male)—usually a remote figure who, while comfortable in the world of work, was not comfortable in the world of intimacy.

Because most little girls never have to break ties with Mother the way boys do, they have the opportunity for more practice in developing relationship skills. They have less opportunity, however, to define themselves as separate.

While most boys accomplish the task of seeing themselves as separate individuals, they learn to suppress feelings and have difficulty responding to the feelings of others. Instead they are prepared to succeed in the world of work, where emotions are considered a liability and autonomy is essential.

Is it any surprise, then, that men—who define themselves as separate—tend to have trouble being related, while women—who define themselves as connected—tend to have difficulty being separate?

"Why Can't a Man Be More Like a Woman?"

It makes sense that, given these differences in early bonding, women structure relationships in a distinctly different way and have quite different needs for intimacy. Carol Gilligan uses the metaphor of the *web* to describe the way women structure relationships. Unfortunately these differences provide a chronic source of shame for women attempting to create healthy relationships.

When a woman approaches a man for more closeness, he may withdraw, even push her away, afraid of losing his autonomy. And his discomfort with expressing his vulnerable feelings—including his love and need for her—along with his difficulty in responding to her feelings, *may leave her feeling unloved, but is not proof that she is unlovable.*

Nor is it proof that he loves or needs her any less than she loves or needs him. If we women could truly comprehend this, we could be spared the considerable anguish of concluding that the failure to connect is our fault or that we are too needy.

Each sex perceives a danger that the other does not see—men in connection, women in separation. Men, fearing that connection may engulf them, move toward more autonomy. Women, fearing loss of identity through separation, move toward more connection. We are dealing not merely with a gender gap but with a gender gulf. Is it any wonder both sexes often end up hurt, confused, and *misunderstood*?

The Web of Friendships and Family

One of our greatest assets is the ability to form deep friendships. Yet the fact that women tend to turn to each other to fulfill their need for closeness can be a source of shame. They are looked upon as being too needy, too "dependent," or immature.

Some years ago, the psychiatrist of a close friend of mine warned her that she and I were becoming too dependent on each other. We were both single mothers, our children played together, and we exchanged child care. We were a support system for each other and shared many wonderful moments of laughing and crying together. I felt both ashamed and angry that he was depicting the friendship I treasured in such a demeaning way.

In a psychological study on love, women report loving their best friends as much as they do their lovers.[2] Yet our easy intimacy with friends troubles us. Many women feel ashamed of their normal dependency needs, not knowing these needs are common to all healthy men and women. Why should this be?

Clearly the viewpoint of psychological "experts" has permeated our thinking. According to standards devised by men— based on studies of men—dependency needs are seen as indicating weakness. Autonomy, not the ability to establish relationships, has been the accepted measure of maturity. Consequently most men are threatened by their own dependency needs and frown on these needs when they appear in women. Men tend to equate women's healthy need for relationships with dependency and therefore consider women less adult.

Yet the need for intimate connection with others, the need to have our feelings listened to and our experiences understood, are basic human needs, as is the need for help in coping with life's inevitable problems. While women are quick to acknowledge and even put themselves down for having these needs, many men have difficulty admitting to them at all—for fear of appearing weak or unmanly.

A woman takes care of a man in such a way that he is spared having openly to acknowledge or express his needs and thereby lose face. Because she is the nurturing one, his needs get taken care of better than hers.

Perhaps it's no surprise, then, that men who lose their spouse through death or divorce have higher rates of depression, death, and suicide than women in the same situation. In spite of popular views about women's dependency, the single life seems to be harder on men than on women.[3]

Karen, an elegantly dressed homemaker, was sure she knew what her problem was when she came for her first appointment. She wanted to work on her "codependency." When I asked her what she meant by the term, she told me, "I'm too much of a giver, too emotionally dependent on David, my husband." She stopped and looked at me.

"Please go on," I prompted.

"I miss him a lot when he's on the road. He doesn't miss me much. And I want so much to please him. I love making his favorite meals, doing little special things for him. Isn't that being too caretaking?" She paused for a moment to examine her long red fingernails. "Sometimes he's really mean to me, telling me what to do and how to do it. When I'm upset over a fight I had with my mother, he takes her side sometimes. Other times he says I should stand up to her more. The funny thing is, I don't stand up to *him* enough. Sometimes I think I should leave him, that I don't deserve his treatment—that I'm being a sick codependent. Other times I just love being with him and can't imagine my life without him."

Karen learned to accept and even appreciate that she needed her husband and that her pleasure in taking care of some of his needs was nothing to be ashamed of. She discovered, however, that she got in trouble if she consistently put his needs ahead of her own. As we worked together, it became apparent that she thought she needed David in order to survive—one of the mating myths we talked about in the previous chapter. When she began to trust in her own competence, she took another look at her marriage and chose to stay because she wanted to, not because she *needed* the marriage for her survival.

She worked on asserting herself more with David: "I want you just to listen to my feelings about my run-ins with Mom. When you take her side, I feel hurt and abandoned by you." Regarding his need to tell her what to do, she said, "I'm open to hearing about your possibly better way of doing things, but I will decide for myself what I think is best for me." She learned to use "I" statements more than "you" statements. ("I feel, I want" works better than "You are unfair, mean, bossy.")

Karen came to see and accept that she and David were dependent on each other and needn't be ashamed of it. Couples are actually interdependent, needing each other for companionship, support, nurturing, and reassurance that they matter to someone. What Karen mistook for codependency was a mixture of normal dependency and excessive caretaking stemming from her learned role about appropriate behavior for a woman in a relationship.

Codependent: A Shaming Label?

What is codependency, anyway? This vague term, aimed mostly at women, covers a wide range of behavior, from simple caretaking to a pathological focus on others. Unfortunately what began as a classification for people (usually women) who stayed with alcoholics or drug addicts has now become a shaming label that keeps countless women trapped in self-blame for carrying out a feminine role passed on by generations of women and reinforced by society.

Because it has been used to chastise women for their difficult and complicated choices, this term has probably done more damage than good. Women have to be careful not to blame themselves for persisting in patterns of relating that were established centuries ago, when it was considered their proper duty—if not an economic necessity—to accommodate and/or stay in relationships regardless of the burdensome conditions.

Consider these definitions. According to psychiatrist Charles L.

Whitfield, author of *Healing the Child Within,* codependency is "any suffering and/or dysfunction that is associated with or results from *focusing on the needs and behavior of others.*"[4] Experts attending the First National Conference on Codependency defined it as "a pattern of painful dependency on compulsive behaviors and *on approval from others in an attempt to find safety, self-worth and identity*" (emphasis added).

Given these definitions, what woman isn't codependent? When authors like this describe what they consider a disease of epidemic proportions, they are in fact describing traditional feminine behavior!

Is Femininity a Disease?

"Defining femininity as a disease" writes lawyer Wendy Kaminer, in a *New York Times* article, "overlooks the ways in which women are trapped in abuse by circumstance, not weakness. Charging co-dependent wives with complicity in their husbands' addictions may be . . . another way of 'blaming women' for the crimes and failures of men." According to Kaminer, feminists would tell us nonliberated women aren't sick, they're oppressed.[5]

These oppressed women hope to alleviate profound feelings of worthlessness the only way they know how—by establishing a relationship at almost any cost. But I've had many clients who accuse themselves of being codependent whenever they choose to put another's needs ahead of their own, even when they are only being considerate or giving. Or when, like Karen, they do what they were socialized to do: overfocus on others.

The term *codependence* implies that a woman shouldn't take pleasure in caring for other people. I think we do a great disservice to ourselves if we cast off the role of caretaker as no longer valid. Taking care of others, in the highest sense, can be a deeply satisfying activity. Calling ourselves codependent and sick does nothing but add shame to our already damaged self-image.

Having said that, I should add that the *concept* behind "codependence" is not all bad. It has served an important function in alerting women to the myriad ways they give up their power in a relationship. Without the label and the implication that the codependent is sick, bad, or wrong, women could more easily explore without shame their tendency to give up parts of themselves for the sake of their relationships. And these age-old social roles should be challenged.

Some of us sacrifice more than just parts of ourselves; we give ourselves up entirely in unhappy situations—choosing partners who are alcoholic, workaholic, or abusive. Why would women choose relationships that are unnurturing or even destructive?

Some of us are convinced we can't survive emotionally on our own. Often we genuinely care for the other. Partly we feel we don't deserve better. We also hope to build up our self-esteem by proving how much the other really needs us. Or we feel useless when there is no one to take care of—when we're not being used. Or we are locked into a familiar pattern of relating, rooted in childhood. If we were mistreated as girls or saw Mother being abused, we learned at an unconscious level that such treatment was an expected and acceptable part of being in relationship. And we developed our own set of coping skills to deal with these familiar behaviors—ways of relating that have become part of our repertoire.

Because women have so many reasons for choosing the relationships they do, we need to respect the complexity of women's choices and not be too quick to judge each other or ourselves. While change may be desirable, it may also threaten the very fabric of the partnership. Some women simply aren't able—economically or emotionally—to take the chance.

Why We Continue to Hold Back Our Power

Historically speaking, women have focused their energies on developing their relationships rather than developing themselves. In order to find or keep a relationship, many women felt they had to suppress their strength, their individuality, their ability to function capably on their own.

Today women are breaking with tradition by shifting their focus to include listening to their own needs as well as those of others. As one woman put it, "It's time I painted myself into the picture." But such changes do not come easily or without deep apprehension. We are confirmed in our fears when, for example, our mates object to our going to work, taking courses, or getting into therapy. Some of us hold our own under such pressures, but many more give in, for not far beneath the surface lie fears of losing him if we become too strong.

Women succumb to such pressures and defer to male authority for complex personal reasons. Our dependent role allows us to feel secure and protected. In assuming the role of the dependent partner, a woman also takes care of the man by allowing him to take care of her. These kinds of "bargains" are made at an unconscious level. It goes like this: By taking on the role of the dependent person in the relationship, we diminish his fear of abandonment because we "need him too much to leave." We ensure that *he* won't leave by taking care of his needs (even putting them first). It's a kind of abandonment insurance for each.

There is one problem with this arrangement. His dependency remains unacknowledged, while ours is not only taken for granted but becomes something to be ashamed of. "What's wrong with me?" we ask. "I'm too needy."

Many women feel trapped in unhappy marriages because of economic or emotional dependency.

Kate, a bright mother of four, is considering separating from her husband. "I'm afraid I can't make it on my own, emotionally and financially," she says. "And I'm terrified of holding down a job. Who'd want me?" Although she already has many skills, sharpened during twenty-five years of running a household and raising four children, few of them are immediately marketable.

Yet there is a real basis for her lack of confidence. Women's talents for child care and home-management skills are not highly valued by society. Kate earns no wages for her labors. While some unemployed women have equal access to the money, others, like Kate, have to ask for it, which feels terribly demeaning to her. Or she gets handouts, at the whim of her husband. Kate says, "This is what he tells me: 'Here's fifty dollars. Go buy something for yourself.' I feel like a damn kid."

Kate hasn't yet given herself permission to take a stand on being an equal partner regarding financial decisions in her marriage, but her entering therapy is a step in the right direction, even though he's paying for it. She becomes vulnerable to his possible threat to withdraw this financial support should her changes rock the boat too much. Her economic dependence contributes to her emotional dependence, relegating her to a childlike position.

"Besides," Kate says, "I'm intimidated because I haven't had the experience in gaining the skills I need to deal with the world. I've always depended on Kevin to balance the checkbook, take care of our insurance, know when to change the oil."

I ask if there is anything else scary about surviving on her own.

"I'm terrified of being lonely."

I suggest that maybe she's missed the opportunity of learning to enjoy solitude.

"Could be. I got married right out of college. I've never lived alone."

Kate may be conforming to others' expectations rather than checking in with her own experience. For instance, she actually enjoys the quiet and does just fine when her husband is away, but she hasn't let herself know that she could take care of her own social and intimacy needs if they were to divorce.

Until Kate is assured of being able to make a living for herself— she doesn't feel she can count on her husband to help her while she gets on her feet financially—she will not be able to leave. (It's possible that men's awareness of the power their superior economic position gives them plays a big part in the resistance of businesses to paying women an equal wage.)

Women's Strong Points

Rather than being ashamed of the high priority our relationships have in our lives, we need to claim our abilities in this area. As women our capacity to create deep and abiding relationships depends on having concern for others' welfare, being interested in their experience, nurturing them, fostering their growth—all extremely important strengths. In problem solving we are often willing to compromise, to engage in cooperative efforts to work toward consensus. We have fluid boundaries that allow us to tune in to the feelings of others, and we frequently consider other people's needs and feelings before we take action.

We have the capacity to trust enough to become vulnerable— to express our feelings and to be open to the feelings of others. Our vulnerability creates a bridge to the other person; our empathy allows us to cross over and experience what it's like on the other side.[6]

Our relationship skills should and do give us good feelings about ourselves. Yet when we try them on our mate, we often feel inadequate for not being successful with them. As Kate puts it, "I want to encourage Kevin to see the doctor for his allergies or call his mother. He resists. He doesn't like me telling him what to do. When he's emotionally hurting, I want to be there for him, yet he's uncomfortable talking about his pain. Sometimes he withdraws or lashes out at me. It's almost like he's learned that it's weak to be sad or scared.

"If we have an argument, I want to talk things out, but he thinks talking things over will only make them worse, so he ends the conversation by going to work in the garden or watching a game."

The more we pursue, the more he withdraws, leaving us feeling we have failed at the very thing we long for and are trained for: the creation of a loving relationship. And even though we make a lot of fuss blaming him, deep down we blame ourselves.

"Can I Be Me While I'm with You?"

Because a woman tends to blame herself for her relationship troubles, and because having a relationship seems so crucial, she is usually willing to mold herself into the kind of woman she thinks a man wants. She accommodates, deferring to his needs and wishes at the cost of her own preferences. She concludes, "If I can just be who he wants me to be, he'll love me." This often calls for playing a part, putting on a false front.

The strain of this became dramatically clear to me the day Lydia came in, upset because she had had a mild anxiety attack. She had just begun a new relationship. "This time I'm consciously trying to be myself, not accommodating, not dropping everything when he comes over, not pretending to be flawless like I used to. I was so proud of myself. I didn't stay up till two A.M. cleaning and baking so everything would turn out perfect when he came for the weekend. I don't understand why I'm so anxious, because this time I'm not trying to be perfect."

I suggested it might be scary to offer her less-than-perfect self.

Her relief was immediately evident, and she sighed. "I get it. I shouldn't beat myself up."

In her next relationship, much later in her therapy, Lydia was able simply to be who she was and with much less accompanying anxiety.

Being ourselves is no easy task. Many of us don't know what we feel or think, don't trust ourselves; we have weak boundaries. We try to connect with others without a sense of who we are and what we want. Like Lydia we are afraid that if we are fully authentic, we will jeopardize our relationships. We give up ourselves in order to keep the relationship.

When our boundaries are too weak and we let ourselves be defined by others in our life or taken over by their needs and wants, we lose respect for ourselves at a deep level.

A Life of Our Own

They may not put any pressure on us. They don't need to. The pressure comes from within. A woman's need for connection and her diffuse boundaries—while assets in connecting—can be liabilities in maintaining separateness. As Lillian Rubin so aptly puts it, she is afraid of losing a part of herself, not just because he "is taking something from her but because, unless she's constantly vigilant, she's all too likely to give it away."[7] It's often a relief to women when their partners are temporarily out of town. They can relax their guard, be themselves, put themselves first for a change.

No Rights of Her Own

Some shame-prone women need to maintain their relationship at a price. Take Margie, for instance, who lives with a man and her eleven-year-old daughter. "I have to give up myself to be in this relationship. He wants a nonmonogamous relationship, but I want a monogamous one. I'm comfortable sleeping with only one person at a time, thank you very much. But he's different. I go along with it—the way he wants it to be." Margie doesn't feel entitled to have things her way. Instead she accommodates his needs. Her increase in migraine headaches testifies to the cost she pays to keep her man.

One week Margie was visibly agitated when she came to her appointment. She started right in, words tumbling out: "Last

Saturday I came home from work to have lunch. Both my daughter and my boyfriend were there, just sitting at the table. I made all our lunches and sat down. I had ten minutes to eat. They had all afternoon. There I was taking care of everybody again. I'm so tired of putting my needs last.

"Then Sunday night I'm fixing dinner. I'm thinking, *Here I am, cooking one more meal.* I'd been cooking all weekend. He walks in, having been on the phone with his ex-wife. 'Where have you been?' I ask. 'Talking with Jane.' I could feel the dynamite inside me explode." She stopped for one quick gulp of air and rushed on. "I didn't say anything all night. Later in bed he wants sex. I said, 'I'm not interested—can't you tell something's bothering me?' He had had no idea I was upset. He was so angry, he left the house. I felt terrible. Immediately I began attacking myself: *You're too sensitive. You're too paranoid.* I felt so alone and empty. Do you think I should have talked to him?"

"What do you think?" I responded.

"I was afraid that he'd feel encumbered by this too-sensitive person he had to be so careful of—afraid that he might leave for good."

Margie needs to know that she can take care of herself emotionally and financially before she will be able to take a stand on the crucial issues that are eating away at her relationship.

Not only do we have trouble standing up for ourselves or expressing anger, we have a hard time even putting our needs ahead of others'.

Fear of Conflict

Because we have learned in our families and from society that it is risky to be a powerful woman, we deny our anger, our wants, and our competence. Because we don't feel powerful, we tend to avoid open conflict. This makes sense if we consider that conflict usually ends up with a winner and a loser, and nobody wants to be a loser.

Small wonder that women are known for trying to defuse explosive situations, while men are more likely to turn up the heat.[8]

We have many shame-related reasons to avoid conflict. As women we have taken on the responsibility of keeping the peace in our relationships. Conflict therefore becomes a personal fail-ure—proof of our inadequacy rather than something normal and inevitable. We also avoid conflict because we're afraid of looking too emotional or irrational.

Conflict also threatens intimacy. We're afraid that conflict will damage the bond we've worked so hard to create.

If we initiate conflict by disagreeing or questioning male au-thority, we might be considered audacious. "How dare you ques-tion my idea, my action, or challenge my position? I have decided. And that's it."

And of course among some couples the threat of violence keeps women silent.

Besides being discouraged by male attitudes and male anger, women believe they lack essential assertive skills necessary to disagree openly and effectively. But *assertive* does not mean *aggres-sive*. To be assertive is simply to communicate your wants, needs, or thoughts in a way that is clear but not hostile. It helps to indicate, as Leah did, what your bottom line is and what action, if any, you plan to take. The goal is not to overpower the other but to empower yourself.

This is a difficult task for women who not only have trouble knowing what they need but who also believe that expressing needs openly is selfish and threatening to the balance of the relationship.

Internalized shame can silence us. We hold back because we don't trust our reality, our perceptions, our right to take care of ourselves. Afraid to be wrong, afraid to be abandoned, we stay silent, like Margie, who was sure her boyfriend would leave for good if she openly expressed her anger.

In order to become a person in our own right, we need to be able to tolerate conflict. "Without the capacity to bear conflict, an individual is in danger of being defined by another or taken over by another's identity," warns psychologist Judith Jordan. We need to speak our minds, trust our experience, while honoring the experience of the other—essentials for engaging in growth-producing conflict.[9] Women who avoid conflict often end up nagging and complaining fruitlessly or exploding when the ten-sion builds. It is from the resolution of healthy conflict that people grow and relationships improve.

What's Possible

Now that we have explored the dilemma facing women in their attempts to balance their need to take care of others with their need to take care of themselves, their need to connect with others and their need to stay connected to self, let's look at possible ways we can create relationships that reduce rather than increase our shame, relationships that nurture and empower us.

- We can try to see problems (and especially conflicts) as opportunities from which to learn and grow.
- We can take a look at our hidden expectations and assumptions, especially those about gender roles.
- We can give ourselves permission to have feelings, needs, and wants and to trust in our capacity to think for ourselves and know what we know.
- We can consider: What would be the most dangerous thing about being fully ourselves?
- We can listen to our partner and insist that our partner listen to us.
- We can accept that we will never have perfect understanding.
- We can be willing to change ourselves and give up trying to change the other. We can be patient with each other. We know that change does happen.
- We can take time out to be together, to nurture the relationship.
- We can love ourselves and know we can take care of ourselves.
- We can be in our relationship on the basis of choice, not survival.
- We can accept that we are different from our partners, that each of us is unique.

There is nothing more important to most women than their relationships. Yet the ability to form and maintain an intimate connection rests on a solid sense of self. Without this crucial component we are indeed limited in our capacity to create the very relationships we long for.

On the other hand there is nothing more useful in developing a sense of self than being in a healthy relationship. Our relationships provide us with the opportunity to strengthen our ability both to know and define ourselves and to love and care about others.

Fortunately when we attend to, honor, and nurture both ourselves and our relationships, we grow in our capacity to deeply fulfill these dual needs. Ideally these needs can be mutually enhancing—creating a relationship that encourages a self-definition that includes responsibility for ourselves, the other, and the relationship.

PART FIVE

SHAME
AND SEXUALITY

CHAPTER THIRTEEN

Body Shame:
Beauty vs. Beast

*The idealization of female appearance camouflages an
underlying belief in female inferiority. . . . Beauty helps
to balance woman as a misbegotten person. It disguises
her inadequacies and justifies her presence.*
—RITA FREEDMAN

"I'm back on a diet again," says Natalie. "Seems like the story
of my life. I look in the mirror and I want to gag. I can't go
for that promotion for supervisor until I lose thirty pounds. No
one will take me seriously the way I look now. I know when people
look at me, they think I'm out of control and lazy. My fat body
betrays me wherever I go. And I certainly can't start looking for
a man."

Natalie's weight problem began in childhood. "I started dieting
at ten. When I turned twelve, my mother decided I was still too
plump and put me on diet pills. I sure got the message my body
was not okay. And yet my mother used food as a reward. If I came
home from school with a good grade, she'd say, 'Let's go out for
ice cream.' If I came home upset, she'd bake cookies for me."

"Sounds like you got some confusing double messages," I say.

"Yeah. To this day I use food to reward or comfort myself, but I'm always dieting too."

Although body shame is common to most women, it is especially debilitating to those of us who are shame-prone. It often masks underlying feelings of low self-worth. Because Natalie feels insecure and unlovable deep down, she focuses on her large body as the reason not to take risks rather than facing her feelings about herself.

Our bodies are our ambassadors; they represent us in the world. Most of us think we *are* our bodies. Our bodies are central to our self-concept and interact with it in complex ways. If a woman feels deficient as a person, she will include her physical appearance in her negative self-appraisal. Conversely, if she believes her body is flawed, she usually feels flawed as a person.

Yet not all women dissatisfied with their bodies are overweight. "I hate my body. I'm too fat," says Connie, a beautiful woman with a normal body. "And something's wrong with my skin. I thought you got over pimples when you grew up. Not me. I break out every month and I'm almost forty! I'm so ugly. Yuck."

Because Connie has a distorted body image, she sees herself as fat even though her weight is normal. She compares herself to beauties in glossy magazine photos and falls painfully short. Because she doesn't accept herself, she can't accept her body.

Where Does Body Shame Come From?

Both Natalie and Connie are victims of our culture's obsession with beauty. By the time a girl reaches adolescence, her ability to conform physically to the standards of beauty has become a crucial element (maybe the most crucial) in her self-esteem. Both her family and the prevailing culture teach her what to value and what not to value in her body.

Lessons from Home and School

Because little girls are told from infancy that they are "pretty" and little boys are not, they learn early on that their appearance is an important way to please. Even teachers comment more often on the appearance of girls than of boys. Their strength or coordination earn few comments. As cheerleaders, pom-pom and song girls we add decoration to sporting events in addition to team spirit.

Many girls learn to become obsessed with their bodies and dieting by observing their mothers around food. Sometimes insecure mothers think there is something wrong with their daughters' normal bodies and become preoccupied with how they look.

PEER PRESSURE

We learn that being attractive is the key to being popular.

Janelle, a woman who had had several hospitalizations for bouts of major depression, told me of her harrowing experience at the hands of her "friends" when she was thirteen.

"One day we sat at the kitchen table and played a game we called Reform. It went like this: We would take turns going around the table telling each girl one thing she needed to reform about her appearance. They would say silly things like 'your eyes are too blue' or 'your hair is too long.' But each time they came to me, they'd say real things." Her hand darted quickly through her dark hair.

I asked her to go on, suspecting what she meant by "real things."

She took a deep breath and plunged ahead. "Well, they told me I had B.O. And bad breath. I had hairy arms. And I should stop biting my nails and—" At this point she started to sob and couldn't go on.

Though I knew her family had been troubled, I couldn't help wondering if these children, cruel as only children can be, didn't push this already wounded girl beyond the point where she could salvage even a shred of self-love.

POPULAR CULTURE

Besides being influenced by parents, teachers, and peers, we pick up messages from the media that promote body shame. Television presents flawless women in commercials and programs. Women's bodies are used to advertise every imaginable product.

Women's magazines make us feel it's possible to have a gorgeous face or body if only we buy that eye makeup or start the latest diet. It takes Connie over two hours every morning to put on her makeup, fix her hair, and try on numerous outfits in search of the right one. Then, when she compares herself to the slim media beauties, she shames herself with, *You're just not trying hard enough. It's your own fault.*

Advertising lowers our self-esteem as it raises our anxieties about (a) catching and keeping a man; (b) succeeding at work without letting stress threaten our hard-earned good looks; (c) eating without getting fat; and (d) aging without turning ugly.

Because we can compare our bodies only to slick magazine photographs or skinny, full-breasted actresses in movie love scenes, it's no wonder we suffer by comparison. One of our problems is that as females we have been limited in our knowledge of other females' bodies, except for what we see in the media.

Even very young girls, with nothing to hide, are quick to cover up as they dress and undress for P.E. Taught to be modest from an early age, many women automatically turn their backs to other women as they put on their bras. We end up with no idea of the diversity of normal women's bodies. Until we really look at other women, we won't be able to shake the stereotypical ideal.[1]

Our culture's worship of beauty leaves women feeling they can never quite measure up, giving them perhaps the most potent weapon in their already self-destructive arsenal of *shoulds*. Though our culture undervalues and even denigrates many aspects of a woman, its contempt focuses most intensely on what is uniquely feminine about her, her body and her sexuality, which then become targets for abuse, control, and exploitation.

What chance has a woman got to love her body when her culture views it as fat, aging too fast, and desperately in need of mouthwashes, antiwrinkle creams, and deodorants for armpits and vagina? Displayed for men's admiration and women's envy in advertisements and films are ideals of beauty impossible for most of us to achieve. Small wonder we see our body as the beast, the enemy.

The Politics of Beauty

Throughout the ages society has viewed women's bodies as ornaments while it has considered men's bodies as instruments of power. It is interesting to note that throughout history standards of beauty have rejected woman's *natural* body to idealize one that is not only unnatural but often defective. For instance the Chinese bound girls' feet, crippling them, while Victorians squeezed women's bodies into corsets tight enough to damage internal organs. We may have come a long way, but we are still in bondage to beauty, wearing high heels that shorten our calf muscles, having silicone implants inserted in our breasts, starving ourselves (sometimes to death) in quest of bodies that will make us feel good about ourselves.

The beauty industry both creates and feeds on our shame by setting standards of beauty that are largely *unattainable*, keeping us forever dissatisfied with our natural body, convinced that it is flawed and needs to be fixed.

Even those rare women who succeed—the true beauties— usually manage to find something wrong with themselves, some fatal flaw that becomes the focus of self-hate. Or, like Marilyn Monroe, they become convinced that their external beauty is all that attracts people, not their inner worth.

Beauty Is as Beauty Does

Another way our culture shames us is by showing both contempt and idolatry toward women as it sets up standards of beauty that are not only beyond our reach but are always changing. Rather than being an abstract, permanent ideal, beauty seems to fluctuate as women's role changes from dependence (being reproductive at home) to independence (being productive in the workplace). During eras when women stay home, maternal shapes are popular, and fashions promote garments to enhance women's roundness, such as the corsets, cinch belts, and padded bras of the postwar forties and fifties when women left the munitions factories and turned their homes into baby factories. Yet during the 1920s, when they won the right to vote and went to work in large numbers, women adopted boyish styles, bobbed their hair, and bound their breasts to make them flat.

Thinness and fleshiness carry symbolic meanings.

"When I go to work, I want to be thin, because it makes me look more competent, like I'm in control, and self-sufficient," says Connie. "I see fat people as greedy, not very capable, and out of control."

Fat suggests a lack of definition, an unending availability, perhaps because we associate fleshiness with maternal nurturance, to
the point of unbounded giving. Thinness, on the other hand,
suggests tightness, firmer boundaries, clearer body definition, assertion. It's as though both the beauty industry and women believe we need to suppress our femininity in order to be taken
seriously in the world of work. Today's woman—double-duty
wife-mother and career woman—faces a dilemma because of
these contradictory demands and expectations. What should she
be? Boyish and independent or feminine and maternal? Why not
both? Why not be herself?

Taming the Beast

The beauty industry's solution to this dilemma is the unlikely
Barbie-doll combination of large breasts and thin hips and thighs.
Our ideal woman has big breasts consistent with a strong pro-
mother sentiment in our society, yet she also has a thin, firm
body—one that denies her femininity, enabling her to compete in
a man's world. What is a woman to do?

Carol Tavris spells out the modern woman's predicament: "If
she accepts nature's body—the one with breasts, fat deposits, and
curves—and throws away the diet books, she risks being regarded
as incompetent and best suited for motherhood. If she wishes to
enter the business and political world, she struggles to have a
man's body, one without those nurturing, feminine breasts."[2] We
resolve this dilemma by the way we dress, says Tavris. We try to
be both professional and sexy at the same time by going to work
in a "masculine" tailored jacket and a "feminine" miniskirt.[3]
Small wonder that most young women are profoundly discon-
tented with and confused about their bodies.

Another solution is to alter our bodies to conform to the ideal
by surgically ridding ourselves of fat or reshaping offending fea-
tures. We have been flocking to plastic surgeons for implants to
increase our breast size and liposuction to give us thinner thighs,
hips, and stomachs. So commonplace has it become that Frances
Lear predicts that "plastic surgery is going to become as important one day as a résumé."[4]

Exercise offers another means of perfecting our bodies. My
guess is that most women work out as much to improve their looks

as to be fit. Failure to achieve today's popular firm, lean look leaves us feeling discouraged and ashamed of not working hard enough—as though anyone's body could conform regardless of individual genetic differences. Although exercise can give us the confidence of having a strong, powerful body, it can become compulsive when women spend excessive hours at it.

Connie works out twenty hours a week because she is pushing forty and finds her normal body repulsive. Since she doesn't like herself, she focuses her self-loathing on her body, the part of herself that observers can immediately judge and find unacceptable.

"I won't let my husband see me naked any longer because I'm so ashamed of my body," she says.

I ask what that might be about.

"I must have been really young when I got the message that people valued me for my appearance above all else. I'm so terrified of losing the visible proof that I'm lovable."

The Cult of Thinness

We have become a culture that worships a thin female body. The beauty industry has succeeded in convincing women that any fat is bad and shameful.

Besides needing not to be too feminine in order to compete in the marketplace, we attack our fleshiness in part because our culture equates fleshiness with devalued feminine attributes such as emotionality and the need for close relationships. Thus a woman is subtly socialized to be ashamed of her femininity and fears that her "excess" weight exposes these so-called feminine inadequacies. By controlling it she hopes to hide her defectiveness.[5]

We desperately long for the ideal thin and firm body—the ticket to love, self-esteem, success. As we read magazines whose covers feature both the latest diet exhorting us to be thin and luscious desserts tempting us to eat, we are caught in a double bind—one we can never escape. Even elderly women cite weight as one of their greatest worries.[6]

We associate being thin, staying on a diet, and avoiding certain foods with being virtuous. Listen to this common trap we all fall into: I meet a woman I haven't seen in a while. "You look great,"

I say. "You're looking thin. Have you lost weight?" There it is. How often do we hear this question as a compliment, as if we've done something especially praiseworthy. What happens next time I see her and she's gained it back? Will her self-esteem drop a few notches?

Diet and Shame: Constant Companions

Natalie, the woman who's been dieting since she was ten, lost thirty pounds and was pleased with herself until she began to regain it. Facing a holiday reunion with her family, she tells me, "There's no shame worse than getting fat again after you've lost weight." She came to one of our sessions close to tears. "I've been *bad*. I ate two pieces of Geri's birthday cake. And just when I've been so *good*."

Is she saying she's a bad person?

"I just can't feel good about myself when I eat foods I know are going to put the weight on. But I just couldn't resist it. Then when I got home, I started grazing. Why can't I have more willpower? What's wrong with me? And when I go to Weight Watchers each week, I find out if I'm good or bad. If I've lost weight, I'm good, and everyone applauds. If I haven't, I'm bad and feel ashamed."

Controlling weight by dieting is a major shame-laden issue for many women because most fail again and again at this difficult and demanding task. The diet industry sets us up for failure by promising answers to our anxieties about being too feminine in the workplace. It also lures us into believing that all that stands between us and happiness is our weight. We are led to believe that if we work hard enough at it, we will succeed. And if we don't, *it's our own fault.*

That's why so many American women are either ending a diet ("I got hungry and bored"), just starting one ("This time it'll be different"), or between diets ("I should be dieting"). Our ability to govern our appetites determines how we feel about ourselves—a mentality that threatens our psychological well-being.[7]

Even women who stay on their diets and lose weight often find, like Natalie, that they gain it back and more, because the drastic reduction in calories changes their metabolism, causing more of what they eat to be converted to fat.

The Diet Ritual

Why are so many women compelled to diet? Dr. Judith Rodin, founder of the Eating Disorders Clinic at Yale University and author of *Body Traps,* suggests that dieting goes beyond the need to lose weight to become an important ritual, "a form of self-cleansing, physically and spiritually—a promise of a better life, a better self."[8]

Dieting provides shame-based women with something specific they can do to improve themselves in the face of so many loathsome things about themselves they feel powerless to change. Depriving ourselves of food also unconsciously provides a way of atoning for all the ways we've been selfish and bad.[9]

Obsession with weight starts at an early age. As early as eight and nine, girls think they're too fat and start dieting because their good feelings about themselves already strongly depend on having the ideal body weight. Researchers found that 81 percent of the ten-year-old schoolgirls in their study had already dieted at least once.[10] Then, to make matters worse, by puberty girls naturally gain in body fat, adding 20 to 30 percent more fat than boys. This is nature's way of preparing them for their reproductive role, since fat stores estrogen. At the same time boys add muscle and lean tissue. While these physical changes move boys *closer* to the ideal of being muscular, they move girls *away* from the ideal of being thin.[11] These changes give rise to a devastating contradiction of forces for adolescent girls.

"Mirror, Mirror, on the Wall"

By adolescence, girls have become acutely aware of the importance of looking good. In the eyes of a developing girl boys suddenly graduate from being "yucky" to being "fine," from being playmates to becoming powerful judges of her worth.

Consider Tiffany. Once a spirited, self-confident girl who was obsessed with horses, by fourteen Tiffany has shifted her focus to boys and her appearance. She has become exquisitely aware of every real and imagined flaw as she competes for the desired male stamp of approval. Now she anguishes over every zit, every extra pound, every hair not exactly where it should be.

Simone de Beauvoir writes about the growing alienation a girl feels toward her body as she becomes aware of her status as object: "When the breasts and the body hair are developing, a sentiment is born . . . which is originally shame; all of a sudden the child becomes modest. . . . [Her body] becomes an object that others see and pay attention to . . . it is no longer the straightforward expression of her individuality, it becomes foreign to her; and at the same time she becomes for others, a thing."[12]

Now she becomes more vulnerable to depression and eating disorders. As studies consistently show, concerns about appearance leave girls more prone to depression.[13] And it should come as no surprise that eating disorders begin in adolescence—the average age of onset is fifteen. One out of five girls has or will have an eating disorder. Ninety-five percent of those suffering from bulimia—the binge-purge syndrome—are females. Fueled by shame while at the same time increasing shame, eating disorders clearly are a feminine issue and exact a high price. Aside from assaulting emotional well-being, anorexia and bulimia present serious physical risks.[14] For these reasons people who suffer from eating disorders should seek professional help.

Those who eat too little often wish to postpone their fate as females—to forestall the natural development of their sexuality. Starving themselves keeps them looking boyish and often delays menstruation.

Anorexics look to others for admiration and relish a feeling of being special for demonstrating so much control over their appetite and their body—often the only domain that is within a girl's control.

Bulimics harbor intense feelings of shame about their disorder. To eat to the point of bursting, to make yourself vomit, to know you are out of control, brings shame with little relief. For many the only apparent remedy is the cleansing and self-punishing purge and then eating again to deaden the bad feelings. And so the vicious cycle goes on.

Randy, a twenty-three-year-old graduate student, waited many months before she brought up her concerns about her eating problem. Speaking so fast that I could hardly follow, Randy began telling me about her secret.

"By the time I was fifteen, I began to be totally obsessed with how fat I was. Even though the doctor and my parents told me I was just right, I didn't believe them. So I started to diet."

"You couldn't feel good the way you were?" I asked, already knowing the answer.

"Not at all. And I did lose about ten pounds, but all I could think about was food. Finally, after a few months of this, one night after a fight with my parents I snuck downstairs after they were asleep and ate a whole box of cereal, two packages of cookies, and two candy bars. I felt terrified that I was going to put the weight back on, so I put my finger down my throat and it all came up. That made me feel better. In fact I was rather elated. I had figured out a way to eat and not get fat.

"But pretty soon I was gorging on food every day, sometimes more. I can't tell you how ashamed I am even telling you this. When I heard about it on a talk show, I realized I hadn't invented this despicable habit myself. Now, eight years later, I'm a wreck. I live alone in my apartment, and I only go out to class and to buy—" She stopped and covered her face. "Sometimes I even steal food. I'm so disgusted with myself. I even think about killing myself." She paused, sighed deeply, and then plunged on. "Every morning when I wake up, I promise myself that I'll quit today, but by the end of the day, especially if someone has slighted me or I've been upset about something, I'll do it all over again."

In addition to her individual therapy Randy joined a group for women with similar problems and was eventually able to overcome her disordered eating. She found other ways to meet her needs. She learned to appreciate her natural body and to understand and find healthier ways to manage her anxiety and other uncomfortable emotions. Most important, she learned to love herself.

Problems of the Overeater

Compulsive overeating without purging brings a double humiliation that comes from failure to meet the cultural ideal of slenderness along with the inability to hide the evidence of lack of control.

Why do women overeat? I believe the two most important reasons women eat to excess are to nurture themselves and to dull emotions. Their low self-worth and shame keep them locked in this maladaptive behavior: They are the first to take care of others' needs, the last to take care of their own. Because they feel undeserving, they don't let others nurture them, nor do they nurture themselves. Because these women have weak boundaries, they can rarely say no to others or yes to themselves.

FOOD AS NURTURANCE

Some of us eat as a way of rewarding or comforting ourselves. Natalie, highly stressed with a demanding job and baby, confesses, "Sitting down to eat is the only pleasure in my day."

Rodin advises developing a *specific* list of alternative things to try instead of always depending on food as an answer to our emotional needs. One of her clients learned to manage stress by jogging and to deal with boredom by playing the piano. The point is to identify the specific function the food is serving and to make a specific plan to find substitutes.[15]

It is possible to find other ways to nurture ourselves besides eating, such as calling a friend, taking a bubble bath, or buying some new perfume. Or we can let ourselves have that muffin without feeling guilty.

If we are too accommodating, it's important to ask ourselves, *Where am I giving in, not asserting my wants and expressing my feelings? What stops me?*

Natalie and I found that she was giving up her power in all areas: at work, with friends and family. "I never say anything when friends or people in the office borrow my stuff and never return anything. And I hate going every Sunday to Mother's for dinner. I'd love to have Sunday home just with Jim and me and the baby. But I don't dare bring it up."

I ask what would be so bad about saying something.

"I'm afraid I'd hurt my mother's feelings."

"I know you care about her, but do you think you're responsible for how she handles her feelings when you are asserting yourself?"

"Well, if you put it that way, I guess not. I'd need to be tactful, though."

The next session Natalie said, "I told my mother, 'I love you a lot, Mom, but I need to have Sundays to be with my own little family.' She was hurt at first, but she felt better after we compromised. We're just going to go once a month and see how that works."

EATING DEADENS EMOTIONS

For many shame-bound women there are often unexpressed or even unfelt emotions lying beneath the surface such as anger, grief, hurt, and loneliness. Eating can numb these unacceptable feelings. When we consistently put others' needs ahead of our own, we often end up angry, with no acceptable outlet to express it. "I guess stuffing my body has been a way to stuff my anger," says Natalie.

Sometimes we eat to ease anxiety or deny unacknowledged pain. It's not uncommon to find that obese women have been sexually abused.

Sometimes fat protects us. "I stay fat because then I don't have to deal with men," says one woman. "If I were thin, there wouldn't be anything left of me. This way I know I exist," says another.

If we are to regain control of our eating, we must look at areas where we may be using food to dull or even block psychic pain. Natalie and I looked at the underlying emotions that her eating might be covering. As she allowed herself to feel and express her long-repressed emotions, she started to feel better about herself. She began to stand up for herself more. As her self-esteem improved, she came to accept her less-than-perfect body. "I know I'm on the plump side," she now says. "But this is *my* body. I like it the way it is. I know if I start getting too heavy, I can eat less. I walk every day, and I feel great."

Age Shame

Like adolescence, middle age is a time of body crisis that forces us to confront major changes. Our skin loses its elasticity and becomes wrinkled. As our metabolism slows down and we enter menopause, we add fat. The increase in weight most menopausal women experience is our body's attempt to keep a healthy balance of hormones, because fat stores estrogen. Since women's beauty is so often used to justify our existence and to enhance both the male and the female ego, it's no surprise that the fading of our youthful beauty ushers in new shame-based anxieties. We see the natural aging process as a negative force to be eluded if at all possible.

Society treats aging in the two sexes quite differently: While men grow distinguished, women grow old. This double standard turns aging into a painful process for a woman partly because it threatens to destroy those aspects of her that our culture most values: her youth and beauty and her reproductive capacity.

The beauty industry is quick to play on the aging woman's anxieties. Consider this Oil of Olay advertisement: "I don't intend to grow old gracefully. I intend to fight it every step of the way."

Some women resist this kind of age-shaming.

Consider Allison, a vibrant woman in her late forties, who was strolling through her favorite department store one day when she was offered a free facial. Halfway through the procedure the cosmetics clerk picked up a jar and announced, "Now for the antiwrinkle cream."

"Stop right there," Allison said. "I don't mind having wrinkles. My mother is seventy-seven. Her face has lots of wrinkles, and she's beautiful."

What's so bad about wrinkles anyway? Why the fetish about preventing them with useless creams? What's wrong with nature's way? Look at Jessica Tandy, a wonderful example of a woman aging powerfully.

Am I saying appearance shouldn't be important? Absolutely not. Looking good does matter to most of us, not only because of its many advantages, but because it pleases us. Let's just call it healthy narcissism. There's nothing wrong with appreciating beauty and wanting to enhance our appearance. It becomes a problem only when it takes too much time, energy, and money or when our focus on it comes from deep feelings of inherent defectiveness, leading us to reject our natural selves.

Body Image

Our body image (how we see ourselves in our mind's eye) often has little to do with objective reality, yet it determines how we feel about our bodies and ourselves. I have heard women I consider good-looking, even beautiful, bemoan flat chests, "thunder" thighs, fat stomachs, bad skin, or "impossible" hair. Our evaluation of ourselves appears to be fairly independent of our actual physical attributes.

When women vulnerable to shame look in the mirror, what

they *think* they see usually convinces them they look bad. Yet less physically attractive women who have good self-esteem are more likely to have a positive body image. For example, older women with a strong sense of self-worth are able to maintain a positive body image regardless of their actual appearance.

The relationship between the value we place on ourselves and the way we view our bodies is complex. Because shame-prone women lack a reliable sense of their bodies, they find it especially difficult to have a solid sense of self.

Betsy, a secretary who has battled weight problems for years, says her whole perspective on life changes with her fluctuating weight. "If I'm up twenty pounds, I feel fat, depressed, and so undesirable I just want to stay home. If I'm down twenty, I feel attractive, I'm happy, I'm ready to go."

Is Body Shame a Sex-Linked Characteristic?

Exaggerating our flaws and seeing ourselves as less attractive than we are is a predominantly female affliction. One study found that one out of three women is "strongly dissatisfied" with her body, while only one man in ten is "strongly dissatisfied" with his.[16] A survey of over thirty thousand women by *Glamour* magazine found that 75 percent of women between the ages of eighteen and thirty-five believed they were fat, yet only 25 percent were actually overweight. *And almost half of the underweight women considered themselves too fat.*[17] Men tend not to see being overweight as a serious problem.

Some of us obsess over one part of our body that we think is too fat or the wrong size or shape. We let these so-called flawed parts dominate our entire self-concept.

"When I walk into a room full of people, I wish I were invisible," says Abby. "I feel like everyone's looking at me, judging me, seeing all my flaws, especially my big ass. That's why I try to get places early, so I can just stay in my seat."

A woman who is embarrassed about her body is often self-conscious. Because Abby believes that people are constantly scrutinizing and evaluating her, she frequently checks in mirrors to reassure herself that every hair is in place and her makeup is fresh, hoping her looks will shore up her flagging self-esteem. Too often her internal shame influences her external view of herself.

Because our body image stays fairly constant, it rarely improves with dieting and cosmetic surgery. (We've all heard the expression, "There's still a fat person inside this thin body.") We need to realize that our body image is usually not based on reality; rather it's an image we create in response to our environment, and we can often find its roots in our culture and in our childhood.

Inaccurate body images and resulting body shame create a deep alienation from our bodies. At the extreme many obese women have little sense of their bodies below the neck.[18] Most of us are unaware of the stress we carry in different body parts. When we start to tune in to our body, we become aware of holding patterns, places we are tight, times we forget to breathe. Increasing body awareness allows us to loosen muscle tension. It also informs us about feelings we may be storing. We each have our own favorite places to pack in emotion and tension: jaw, stomach, shoulders, back, chest, legs. Physical exercise and massage are ways to get to know and appreciate our body.

What Keeps Us Hooked?

Why are women so preoccupied with their appearance and so vulnerable to influences from the beauty and diet industries?

A route to power and success.   There's no doubt that appearance is an important factor in making it in the world, enhancing everything from our popularity to our earning capacity. For instance fat people are hired less often and often earn less (most states have no laws against weight discrimination). One fat woman went to court because she was kicked out of nursing school on the grounds that she was too fat to perform her duties. She went on to earn her nursing degree from another school and today holds a management position in a hospital.

The attainment of beauty has traditionally been a means for women to exercise power. And our appearance is the most concrete and visible accomplishment allowed a woman in our society. It also gives us a chance to excel in one of the few areas that not only avoids threatening men but pleases them. It also redirects our competitive feelings into acceptable arenas.

A way to ease anxiety.   Connie's husband always lets her know when she starts to get "too fat." Fearful of losing him to a more attractive woman, she watches the scale, goes hungry most days, and wonders why she doesn't feel like making love. But she *is* trying to please him. (His recent hiring of a cute new secretary has added to her need to work harder on her body.)

An antidote to shame.   Beauty and thinness become all-important because they promise a way to overcome the feelings of defectiveness arising from being female in our society. Focusing on our body also allows us to avoid looking inside and facing painful feelings of low self-worth. By asking the question How do I look? rather than How am I doing? we can allay these deeper anxieties about not being okay. Scapegoating our body gives us reasons to "explain" social oversights or possible rejections *(They probably didn't invite me to their wedding because I'm fat)*. It also gives us an excuse not to take risks. Like Natalie we say, *I'll get a better job when I lose thirty pounds.*

A means of control.   When a woman can blame her body, she gains a feeling of being in charge of herself. For instance, when she is ashamed of failing in a relationship, it's a relief to place the responsibility on her body—the one area she *can* control. "When I lose fifteen pounds, then I'll be happy," says one woman.

A reduction of guilt.   As we've discussed in earlier chapters, sometimes we allow ourselves to have more than our mothers. Failing to control our weight and constantly dieting give us something to lessen our guilt for surpassing them in other areas.

Who Owns Our Bodies?

Our bodies are exploited for many purposes. They are used as ornaments to decorate playing fields, restaurants, bars, and offices; to sell products; to enhance the male ego; and to satisfy male sexual and aggressive urges. Our bodies are objects for men to view, use, and rate. "She's a 10" is supposed to be a compliment, not the insult it really is. Our natural body functions (menstruation, childbirth, and menopause) are treated as if they were medi-

cal problems. Our right to choose whether to continue an unwanted pregnancy rests tentatively in our hands as our legal
system continues to add humiliating constraints.

*"If even our bodies—their health, their freedom, their adornment, their
uses—are not our own, what is?"* asks Gloria Steinem (emphasis in
original).[19]

Lack of ownership of our bodies may result in an aging American woman's face being operated on to keep her husband's interest or an African girl's clitoris being cut out to ensure her
marriageability.[20]

Yet we also relate to our *own* body as object, something to
please others, a thing to be used to shore up our faltering self-
esteem or to bring power and success. When we use our body to
these ends, we lose touch with its natural needs for rest, food, sex,
or touch.

We can't win in this beauty and body game, but we can stop
playing. We can begin to set our own more generous standards of
beauty and refuse to be manipulated for gain by the beauty
industry. We can expose the myth that equates youth and thinness
with beauty. We can learn to become comfortable with our new-
found powers and let go of needing to downplay our femininity in
order to be taken seriously. We can embrace the naturally
rounded female figure instead of starving ourselves in pursuit of
the thin, boyish look. We can be both powerful and female without compromising either vital aspect of ourselves. We can reclaim
ownership of our bodies.

It's important to remember that when we are absorbed with
becoming beautiful or having the perfect body, we are buying in
to the notion that our natural bodies are defective. We also need
to avoid falling into the trap of either/or thinking. *(Either I'm thin
or I'm fat. Either I'm beautiful or I'm ugly.)* We need to accept, even
welcome, diversity and learn to love our own unique face and
body.

We need to recognize that we are never going to have the body
we want, that we can never make our body perfect. We need to
stop attacking our self-worth because we have a nose larger than
average or we are taller, shorter, or fatter than average. We must
remember that there is a wide range of body types and sizes, and

we need not feel ashamed of our innate differences. It will help to look at what we were like as little girls, to consider family body types, and to ask ourselves whether it is really *natural* for us to be thin.

Most of us have a distorted body image that leaves us overly concerned about imperfections and exaggerating our size. We need to silence our Inner Critic by answering its attacks with positive comments *(I look great. It's okay not to be perfect. I love myself the way I am)*. And when other people offer compliments, we can take them in, accept them, enjoy the good feelings.

We also need to look at our particular benefit in hanging on to our body shame. Is it easing our guilt for having a better life than Mom? Is it giving us an excuse not to risk, go for that job, have a relationship, play, or exercise? Is it a way to feel in control? To avoid our deeper shame?

By loving the Beast, Beauty freed him from the witch's curse and revealed him as the Prince (and soul mate) he really was. By loving our own bodies, we, too, can remove the curse put upon us by society and reveal the natural beauty and wholeness that are our birthright.

CHAPTER FOURTEEN

Shame
as Old as Eve

*Shame, which is considered to be a feminine characteris-
tic par excellence . . . has as its purpose, we believe,
concealment of genital deficiency.*
—SIGMUND FREUD

Josie, a tall, attractive thirty-three-year-old bookkeeper, always
comes to our sessions in baggy sweatsuits. She tells me she
dresses like that to conceal her breasts. "Besides," she says, "I feel
so big, bony, and awkward. I don't feel attractive. I don't even feel
feminine." Tears well up as she continues. "Mother wouldn't let
me wear sweaters that revealed the shape of my breasts. I don't
think she liked sex."

I ask her how she got that idea.

"For one thing she never looked feminine or sexy. For another
she told me sex is a duty. And she didn't give me much information. 'Your husband will tell you all you need to know,' she'd say.
What a joke. I cried myself to sleep on my wedding night, it was
so awful."

Josie is torn between being sexual and being a good girl. By denying the external evidence of her sexuality, she eases the internal conflict raging inside her. It's no surprise that passion comes to her only in her fantasies.

As we've seen throughout this book, many women deny their own experience in order to be connected to others, and nowhere is this more common than in the area of their sexuality. Their shame is so constricting that even in a therapeutic setting few can discuss sex comfortably, most not at all.

Even for healthy people "there is shame aplenty in normal sexuality," according to Donald Nathanson's theory of sexuality.[1] In addition to all the learned negative associations we acquire around sex, Nathanson says shame is linked to sexual activity because it arouses our excitement and feelings of joy, those positive emotions that when even slightly thwarted will trigger our inborn shame response. Nathanson believes that when our partner fails to resonate perfectly with us (as will even the most intuitive lover), we will inevitably experience shame.[2] "To know sex is to know shame, just as to know shame one must understand sex."[3] And to know a *woman's* shame, we must understand the social and psychological factors that shape her sexual experience.

Myths About Woman's Sexuality

Josie is a product of a culture that historically believed a woman didn't have sexual feelings and valued her for her reproductive capacity and her ability to arouse a man. Being treated as an object is a deeply shaming experience.

I have compiled the following myths about natural female sexuality that stem from this cultural view of woman as sexual object:

- Female anatomy is inferior to male anatomy.
- Women's sexual desire isn't as powerful as men's.
- What desire we do feel must be awakened by a man.
- Our job is to accommodate and satisfy the male sexual urge.
- There are two kinds of orgasms. We should strive for the "preferred, mature" variety, always remembering the man's is more important.

- Asking for what we want in bed isn't ladylike.
- Men can't control their urges, so if we provoke them, whatever happens is our fault.
- Our natural functions (menstruation, childbirth, menopause) are forms of sickness.

Although we are slowly exposing the destructiveness of these myths, we need to remember that most of our mothers and grandmothers passed them on to us as truths. Small wonder that many of us are dissatisfied with and ashamed of our sexuality.

Where did these myths come from? For centuries male-dominated culture defined woman as inferior, even the source of evil. Historically Christianity has promulgated the belief that women's sexuality was sinful except for the purpose of making babies. Ideally it could be dispensed with entirely: the Virgin Mary gave birth to Jesus untainted by sex.

Viewing woman as evil gave man an excuse to control her sexuality, thus ensuring that her offspring belonged to him and guaranteeing their inheritance.

As object for man's sexual outlet and producer of his children, woman was herself considered property, and as such she lost value if she wasn't a virgin on her wedding night. It was important never to have "belonged" to another man. Yet no such requirement impeded the groom. We see the legacy of this attitude in today's double standard. A man who has many sexual partners is "sowing his wild oats"; a woman who does the same is "promiscuous."

Freud's distorted yet authoritative picture of the female's inferior sexuality confirmed established Judeo-Christian views of woman as sexual object. Freud was right about one thing at least—anatomy is destiny.[4] The fact that we are female has had enormous impact on our role in society, our lives, and our happiness.

Freud perpetuated the myth that we are biologically inferior because we lack a penis.[5] What we now know as our principal organ of pleasure, the clitoris, he considered insignificant. Freud taught that healthy feminine development required that a girl at puberty give up attachment to her clitoris and shift her orientation to her vagina. (Doesn't scorning the clitoris and elevating the vagina create the illusion of woman's dependency on man for sexual satisfaction?) Women who failed to renounce the clitoris were immature, neurotic, or resisting their femininity. The key to female psychology, according to Freud, was penis envy. Lacking that ideal organ, how could the girl not feel castrated?

Although Freud made an enormous, even revolutionary contribution to the understanding of the human psyche, his blind spots, related to his Victorian-era upbringing and his own psychological shortcomings, gave scientific support to the view of women as inferior.

Is Pleasure Beside the Point?

Historically woman has been viewed as existing for man's pleasure, a passive-receptive creature who must deny her own sexual feelings. Since her role was to bear children and to satisfy male desire, her sexual pleasure was unimportant.

The belief that female sexuality was a disgusting or dangerous thing to be extinguished led nineteenth-century doctors in Europe and America to perform clitoridectomies. This practice continues today, especially in African and Far Eastern and Middle Eastern countries. Genital surgery to eliminate sexual feelings is the ultimate attempt to negate a woman's sexual will. The World Health Organization roughly estimates that between seventy and eighty million women and girls living today suffer from the effects of genital mutilation.[6]

Although society has historically defined woman as not having strong sexual needs of her own, she was expected to be available for sex when her man needed her. The double messages we receive about the appropriate expression of our sexuality keep us locked in shame. Men see us as both madonna and whore. If we climb up on the pedestal and deny our sexuality, we stay safe. But if we descend to express our sexual urges, we risk being shamed.

The advice our mothers gave us reflects these confusions:

- "Sex is dirty, so nice girls don't do it."
- "It's sacred, so you'd better save it for the one you love."
- "It's your womanly duty to service your man, so don't enjoy it too much."
- "On the other hand don't be frigid."
- "If we got what we didn't ask for, it's because we were asking for it."

Is It Lust or Is It Love?

Having sex that is not grounded in love leaves some women feeling shame. While we need to honor our need for connection with our lovers and may choose not to have sex when we are feeling too much emotional distance, we can also enjoy lust without love.

"I got something clear this weekend about sex and love," says Kitty, a divorced real estate agent in her early thirties who had been dating a man for several months. "I think I've been getting them mixed up. I was feeling turned on, and I thought, *You really love him.* Then I thought, *No you don't. You like him and you like sex with him.* It's like I have to justify my lust.

"Looking back over some of my relationships, I realize I've talked myself into thinking I loved the guy so I'd feel okay having sex. So I wouldn't feel like a slut." She blushes. "It's hard to admit to you that I'm seeing him mostly because I like the sex."

I ask where she might have learned to feel ashamed of her sexual feelings.

"My parents made me feel like a tramp," she says. "When I was fifteen, I discovered the joys of kissing, but my dad caught me necking in the garage with my boyfriend and told me I was cheap."

Her mother told her, "Women don't *really* like sex, they endure it." Although stories like these are becoming rarer, my guess is that even today most mothers, ashamed of their own sexuality (or at least uncomfortable acknowledging their pleasure), give their daughters limited information and fail to mention that sexual organs exist for more than making babies.

Most women learned as little girls to be ashamed of their genitals. Some were even instructed to use a separate washcloth for washing "down there." Whereas a penis is proudly erect and associated with power, a vagina is hidden, associated with passivity—and bad smells. As far back as we can remember, we have suffered the mortification of dogs sniffing our crotch.

Names for our genitals can evoke shame:

"I remember the first times I heard 'cunt,' then 'gash' and 'slit' and 'beaver,' " one woman said. "I felt so ashamed—not of the kids saying those things but of myself as a female."[7]

"Nice Girls Don't Get Turned On"

Darlene, raised Catholic, had learned that sexual pleasure was bad. "I'd go to confession every week and ask for forgiveness for French-kissing my boyfriend. I never masturbated until I was thirty. I never had orgasms in my first marriage. Every time we made love, I would see all the nuns standing by me, telling me it was wrong except to make a baby. For twelve years I never found pleasure. I didn't talk to other women about anything—couldn't ask, 'Do *you* feel that way too?' My shame was huge—billboard size."

Today sex education in schools is inadequate and unenlightening about girls' physical and sexual development, narrowly focusing on menstruation and reproduction, rarely acknowledging a teenager's often powerful sexual urges.

"All I hear is 'Don't get a disease, don't get raped, don't do it, but if you do, don't get pregnant,' " says Heather, sixteen. "How come they don't tell me anything about these incredible feelings I get when I'm with my boyfriend? Sometimes I think I'm bad to feel like that."

We discuss her feelings about having a full sexual relationship with her boyfriend. I ask her if having sex is something she wants to do or if she's considering it because he's pressuring her. Girls often say yes to accommodate or to get nurturing.

"I really do love him and we've been together a long time. I think I'm going to be ready soon. I think I'd better get on the pill. My mom said she'd come with me to Planned Parenthood if and when I'm ready. But I'm afraid he might think I'm a slut—you know, like I *planned* to have sex."

"Is it being a slut or being responsible?" I ask.

"Responsible, I guess. I sure don't want to get pregnant."

I ask how she will handle protecting herself against AIDS.

"I'd be too ashamed to make him wear a condom. He'd think I didn't love and trust him."

The shame women are made to feel for knowing about or, even worse, carrying condoms and insisting that a new sexual partner wear one isn't just harmful to their psychological health, it may threaten their lives. AIDS is more readily transmitted from male to female than female to male, so the woman who has sex without a condom is much more at risk. (Even having sex with a condom is not fail-safe.)

Girls faced with Heather's dilemma often end up having sex without birth control. Those like Heather, who have sex only after carefully thinking it through, are more likely to use birth control and practice safe sex.

The culture's refusal to acknowledge the importance of girls' sexual pleasure leads many girls eventually to disavow their own experiences. They either feel nothing, or, believing that sex is bad and dirty, they find it easier to be "swept away," to deny the power of their own desire, taking no responsibility for it. Either path leads to shame. When they can't claim their feelings and consequently can't be in charge of them, they set themselves up for irresponsible decisions.[8]

Some girls are so highly pressured by boys that they give in before they are ready and consequently feel guilt and shame. Buying temporary closeness, they often end up hurt when the boy drops them. Yet it's tempting to use sex to enhance self-esteem. Making love can reassure us that we matter.

The Myth of the Vaginal Orgasm

Although many women have suspected or known the clitoris was the true center of their sexual pleasure, we have historically deferred to male experts who told us we were wrong. The woman was supposed to climax through intercourse alone, and if she didn't, she was deficient, abnormal, frigid.

Herein lies a problem. As writer Alix Shulman puts it, the "penis and the vagina together can make either babies or male orgasms; very rarely do the two together make female orgasms."[9] Mothers seldom teach their daughters about the clitoris—*the only organ whose sole purpose is sexual pleasure*.[10] Treating this primary organ as if it didn't exist can create shame about our sexuality. How do we reconcile our bodily experience with our culture's denial of its existence?

When we do find our clitoris on our own and discover how good it feels to touch ourselves, we usually feel ashamed. One woman's mother told her she'd become sterile if she masturbated. Another woman says, "Nobody told me it was bad; I just knew it was bad. I was also sure I was the only one. I felt so ashamed that each time I got a new pair of pajamas, I would promise myself I'd stop masturbating. Didn't do any good."

We're now learning that masturbation has beneficial effects. For instance women who learn to masturbate are more orgasmic with a partner than women who don't.[11]

It wasn't until 1966 that sex researchers Masters and Johnson gave us startling new information: *All* female orgasms begin in the clitoris and occur by direct stimulation (hand, tongue or penis) or, less commonly, by indirect stimulation (from the thrusting penis). Furthermore most women require direct stimulation of the clitoris.[12] All those women who felt ashamed of not measuring up were suddenly exonerated.

Yet many of us still hold on to the old shame-producing beliefs that we're abnormal if we can't have an orgasm from intercourse. Why would this be? Perhaps because it's so deeply ingrained in us to disavow our own experience, especially in the face of our partner's adherence to the old thinking. We also don't talk freely with other women, missing opportunities to confirm the truth.

Even Masters and Johnson told us that a woman has an *orgasmic dysfunction* if she can't have orgasms through intercourse alone (emphasis added).[13]

As if that weren't enough, eighteen years later the American Psychiatric Association, in its widely used diagnostic manual, continues to reflect this notion of the deficient woman in its comments about diagnosing Inhibited Female Orgasm. Women who require manual clitoral stimulation to climax represent a "normal variation of the female sexual response" but it goes on, "In some of these females, this does represent a psychological inhibition that justifies this diagnosis."[14]

Are they trying to have it both ways? Given that orgasms originate in the clitoris, how can a woman who climaxes through manual stimulation but not through intercourse possibly be considered dysfunctional? Is orgasm through intercourse still considered the ideal? It sounds as though these doctors think so. This attitude confirms women's belief that we are anatomically and psychologically impaired when we can't climax through intercourse alone. Anyone can see that Freud's ideas about women being deficient die hard!

Faking Orgasms: A Costly Way Out

Some women, feeling inadequate for not having orgasms through intercourse alone, try to escape this shame trap by faking. (According to *The Hite Report*, more than 50 percent of women fake orgasms.)[15]

Although faking orgasm may be one more way we are alienated from our bodies, we need to be careful not to judge ourselves for using this solution to a complex problem. The last thing we need is to feel ashamed once again for the way we handle our sexuality in a culture that teaches girls early on to misrepresent much of their experience, to accommodate, and especially to deny what their bodies are telling them.

Unfortunately faking orgasm has the side effect of adding to the shame of our sexual inadequacy the shame of lying to our partners. Shame from this kind of subterfuge is self-perpetuating. Once a woman has faked an orgasm, she may be obliged to keep on faking. The longer she fakes, the more difficult it becomes to tell her partner the truth about what she needs to be sexually satisfied. Often it is her healthy sense of shame for not only deceiving her partner but using her own body as a means to an end that finally allows a woman to divulge her secret.

Josie was one of those women. After we worked on helping her understand the problem and why she had chosen that solution, we explored together some possible approaches to telling her husband that she hadn't been having quite as much fun in bed as she'd been pretending to have.

Josie told Don that she loved him deeply and that she wanted to make some changes in their sex life because she'd been learning some things about her sexuality that made her realize they were missing out on some great sex as a couple. She proceeded to tell him that she'd been faking orgasms, that she'd always felt abnormal, and that that's why she did it. In addition she'd wanted to please him, and she knew how important it was to him that he satisfy her.

Several months later Josie reported, "Although it was embarrassing to talk about it, I couldn't go on the way we had. I'm so glad we talked, because the pressure's off now. Even though he still doesn't trust me completely, he's beginning to understand. Now he stimulates me with his hand, or I do it myself. We're both getting satisfied, and I no longer feel flawed for not coming or ashamed of being a fake."

We can begin to take charge of our own sexual gratification by sharing our knowledge with our partners. Many men *do* want to be sensitive lovers. In fact some overly conscientious men have gone so far as to assume the entire responsibility for bringing their partners to climax. (They also worry about not being big enough, climaxing "prematurely," or being unable to maintain an erection.)

Sex Is Sexist

Though some lovers today understand that the pleasure of a clitoral orgasm is a legitimate end in itself, not necessarily a prelude to the more "desirable" orgasm through intercourse, most men and women *still view penetration and ejaculation as the desired culmination of the sex act and a woman's clitoral orgasm as secondary.*

Kitty tells of her experience with her former husband. "I was ashamed that I couldn't have a *regular orgasm* when he was in me, like a normal person. He'd have to play with me so that I could climax. He sure let me know I was lacking. One time he yelled at me, 'I'm so sick of you not climaxing,' I was sure the neighbors could hear. And I couldn't leave him, because he made me feel so sexually defective. Who'd want me? I got the sense that he was staying with me only out of generosity. Funny thing, though, when I finally got the strength to leave, he was the one who fell apart.

"Now with my lover I don't feel like such a sexual freak anymore. But sometimes I feel like when I have my orgasm during foreplay, he thinks it's just that: foreplay. But for me it's often the endplay. And sometimes his orgasm is like afterplay. I feel selfish saying that.

"It's not like I always want to stop at that point," she continues. "I like him in me—it feels wonderful—and I like to give him pleasure. It's just that I've been pretending for a long time that I'm always waiting for the real sex to start.

"Then there are the times when all I want is to cuddle *without* sex, yet I'm afraid to say so because I think I should be taking care of his needs, not my own," says Kitty.

What's so bad about making her needs as important as his?

The Right Way to Do It

There are other ways a woman's feelings of sexual inadequacy are triggered by not having the correct sexual response. Shame about not doing things "the right way" often generalizes to feelings of being flawed as a person.

"When I hear of other women making love all night, I wonder what's wrong with me," Kitty says. "I don't like oral sex, but I feel like such a prude. How come I'm so uptight? And why can't I have multiple orgasms like Sally?"

With the sexual revolution and the advent of birth control, many women feel there's no excuse for lack of sexual desire, not realizing that many things can kill or diminish desire. Some women lose interest in sex when they believe their responses are faulty, failing to realize that the fault may lie in sex being defined as intercourse and male orgasm. The sequence of lovemaking is often determined by male desire: little or no foreplay, penetration, and ejaculation. A done deed.

I often tell couples that the most crucial foreplay is *emotional foreplay*.[16] In order for a woman to want to make love, she needs to feel cared about. This is normal.

Anger (whether chronic or fresh) and resentment (long-standing, even buried) can kill desire. "You can't make love under a blanket of resentment" goes the wise old saying. Many women resent the imbalance of power in their marriages and find that unconsciously withholding sex or not being very responsive are ways they can exert their power. Exhaustion also robs us of sexual desire. "When I crawl into bed, I can't face one more demand on me," Josie says.

On the other hand, if our need is greater than our lovers', we may feel oversexed or too needy. If they are less interested than we are, we worry that we have lost our desirability.

Even if all conditions are favorable, our belief that sexual feelings are shameful can hamper desire. By the time we are grown women, some of us have lost touch with our passion, left behind in adolescence or never kindled due to potent cultural prohibitions. We don't allow ourselves sexual pleasure, don't have orgasms. Others of us can feel sexual only with an illicit lover, as though our sexuality were split off from the rest of us.

Our patriarchal culture considers lesbians or bisexuals abnormal or sinful, so women who choose other women as lovers carry an additional burden of shame. While many lesbians guard their secret to ward off shame and protect their jobs, "coming out" often alleviates shame and empowers them.

As women of all sexual orientations begin to define their *own* sexuality instead of depending on men, as they break the taboo about asking for what they want and start claiming the right to sexual pleasure, their self-esteem improves. And in the process they learn there's *no right response.*

Rather than blaming our lovers for their inability to understand our sexuality, it's time we spoke of what we've always known but never trusted. Now that we have more knowledge of the way our sexuality works—and especially since we are able to talk more frankly with other women about our experiences—we can look forward to the possibility of more pleasure and more self-confidence in our sexual lives.

Menstruation and Menopause: Feminine Failures?

Two major turning points in a woman's sexual development are adolescence and middle age, both times when the ticking of our biological clocks ushers in changes that can deeply affect the way we see ourselves. "Menstruation is *failed* conception; menopause is *failed* reproductive functions," writes social psychologist Carol Tavris. "Ultimately, the belief that menstruation and menopause are problems for women is part of a larger assumption that female physiology itself is abnormal, deficient, and diseased."[17]

We need to honor our natural functions as powerful and significant benchmarks in our psychological and spiritual lives rather than as reasons to consult a doctor.

MENSTRUATION: CURSE OR BLESSING?

Menstruation has been surrounded with stigma for centuries, based partly on men's fear of the evil powers of women to pollute and contaminate. Even today many women still see themselves as sick or dirty while menstruating—remnants of old taboos.

Women tend to dismiss the sometimes intense feelings that accompany their periods.

"I'm so upset with the condescending way my boss treats me,"

Josie says. "I can put up with it during the rest of the month, but I can't seem to ignore it when I'm getting my period." She starts to weep. "Here I go again. It's just my PMS talking. I'm so ashamed that I can't control my emotions. My husband is always making fun of me when I'm on the rag."

The menstrual cycle has been used as a rationale for not putting women in positions of great power, on the assumption that menstruating women are irrational or less competent. Yet research consistently shows no significant link between hormones and performance. Journalist Susan Brownmiller, in her book *Femininity*, points out that suicide, violent crimes, and dangerous psychiatric disorders are four to nine times more prevalent in men. She asks, "Should we theorize then that raging hormonal imbalance is a chronic year-round condition in males?"[18]

For years we were told that menstrual difficulties were all in our head, that we were neurotic or resisting the feminine role. Now we are told we have a medical syndrome. Many of us do have heightened emotions (positive or negative) before or at the time of our bleeding. And some of us have real physical symptoms. Because studies of women have been underresearched, we don't know enough yet about women's physiology to make final conclusions about the complex way hormones affect us. We can learn to take our upsets seriously without immediately filing for divorce or quitting our jobs. We can pamper ourselves by resting more, eating healthy foods, calling a friend. Taking extra care of ourselves helps reduce negative emotional outbursts.[19]

THE PAUSE THAT REVITALIZES

Another crucial, potentially shaming landmark in a woman's development comes at middle age, when her sense of herself again changes along with her body.[20] Menopause informs a woman that her reproductive years are over. While most women feel liberated from family demands as children depart, a few become depressed when faced with an empty nest.

Middle age is a time when we face the loss of our youthful looks. We feel fat. We feel wrinkled. We worry that our partner might abandon us for someone younger and more beautiful—a not uncommon event, given that our culture considers us "used up,"

devoid of sexual appeal, or sees our sexual desires as inappropriate and embarrassing.

Yet many older couples report that sex gets better.[21] And many
older women have lovers and/or enjoy masturbating.

In spite of old wives' tales to the contrary, menopause doesn't
make women clinically depressed or crazy.[22] Although more research is needed, there is impressive evidence that our expectations, emotional stress, life events, cultural milieu, and—most
importantly—self-esteem play a more important part than hormones in determining whether this passage will be smooth or
bumpy.[23]

Most women greet menopause with relief and do just fine.
Those who depend heavily on youthful looks and sexual desirability have the most difficulty. Studies of women in other countries
show that when menopause brings a woman *improved* status, freedom, and power, this stage in her life cycle is not considered
stressful. Women in countries like the United States, where aging
women lose esteem, tend to report more negative symptoms.[24]

Motherhood: Our Highest Calling?

Since the purpose of our sexuality has traditionally been to make
babies, society has promoted motherhood as woman's highest
calling, while regarding women who choose another path as selfish or even abnormal. Becoming a mother is viewed by many as
the ticket to adulthood. Failing to live up to that calling generates
profound shame, as can the lack of motherly stirring when we
greet our newborn. It may take weeks before we find our maternal
moorings. Because most of us mistakenly believe these feelings are
instinctual, we conclude that not feeling motherly is abnormal.

A divorced noncustodial mother says, "People treat me like
some kind of leper when I tell them I don't have custody of my
kids." Women who deliver stillborn, unhealthy, or defective babies also blame themselves. Infertility leaves many women feeling
inadequate. "Even though I know it's not my fault," says Laura,
"I can't help feeling responsible. It's my most important function
in life, and every month I'm reminded I'm a freak." A woman
who had an abortion and later had trouble conceiving believes she
is being punished for her "sin." Even years later women are still

haunted by the shame and disgrace of giving up a baby for adoption as unwed mothers.

The conflict between taking care of ourselves and taking care of another is nowhere more gripping than when deciding whether to have an abortion. For teenagers it is often the first life-altering decision they are called upon to make.[25] Although they may seek advice, they realize that ultimately the decision is theirs and theirs alone.

Reclaiming Our Sexuality

Realizing our sexuality is more defined by cultural myths than by our experience of ourselves, those of us who are shame-prone are the first to assume that our experience is invalid. Understanding that sometimes we are objects to be used for male gratification and exploitation, that our bodies and our sexuality are more for others than for ourselves, we often end up ambivalent about, ashamed of, or out of touch with our sexuality.

I recommend talking openly with friends, exchanging ideas and experiences. Our sexuality isn't a commodity that belongs to our lovers but nature's gift that is ours to actively nurture and to share if we so choose.

We need to expand our definition of sexuality to include more than just sex with another person. We can enjoy ourselves as sexual and sensual beings by savoring how our body responds to various things: a movie, the sight of a sexy man or woman, our own touch, a massage, sleeping naked, nursing a baby, physical exercise.

We need to communicate our own desires and honor our need for closeness and caring in connecting with our lovers. We are beings and we have the power to refuse to be treated as objects. We must remember that while we are givers of pleasure, we are also receivers. It's okay to break the stereotype of the all-giving woman and delight in our own female sexual responses. Embracing our sexuality empowers us to be fully ourselves.

CHAPTER FIFTEEN

Sexual Oppression: Shaming the Victim

MAN WHO STRANGLES NAGGING WIFE GETS SUS-
PENDED SENTENCE

London *A judge has spared from prison a man
who strangled his nagging wife [saying], "You have
suffered through no fault of your own a terrible existence
for a very long time. I do not see that sending you to
prison is going to do you or your children any good."
. . . . [The man] denied murdering his wife . . . but
admitted to the lesser charge of manslaughter on the
ground that her constant nagging provoked him.*
—San Francisco Chronicle,
January 31, 1992

Lottie, thirty-two, works on a road crew. I ask her what it's like
for her. "Terrible," she says. "The first week on the job a
guy kisses me on the neck. One time another guy and I are driving
and he turns to me and says, 'Get your boobs out of the way so
I can see to make a right turn.' They tell dirty jokes and flick their
tongues. You know what one jerk told me? 'Women smell like
fish.'"

"Did you complain?"

"Little good it did. First they said they'd check it out. Then
months later when I came back, they said they hadn't found
anybody who witnessed anything bad. They told me to just ignore

251

it, saying, 'Boys will be boys. And besides, what did you expect as the only girl on this job?' "

Pam, a woman who had been molested by her three brothers, works part-time as a cocktail waitress. She is continually fending off lewd remarks and sexual invitations. "I feel so dirty. Sometimes I feel like a piece of overhandled meat. Men think nothing of patting my behind or slipping a bill into my bra. I know they're undressing me with their eyes, yet I have to wear short, tight skirts and something that shows my cleavage. I'll be so glad when I'm through with paralegal school and can quit this degrading job. I'm sick of being treated like a sex object. When I was trying to decide what to wear to work on Halloween, my boss suggested I wear nothing but a mask and boots and come as Puss 'n Boots."

Like many victims of sexual harassment, Lottie has trouble sleeping. Pam has developed ulcers, and her hair is starting to fall out. Both women have trouble shaking off their sense of shame.

Being sexually oppressed or treated as a sexual object leaves women with a deep sense of anger and self-contempt. While some feminists would argue that all oppression of women is sexual oppression, in this chapter I am limiting my discussion to those areas that more directly reflect sexual or physical oppression.

There are two powerful myths about male sexuality that rely on shame to keep women sexually oppressed:

- *The myth of entitlement.* A man is entitled to sex from a woman (in its extreme form: a father is entitled to sex with his daughter). A man is entitled to stare at, make comments about, or fondle women, even if they are his co-workers or employees. Women are supposed to understand that this is how men are and not take offense. If they do, "it's *their* problem." Their feelings about being treated as sex objects don't matter. Male entitlement or male power is at the root of sexual harassment, wife battering, sexual abuse, and rape, including marital rape.
- *The myth of man's uncontrollable sex urge.* Once a man is aroused, he can't control his urges. A woman has to be extremely careful not to get him aroused if she's not willing to deliver. If she isn't on guard, she deserves whatever she gets. She shouldn't dress in a way that calls attention to her sexuality and she shouldn't start what she isn't prepared to finish.

"I remember a boy I liked called me a cockteaser because I wouldn't go all the way," Joyce says. "I used to get really confused. I still do. I like to flirt with the guys at work, but I feel guilty. Don't I have the right to draw the line wherever I feel like it? Can't I even change my mind if I want? Am I supposed to be responsible for his lack of control?"

Shame: The Most Effective Silencer

One of the most powerful means of keeping a woman silent about her abuse is to hold her responsible for being assaulted. "Secrecy is rooted in shaming the victim and discrediting her story," writes Harvard psychiatrist Judith Herman.[1] When Freud's female patients claimed that as children they had been sexually assaulted by male acquaintances or their fathers, he initially believed them.[2] Later, unable to accept that so many upper-middle-class Viennese fathers would commit incest, he reversed his position, claiming that his patients' reports were simply erotic fantasy.[3] Where might women be today had Freud (with his enormous influence) continued to take them seriously instead of abandoning them?

For one thing we might not have seen little girls blamed for their sexual abuse. In 1982 a man was sentenced to ninety days for sexually assaulting a five-year-old. The judge in the case justified the mild sentence with these words: "I am satisfied that we have an unusually sexually promiscuous young lady, and he did not know enough to refuse. No way do I believe the man initiated sexual contact."[4]

Shame has played a powerful role in keeping women silent about their abuse, be it sexual harassment, rape, incest, or battery.

What Is Harassment?

According to law professor Catherine A. MacKinnon, sexual harassment is "sexual pressure that you are not in a position to refuse. In its verbal form, it includes a working environment that is saturated with sexual innuendos, propositions, advances. . . . In its physical form, it includes unwanted sexual touching and rape."[5] It may include off-color jokes, pinups, or staring at a woman's breasts while she talks.[6]

Sexual harassment in any form is illegal.

Though nasty and degrading, it's not always intentionally so. I think many men are simply not aware of how hurt, offended, or embarrassed women are by male comments and attitudes. "We're just being men, and women should be able to understand innocent male fun." Or if the advances are serious, "Women should just say no." What men don't understand, because most of them haven't been there, is that as second-class citizens in a male-dominated society, women often feel they don't have the right to complain. They fear losing their jobs or they are too ashamed to speak up.

Sexual harassment isn't restricted just to macho blue-collar workers. Dr. Frances Conley, one of the nation's first female neurosurgeons, resigned as a professor at the Stanford University School of Medicine because of sexual harassment from colleagues and superiors that had continued throughout her career.

Even Supreme Court nominees are not exempt from such charges. Until Justice Clarence Thomas's confirmation hearings, *sexual harassment* was not exactly a household word. Professor Anita Hill's televised ordeal dramatically heightened our society's awareness of sexual harassment and empowered us to demand recourse whenever it occurs. Only after these hearings did thousands of women begin speaking of their experiences.

Where Does It Occur?

We're discovering that sexual harassment can occur anyplace a woman works under a man who has the power to hire, promote, or fire her. Or it happens between minister and parishioner, between teacher and student, between therapist and client—in situations where there is an obvious power imbalance. Yet it can also occur between peers, and this form of harassment is widespread in the workplace, in our elementary and high schools, and on college campuses. Men are sometimes sexually harassed by women or gay men, and gay women are occasionally harassed by other gay women.

"Why don't women simply put an end to the humiliating treatment?" some say. "Get another job. Report it. Don't be so sensitive."

Women endure this kind of shame for many reasons. One blames herself for the harassment: "Was it the perfume I wore? The short skirt? Did I send out the wrong signals?" (Just being female sends out the "wrong" signals.)

Another is anxious about her job: "Since the boss is my tormenter, what kind of letter of recommendation will he give me? If I tell, who will take me seriously or even believe me? It's my word against his."

Columnist Anna Quindlen explains: "It is usually one woman against the corporate power structure, against the boss who says she's imagining things and a bulwark of male authority that surrounds him. David against the Goliaths. . . . [Hill] found herself aligned against the most powerful men in America, including the president. Who of us would have had the guts to lift her slingshot?"[7]

Often the harassment itself seems a lesser humiliation than being seen as "the kind of woman who somehow asked for it." Instead the natural tendency is to bury the incident and go on with our lives. In breaking the silence, Anita Hill was accused of being psychotic, of engaging in erotic fantasy, and of perjuring herself to advance her career.

The woman who goes to court rarely gets much satisfaction. Even if she wins her case, she risks grave emotional stress and often financial ruin, to say nothing of her reputation. "I don't want my kids to think of me that way. I don't want to think of *myself* that way," says one woman.

Acceptance of male domination and even abuse are woven into the fabric of what it means to be female. Our culture has trained women to keep silent. At Mother's knee we learned, "There are some things you just have to put up with, honey." And we saw Mother practicing what she preached.

Sexual Violence

The ultimate consequence of the girls-are-asking-for-it-when-they-lead-a-guy-on myth is that we are blamed for being victims of male violence. Our society conveniently views women as temptresses and men as male animals who have no impulse control around a desirable female. This myth absolves the man of responsibility for his actions. Given the prevalence of this attitude, it is only common sense to be aware of male tendencies to misinterpret our behavior.

Adele agreed to give a ride home to a man she met in a bar. After telling her, "You have no right to say no, you agreed to give me a ride," he raped her. She was convinced the rape was her fault. Did she use poor judgment? Yes. Did she ask to be raped? Absolutely not. Her guilt and shame kept her from reporting the crime. I know of women raped by intruders in their own beds who still blame themselves, so deep is their shame and guilt about the wrongly perceived powers of their sexuality.

Acquaintance rape, by far the most common rape experience, reinforces the myth of male entitlement or uncontrollable male urges. In one study of normal male college graduates, 22 percent admitted having sex with women who were unwilling partners. Over 9 percent actually used force.[8]

Many women, confused about what qualifies as acquaintance rape, blame themselves. I've known married women raped by someone they knew who were so ashamed and felt so responsible they couldn't even tell their husbands. Or they kept secret an experience that happened before they were married.

"I've never told a living soul about this, but I had a bad experience once with a guy who was a good friend of my brother," says Carla, age thirty-five. "We were alone in his apartment, we'd been drinking some, when he started to take off my clothes. The last thing I wanted was to have sex with him. But he held me down. I kept struggling. He said things like 'I promise it won't take long. You know you want it.' " She blinks back tears. "I tried fighting him off but finally just gave up because I knew I didn't have a chance. He was much bigger than me. So I just lay there and let him do it. I should have stopped him. I've never felt so ashamed." The tears start gushing.

It was weeks before Carla could refer to this "bad experience" as rape, because she felt it was her fault: "I led him on, I gave in."

Of the over 34,000 women who responded to a sex survey by *New Woman* magazine, 30 percent said they had been raped or forced to have sex against their will by a date, lover, or husband. The results revealed that women with low incomes (under $15,000) and without college educations were the most vulnerable. As many as 50 percent of women in these two groups reported having had sex against their will.

These results led sex therapist Dr. Helen Singer Kaplan and her associate, Willa Bernhard, Ph.D., to conclude that the more autonomous a woman is, the more likely she is to protect herself against sexual and other abuse.[9]

Many women have to contend with the shame of marital rape, the most common form of rape.[10] Diana Russell, author of *Rape in Marriage*, found that one out of seven of the married women she interviewed had been raped by their husbands.[11] Until 1977 husbands, not wives, were protected by the legal system. As of July 1989 fourteen states still refused to prosecute marital rapists. It takes a long time to change historical patterns based on the belief that women are "property" to be used as men please.

Other Kinds of Violence

And then there is battering. Violence is not new to marriage, with wife beating having been permitted, sometimes even sanctioned by political and religious institutions, until the recent past. Statistics show that annually 1.8 million men beat their wives. To be battered or sexually assaulted by anyone is a devastating and humiliating experience, but when the perpetrator is someone we love and depend on, the shame can be excruciating. To make matters worse, society believes that the woman often provokes the man, justifying his uncontrollable violence against her. Again, we see how effectively shame is used to silence her.

Tammy, thirty-nine, married and mother of two young children, works full-time as a lab technician. Her husband sometimes stays out till two A.M., while she is left to handle dinner, cleaning up the kitchen, and putting the children to bed. She falls asleep alone in her bed, exhausted.

Yet Tammy makes no demands on her husband because she doesn't feel she is entitled to better treatment. When she complains, he berates her, shoves her against the wall, and sometimes even beats her. He tells her it's her belligerent attitude that inflames him. She feels deeply ashamed of her inability to leave this abusive relationship, even though she lives in continual dread that he will explode. At the same time, like many battered women, she blames herself for making him angry. "If only I hadn't provoked him. If only I'd nagged him less." And at a deeply unconscious level, she feels she deserves to be punished for being the bad girl her parents always told her she was. Her shame locks her into an abusive relationship.

Tammy and I discussed the different avenues she could take with her husband, including (at a minimum) cutting back on catering to him, calling the police when he batters her, going to a shelter, insisting that he get help, or leaving him.

One night Tammy did call the police, who took her husband to jail. "I was so ashamed, but I didn't know what else to do," she says. They were separated for several months. Her husband joined a group for violent men where he learned how to deal with his rage. They finally reconciled, but only after marital therapy and only when Tammy decided she was ready. By acting in her own best interests, she gained self-respect and he learned that she was capable of setting limits. Both partners have grown from this experience, and violence is no longer an issue in their marriage.

Women abused as children often end up as adults with abusive partners, for many reasons. First, we seek what is familiar. Strange as it may seem, there is an odd comfort in being treated in the same ways we were treated as children. At least we know how to survive. *And maybe,* we think, *I'll get one more chance to prove I can stand up for myself.* Often very real fears of not being able to survive economically keep women in abusive relationships. Indeed many women literally fear for their lives as male threats of "I'll kill you if you leave" are all too often attempted or even carried out. And often our shame keeps us trapped and unprotected ("I deserved it, I was bad. Who else would want me anyway?").

Sexual Abuse: The Worst Travesty

Problems with men brought Fran, then twenty-three, to my office during the late seventies. Her bubbly personality concealed her intensity and vulnerability. She had had a "nervous breakdown" during college, with two subsequent hospitalizations, leading to a diagnosis of schizophrenia. For several years we worked on her many issues, the most important being her love-hate relationship with her father, a man well-regarded in a helping profession. Although she moved away, we kept in touch.

Ten years later, after not having contacted me for several years,

Fran sent me a copy of a letter she had written to her father, confronting him with sexually abusing her. Little did we know at the time of our work together how common incest was. (As recently as the early seventies, experts believed there was only one chance out of a million that a child would be a victim of incest.[12]) Nor did we realize there were major events in her childhood totally beyond her awareness.

"Not quite three years ago now," she wrote her father, "the real reason for my episodes of psychosis began to surface. I used to blame them on my own internal weakness, until I began to have hazy recollections of things: first, your face leaving my bedroom at age fifteen, then overwhelming feelings of shame as I got out of your bed and put on my pants after a nap with you at age four. The memories have continued to come to me—always beginning as vague impressions, dreams, nightmares.

"Although I am healing, the anguish of what I've experienced—the shame and self-hatred of living for years with the belief that I was crazy, the humiliation of psychosis itself and hospitalization, and even more, the agony of being unable to develop normal, healthy relationships with men—has been unbearable. Nothing could make up for what I've been through—or what the rest of the family has been through watching me."

In her letter to her father Fran poured out her feelings of anger and revenge, her fear of seeing him again. Stretching to the limits of her capacity to love, she wrote of her desire to see him heal his own wounds and to possibly reestablish a relationship with him.

Fran's empathy for her dad was unusual. "I have such heartache for the child in you," she was able to write. "I know we share a common pain at the heart of it all, and knowing that sometimes makes me want to excuse what you did to me."

But she honored her own pain above all. She asked him for compensation and sent him a statement of money spent on years of therapy and lost earnings. She also asked him to get into therapy.

When it came to actually sending this letter, feelings of doubt and a desire to protect her father threatened to immobilize her. But in the end her courage prevailed.

Her father denied everything, dismissing her claims as "imaginings." The last time I heard from Fran, she had chosen not to work on a relationship with her father anymore. She now sees all this as "a chapter of my life finally closed so that I can begin to live—fully and appropriately." As a powerful symbol of her new-found strength and freedom, she changed her name—as an unmarried woman—from her father's to one of her own choosing. And she has now found a relationship that deeply nurtures her.

According to most reports, at least one out of every five women has been molested or raped by the time she is twenty-one. Most often the perpetrator is male, usually someone the girl knows. The list of abusers includes fathers, stepfathers, brothers, mothers, uncles, cousins, and grandfathers. Teachers, baby-sitters, ministers, and family friends also sexually abuse children. Abuse happens at all social and economic levels.

What exactly is child abuse? Sexual abuse is any forced or exploitative sexual contact by an adult or child with a child. Besides intercourse, oral sex, and anal sex, it may include any inappropriate touching, lewd looks or remarks, and showing children pornography. Voyeurism is sexual abuse even when it's not sensed by the child. Jody caught her live-in boyfriend peeping through a hole in the bathroom door to watch her daughter bathe.

Traditionally if the instigator is five years older or more, these acts qualify as abuse. But I've known girls who were seduced or raped by cousins, brothers, and friends—all peers. Occasionally the offender can be a girl who sexually abuses a boy or younger girl. Because girls see boys as more important and more powerful, they are more inclined to submit to a male. *It is not only age difference that is coercive but also gender difference, even when age is the same.*

Of course we have to allow for innocent sex play among the very young. For me the key is whether one person exploits or coerces the other.

"When I was a girl," says Theresa, "the boys chased me home and promised me candy if I pulled down my pants. 'We'll let you be in our club,' they promised. But they never did, even though I did." Is this sexual abuse?

Sexual abuse is without doubt the most deeply damaging transgression against a child. With such invasion of the self, a child is overwhelmed with many complex and confusing feelings. The resulting shame, hurt, and anger can take years to heal—if healing ever takes place.

The betrayal inflicts unspeakable wounds to the psyche when

the very person a child depends on for caring and protection is the one who is violating her. Instead of blaming her father, uncle, or grandfather, a girl concludes that *she* must be abnormal, that she has done something to deserve what has happened. She thinks; *How could I have let him? Why didn't I do something to stop it? Maybe I invited it somehow. Now I hate my body for attracting him. I feel like damaged goods.*

We blame ourselves for not getting help, for being aroused by the stimulation (even to the point of orgasm), for getting between Dad and Mom, and for hurting Mom. Older sisters agonize over having failed to protect younger sisters, though to do so would have required exposing their own shame. The list of self-recriminations is endless.

We forget the power that adults, especially parents, have over children. If Daddy says it's good for me or that this is what all fathers do with their daughters, he must be right. When he says not to tell, that if I tell it will kill my mother and that he'll kill me or send me away, I have to believe him.

Some children *do* tell their mothers and get help. Others are either accused of making things up or are reassured that it won't happen again. If it recurs and Mother never mentions it again, what is a girl to conclude? That she deserves this treatment? That she's not important enough for anyone to save her? That she can't trust anyone? Sometimes the knowledge is too threatening for a mother to deal with, and she sacrifices her daughter to keep the family intact or denies even to herself that abuse is occurring. We hear that mothers in some way have been enablers, permitting the abuse to serve their own needs. But I think many mothers are truly unaware of the ongoing abuse, and the victim's intense shame is often what silences her, along with her belief that the abuse is her own fault.[13]

It's important that mothers not be held responsible for failing to meet the emotional or sexual needs of their incestuous husbands. Accountability for sexual abuse lies with the abuser and also with the society that has allowed men to see women and children as objects they are entitled to use for their own purposes.

Coping with Abuse

Some children, in order to numb the abusive experience or block it out entirely, will leave their bodies or develop other personalities that can break up their life experiences into manageable compartments. Experts believe that most multiple personality disorders originate from attempts to cope with the excruciating trauma of physical or sexual abuse.

Fran gained a lot of weight as a teenager in the hope that her father would lose interest in her. Some girls refuse to get involved with boys, for fear of Father's (or Stepfather's or Grandfather's) jealousy. Others are wildly promiscuous, hoping the abuser will realize she has grown up and stop pressing his claims on her.

One of the most common ways to cope is to do as Fran did: she completely forgot about the abuse until she began getting flashbacks years later. When flashbacks occur, some women are flooded with memories, while others experience only vague fragments triggered by a smell, a dream, a TV program, or even sexual contact. Some women never remember, sensing only that something terrible has happened to them. Others never even have a hint.

Some women experience what we call posttraumatic stress disorder, similar to that suffered by combat veterans or other victims of violent crimes or major accidents. It may be years later that nightmares or unexplained panic attacks start. One woman I know was in her late sixties when she started to remember she had been abused by both her father and her grandfather.

The damage may be great or small. Fran lost years of her life and most of her self-respect. Some women confuse abuse with love and stay in abusive relationships. Other women find it difficult to understand why they can't trust, why they drink too much or use drugs, why they stay frantically busy or become workaholics, why they are so anxious or depressed, why they overeat. They wonder why they are sexually numb or continually sexually ravenous. Some are driven to prostitution.

Of course there are many explanations for troubled behavior, and we must be careful not to assume that every woman who manifests these symptoms has been sexually abused.[14]

Is Healing Possible?

It is possible to heal the wounds of abuse, but first we must break through the denial, which requires that we no longer shame ourselves for the abuse. Then we must experience all the grief and anger that comes from being betrayed, exploited, and—in many cases—robbed of our childhood.

We also need to accept that we may still love or care about the abuser. Ironically often the only time we felt loved was during the abuse. Often the abuser is an otherwise kind and caring person.

Sometimes it helps to confront the offender, but we shouldn't expect a specific result such as a confession or apology, because the odds are that, like Fran, we'll be disappointed. While some parents will ask for forgiveness, most will continue the cover-up they've maintained over the years (some having truly repressed the abuse), while others may attack us, calling us insane. Because we risk the possible rupture of the relationship as a result of our confrontation, we need to ask ourselves if we are strong enough at this point to withstand further rejection.

We must never blame ourselves for what was done to us as children, even if we were stimulated by the experience. Though it doesn't seem to be a requirement for healing, some women are even able to forgive their abusers, realizing that forgiveness doesn't mean acceptance. It means, "What you did was wrong, and I forgive you."

Joining a group of survivors helps to break down the sense of isolation and shame that comes from thinking we are the only ones in this situation. Working in a group also helps people begin to trust others enough to be authentic and teaches them that it's usually when they're being themselves that they are most lovable.

The woman who was in her sixties before she began to have flashbacks says, "Knowing makes me stronger. I feel *less* vulnerable, stronger, calmer, more resilient. Finding out was one of the best things that happened to me. I feel bad for the women who never find out and, thus, never understand and outgrow their old, terrible insecurities. Understanding what happened helped rid me of that unnamed shame I've carried all these years."

Although there can be enormous relief in recognizing that we are sexual-abuse survivors, we need to avoid latching on to the abuse as an explanation for *all* our current problems, neglecting the many other contributing factors.

If we are to move beyond sexual oppression of women, we need to challenge the myths of entitlement and male lack of control. We need to educate men and women about harassment. We need to stop treating women as sexual objects in movies, on TV, in advertising. We also need to speak out against violent films and programs that begin to dull our sense of horror by turning unspeakable acts of violence into commonplace occurrences. We need to realize that it's easier to do violence when the victim is seen as a thing rather than a person.

Most importantly women need to stop taking on the blame and shame for their victimization and instead take appropriate action—as Tammy, Anita Hill, and Fran did—to right past wrongs or to halt degrading and abusive behavior. Increasing our own self-respect and sense of personal power can take us a long way toward stamping out many forms of harassment and abuse. We must learn to demand respectful, nonabusive treatment.

We're *entitled* to it.

PART SIX

HEALING
OUR SHAME

The Journey Begins

> *When I speak of an end to suffering I don't mean*
> *anesthesia. I mean knowing the world, and my place in*
> *it, not in order to stare with bitterness or detachment, but*
> *as a powerful and womanly series of choices; and here*
> *I write the words, in their fullness: powerful; womanly.*
> —ADRIENNE RICH

No aspect of our life is immune to shame's contamination. Shame turns us against ourselves—making us our own worst enemy, causing unnecessary anguish. Taught to feel shame by the complex interplay of our culture and our families, we develop various ways of protecting ourselves and in the process often lose access to our natural selves.

The key to healing shame is to create a new relationship with ourselves—one based on compassion, nurturance, love, and respect. It helps to remember there is no right way. We must respect our unique pace and rhythm of growth. We may choose professional help through therapy, we may join one of the many available self-help groups, or we may seek wholeness on our own. I have suggested a few practical exercises in the appendix along with some ideas about choosing a therapist or finding a group.

Let's return to Margo, the first woman to tell her story on these pages. Margo was so used to looking to others to define her that she didn't know who she was. Her mother told her she was selfish, her husband told her she was incapable of loving, and Margo believed them. Not having access to the feelings she had deadened years before, not being in touch with what she needed and wanted, and not trusting her own opinions, she felt empty and unreal. "I feel shallow—not complicated like my friends." She had developed a peppy false self that belied her inner pain. My challenge was to help her regain the self she sacrificed as a little girl in order to be lovable.

Naming the Shame

When Margo first came to my office, frightened and abandoned, she didn't realize that deep down she felt something was wrong with her. She just knew she was hurting. Because shame is largely unfelt, most of us don't recognize its detrimental role as the source of much of our pain. Of course not all pain is shame-based, but when I see a woman like Margo who chronically lacks self-confidence; has difficulty establishing healthy relationships; battles with addictions, depression, or anxiety; or has trouble being assertive, I suspect that shame is at the core of her difficulties. And so it was with Margo.

Her first step in healing was to acknowledge that she felt inadequate and flawed. Painful as this may be, uncovering the truth begins the journey toward wholeness and self-love.

When Margo conquered her fear of the "black void out there" enough to apply for a job, she reported, "I seem to clutch during the interview process. And my face gets beet red. I don't know what my problem is. I just know that deep down I feel like I'm flawed and I'm terrified people will find out."

I suggested that Margo might be feeling shame.

"That's it. That's exactly it. All these years I've had the nagging feeling that something was wrong with me, but I was too ashamed to tell anybody. That explains a lot of things."

After Margo admitted her feelings, she was able to see other areas of her life that were haunted by shame. "I don't like my body. Sometimes I binge. And I feel stupid a lot. Sometimes I even wonder why Bill ever picked someone like me to marry in the first place."

Tracing Shame Back to Its Source

Margo and I explored exactly how she came to believe that she was fundamentally flawed.

"My mother was never there for me," Margo says. "She'd been chronically ill. Lots of surgeries. She was tough to live with—always right about everything. Whenever I had an opinion different from hers, she made me feel dumb or ignorant. When I had problems, she'd fill me with her good advice. I think I learned not to listen to myself because my mother didn't listen to me."

I asked about her father.

"My father wasn't there for me much either. He'd come home from the office, pour himself a drink, and retire into his den. Sometimes I'd go in and talk to him, but I always had the feeling he'd rather be reading the paper. I really loved my dad a lot. But I never felt like I mattered that much to him." She stopped for a moment to tug down her short skirt. A tear slid down her cheek. "All I wanted was some attention. I'd have given anything to have them be really interested in me, what I was feeling, how I was doing. I was just a lonely kid playing with my dolls, but I'd been taught to show a smiley face so that no one knew. The teachers used to scold me for daydreaming a lot."

Understanding that these feelings of inadequacy are learned helps us to realize that they can be unlearned. We're not *really* flawed. We arrived at that conclusion because of what happened to us. Just as we *learned* to see ourselves as defective, we can *learn* to feel whole.

Early in my own healing journey I visualized my family at the dinner table (always a time of tension) and relived my father's criticisms of me—how I ate, dressed, spoke, thought. I could feel again how flawed I felt. Then I had a flash of insight. Those criticisms didn't mean anything about me! They were about my father, about his need to project all his shame onto other people. I realized I was okay. I had simply carried the burden of *his* shame. Once I understood I no longer needed to take on that load, I felt compassion for my father. I knew that he was harder on himself than he was on anybody.

How the Past Shapes the Present

We might ask, "Why explore old memories?" Our present diffi-culties have their roots in our past, stemming partly from our long-held negative view of ourselves and partly from old expecta-tions that can color our present attitudes and feelings. We end up responding to people in our lives the same way we interacted with our family growing up.

Because my father criticized the way I did things, simple things like stirring my tea in the wrong direction or peeling a carrot incorrectly, as an adult I lived in fear of getting nailed for "not doing it right." Even today I feel criticized when my husband cleans up the kitchen and calmly suggests I throw away my used tea bag instead of leaving it on the counter all day. I am quick to remind him that *he* puts empty jam jars back in the refrigerator. (I can always count on my Faultfinder to come to the rescue.) Then I remember that Bob is not my father telling me I'm un-worthy—I don't have to respond as if he were attacking me. I also remind myself that I don't have to do everything right.

It's hard to sort out whether we're dealing with the person in the room with us or reacting as if he or she were someone else, triggering outdated and therefore inappropriate responses. Part of the difficulty lies in our tendency to seek out people who are like our parents. Although Bill had many winning qualities, he was distant like Margo's father, yet capable of being self-righteous like her mother. She resorted to her familiar patterns of being the one to seek contact as Bill sat behind his paper (like her father), and she rarely allowed herself to stick with her own opinions if Bill knocked them down (like her mother).

Our past experiences may also cause us to accept abusive behavior because it's familiar. In extreme cases women abused as children may tolerate abuse today because they were taught to expect it. Some of us confuse abuse with love. We may not have learned that it's okay to set boundaries for ourselves, nor have we any idea *how* to set boundaries. Once we recognize that our childhood abuse was not because *we* were bad, we realize we deserve better treatment. Then we can begin the hard work of learning to protect our boundaries.

When we find that we are repeating old patterns, rather than shaming ourselves why not consider that we are giving ourselves a second chance to deal with unresolved issues? Pam, the woman who had been molested by her brothers, felt cheap being poked at and flirted with as a cocktail waitress. We considered the possibility that she might have chosen this job as a way to reenact being abused, at a less excruciating level, so that she could respond in more powerful ways this time around. Being sexually harassed allowed her to get in touch with the anger and shame she had blocked in her childhood experiences. When she decided she deserved better treatment, she found a job in which she didn't feel like a sex object. This was an important step in her recovery from shame.

For some of us our present-day life sometimes feels like a mine field. We never know when an experience is wired to a hidden bomb. All we know is that we take a step and there is an explosion.

"I used to get so upset when Bill would call to say he was coming home late from the office," Margo said. "I'm ashamed of being such a baby—I was so anxious, I'd almost panic. I don't understand my reaction."

I asked if there was anything familiar about these feelings.

"No, not really," she said, then sat still for a long moment. "Well, I do remember feeling anxious when my dad would come home late from work, because I knew he'd been drinking. Those were the nights he and my mom would get into these terrible arguments. I'd lie in my bed." Her voice became a whisper. "It was so scary. I felt so alone. Sometimes they'd mention my name. I was sure they were fighting about me. It was my fault, I knew it. If only I'd been a better kid." She reached for a tissue and began to cry softly.

Suddenly she stopped. "God. Where did that come from? I had no idea those tears were in there. You know, it hurts to remember, but it feels good to let out the pain. For so long I felt like a tree with its limb broken off and the gaping wound covered over with cement. I guess the cement is starting to crack."

Feeling the Feelings

You can't heal what you can't feel. Even though it hurts, we must first clean out the old wounds before they can heal.

Take Joanie, who went to school with welts on her legs. When she allowed herself to let go of the myth of a happy childhood, her pain was intense. As you may recall, at first Joanie simply referred to the fact that her mother would hit her once in a while.

"I must have done something to set her off. Besides, it wasn't so terrible really."

I asked her to tell me about it.

"She'd come home from work. If I hadn't cleaned the house right, she'd get mad." Joanie began rubbing her throat. "I'm getting a big lump in my throat just thinking about it. She'd get that look in her eye and come after me. She'd grab whatever was there. I remember one time she beat me with a hanger." Joanie was quiet for a long moment. "It hurts so much to talk about. I was so scared. All I wanted to do was die. The worst part was I blamed myself." She began to cry.

Her breath was coming in gasps as she allowed herself to feel the hurt and fear for the first time. "I . . . I didn't dare cry then because it would only make her madder. 'I'll give you something to cry about,' she'd say. As if I had no reason to cry. She'd tell me I was a 'no-good kid.' She'd scream at me, 'Why don't you do what you're supposed to? Why do you insist on making Mama so mad?' I was so ashamed. I knew for sure it was all my fault then. She'd apologize the next day, and I'd tell her it was okay. She felt so bad, I just wanted to make her feel better."

"Sort of like you became the mother. What happened to the hurt little girl? Who took care of *her* feelings?" I asked.

"Nobody. She was so lonely."

I suggested it hadn't been safe for Joanie to have her feelings.

"I can really feel for her now," Joanie said, tears filling her eyes. Then she sat up straight. "This is so stupid. I wish she'd grow up. I'm just feeling sorry for myself. It's done and over with. It doesn't do any good to feel sad."

"Are feelings supposed to *do* something?"

"What's the point of going over old pain?" she asked.

"Seems pretty uncomfortable for you to just let the hurt be there. Like you have to scold yourself, beat yourself up a little."

"My God, that's just the way my mom treated me."

I suggested that she had *learned* to treat herself the way she was treated.

"I hate her. How dare she! I didn't deserve being treated like that."

The gap between her false self and her insides is narrowing as

Joanie becomes more real. Feelings are a valuable resource, not something shameful. Anger tells us what we need to change. Sadness allows us to be empathic toward ourselves. Fear tells us we need to protect ourselves.

Reclaiming Our Lost Child

Experiencing old pain allows us to get in touch with the neglected little girl inside us. Yet getting reacquainted with her can be a painful process that awakens disturbing emotions and yearnings. It also activates internalized parental judgments. *(Don't be so needy, so emotional, so weak. You're bad.)*

It often takes hard work to break the prohibitions against feeling our feelings. When we do, we begin to grieve for the loss of spontaneity, the neglected feelings and needs, the lost childhood we can never regain. When Joanie took care of her mother, she ignored her own feelings and needs. It was more important to make Mother feel good about herself, because Joanie knew at some level that her own well-being depended on Mother being taken care of. It would have been too dangerous, both physically and emotionally, to do otherwise.

Whatever the circumstances, when a girl denies her own feelings and needs, she starts substituting what she thinks she *should* feel. Joanie gave up her own experience *(This hurts. This is wrong.)* and took on her mother's *(I'm a bad girl. I deserve this.)*.

Part of the healing process is getting to know the child we abandoned. I carry in my wallet a picture taken when I was seven to remind me that I still carry that vulnerable little girl in my heart.

Of course the point isn't just to work through old pain. This kind of exploration empowers us to honor as adults our emotional life and our needs and wants, so long suppressed. We develop a voice of our own we can trust. And in the process we become more spontaneous, more playful.

Compassion: The Antidote to Shame

If we are to embrace the little girl inside us, we must first learn to be empathic toward her. In fact developing compassion for ourselves is central to healing our shame. If our parents were unable to meet our needs or take our feelings seriously, or if they actively shamed us, we learned to do the same.

Meg, a CPA, was always the first to put herself down. "I said the stupidest thing to my boss today. How could I have screwed up like that?"

I suggest she's being hard on herself.

"That's the way I feel."

"No compassion at all?" I ask.

"I can't imagine feeling compassionate toward myself. That would seem impossible."

Meg was raised in a family where children were to be seen and not heard. Small wonder she talked about painful childhood memories with little or no feeling.

That is, until one day she recalled the time her bike was stolen at school because she had forgotten to lock it. She was nine. "My parents were furious with me. They sent me to my room without any supper. I don't know what hurt more, losing my bike or having them so mad at me. I cried myself to sleep." Tears fill her eyes. "Poor little kid, how could they do that to her?"

I sit quietly, letting her be with her pain.

Finally she says with a small smile, "I think this must be what compassion feels like."

I ask what she would say if she were her *own* little girl.

"I'd say, 'It's okay, honey. We all make mistakes. I'm sorry you lost your bike. You must feel real sad. Here, come sit on my lap.' "

Even though we can't go back and redo our childhood, it's *never* too late to give that little girl the nurturing and compassion that we longed for and our parents couldn't provide.

At a later session Meg settled in her chair and announced that she had made a large error in doing a tax return. "At first I was mad at myself for being so stupid. When I make mistakes, my self-esteem drops to the bottom. Then I remembered that nine-year-old. I said to myself, 'It's okay. People make mistakes. You're human, for Pete's sake.' This may sound silly, but I even stroked my own cheek to soothe myself. Then I asked myself what I could learn so that it wouldn't happen again. I felt much better."

When we make mistakes, it sometimes helps to consider the possibility that maybe we didn't have enough experience. We don't get a dress rehearsal for life.

We also have trouble being compassionate with ourselves when we don't grow or change fast enough. We think, *I'm so frustrated. What's wrong with me? I should be past all this by now.* We don't realize that healing is like growing a garden. We don't allow time for digging, weeding, and getting the soil ready. We can't expect to have beautiful flowers before we've even prepared the soil.

Learning to Take Care of Ourselves

Besides feeling our feelings and accepting our mistakes, learning to be compassionate depends on allowing ourselves to be in tune with our needs and wants. It took time for Margo to listen to *herself* after so many years of listening to *others* tell her what she should feel, need, want, like, and do. For many reasons we shame-prone women are stunted in our capacity to nurture ourselves. Trained to take care of others, we don't believe we deserve to be taken care of. To act in our own best interests, to be assertive, to be independent, is to risk being "unfeminine, pushy, selfish."

We feel torn between giving to ourselves and giving to others. Margo, like many of us, feared that people would stop liking her if she set limits on her giving. Yet she eventually learned to take her own wants and needs more seriously, without feeling ashamed. She discovered saying no to others was saying yes to herself.

"My second cousin and her family are coming through town this weekend and, before therapy, I would have asked them to stay the night, fixed a great dinner, the whole works," Margo said near the end of our work together. "I would have been too ashamed to put my needs first. But I asked myself what *I* wanted for this weekend. I'm fixing them brunch, and that's it. When they're here, I can *be* with them instead of resenting them because I had to give up my whole weekend for distant relatives."

Taking care of ourselves takes work, something akin to psychic housekeeping. Our house will collect dust because that is the nature of houses. What I mean by "dust" is accumulated resentments, grief, and worries, as well as uncommunicated and/or unmet needs and wants. Fortunately the filter in our furnace traps a lot of this dust, so we can function pretty well. We can check it and clean it out periodically, *if we remember.* We need to become aware of our psychic dust and what it costs us to let it gather and clog up our furnace. We lose vital energy when our furnace can't run at full power.

When we start having doubts about our self-worth, when we don't take care of ourselves, we need to ask ourselves, *Have I forgotten I'm lovable and deserving? Have I been communicating my feelings? Listening to my needs and wants? Acting in my own best interests? Surrounding myself with people who nurture me and whom I can nurture in return?*

Confronting the High Cost of Our Protections

We saw in Chapter Nine how we developed ways to protect ourselves from feeling inadequate, eventually abandoning ourselves to keep our connections with those most important to us. At the time it was the best solution we could find to survive in our family and to ward off shame.

Eventually the cost of rigidly maintaining these protections outweighs their benefits. They cost us in terms of satisfying relationships, fulfillment in our job, and emotional and physical health.

By being alert to the typical patterns that worked for us as children and facing what maintaining these patterns costs us today, we are empowered to respond differently if we so choose.

Personal growth allows us to have full access to all parts of ourselves—good, bad, weak, and strong, and all the ones in the middle. We no longer need to indulge in either/or thinking: that we're perfect or no good, generous or selfish, brilliant or stupid. We even learn that the ability to tolerate mixed feelings is a sign of growth. We can't be free until we embrace our complexity. That's being whole.

We need to acknowledge how *creatively* we responded to our childhood problems. In fact, as we heal, we can grow to appreciate our favorite coping mechanisms, even smile at ourselves.

Roadblocks Along the Way

As we begin to change the way we respond to people, we discover that those close to us are sometimes threatened by our changes.

When we refuse to be shamed or made to feel guilty, when we learn to say a compassionate but firm no, other people aren't always thrilled. When we start taking care of our own wants and needs and let go of focusing on taking care of others, we make waves.

Yet our greatest resistance to change often comes from ourselves because we have a hard time giving up familiar ways of being—ways that have gotten us through life "well enough." Besides, what do we put in their place?

Remember Heidi, the Humble One, who used shame as a defense? Her marriage wasn't happy, she had trouble keeping jobs, and she didn't let herself know her own mind.

"It seemed like I could never satisfy my mother. At times she worried about me; other times she acted as though she didn't even like me. She sent *me* to therapy to get fixed when she and I couldn't get along. It didn't really help. I feel like I was my mother's failed project."

How did she feel about being her mother's failed project?

"I hate it. But if I give it up, who will I be then? I know who this person is, but I don't know who I'd become. I feel like I'm in limbo."

Heidi's seeming incompetence distracted Mother from her own problems, letting her feel like the competent one. Who would shore up Mother if Heidi no longer would?

Heidi was also afraid that her mother might abandon her if she got stronger, because she sensed that being her mother's failed project was the way to keep her mother interested in her.

As we continued to work together, Heidi began to let herself see and appreciate her obvious strengths. She was much more capable than she let on, having run a household and raised five children.

Eventually she was able to let herself know her own mind and her own capabilities. Being someone's failed project no longer fit her new self-image. She decided she could take care of her mother by having an honest and loving relationship with her rather than by cutting into her own self. "Now I can disagree with her strong opinions but still let her have them," Heidi says. "I just say, 'I guess we see things differently, Mom. This is how I see it.'"

She realized that it was unrealistic to worry about Mother abandoning her, that these fears were rooted in her childhood.

And she came to see that her own strength and competence don't really take anything away from others.

There's no question that our present lives are powerfully shaped by our past. It's essential to understand our emotional roots, to be able to say, "I came from a troubled family. I didn't get my needs adequately met." To affirm this can help us be compassionate with ourselves.

Yet there are pitfalls if we carry too far the notion that our present difficulties are largely determined by the past. Maybe we're depressed or angry not because we're an adult child of an alcoholic but because we aren't getting enough help from our partner, or because we're working long hours for too little pay, or because we're housebound with small children. Maybe we have sexual problems not because we were molested as a girl but because we are unable to say what we want, or because we harbor unconscious anger at not having a say about where the money goes, or because our lover is insensitive. Maybe we take care of others too much not because our family was dysfunctional but because we were trained to do so by a society that expects women to put their own needs last.

Talking with Others

Because we have an inner censor that tells us, *Better not say that— you're the only one who feels that way,* some of us stay isolated in our feelings and thoughts, convinced of our unworthiness, afraid of exposure. Shame feeds on itself when there's no one to share our feelings with. Sharing with others becomes a crucial element in the healing journey and teaches us we're not "the only one." As we discover we have many of the same concerns, fears, and doubts in common, our shame diminishes.

Groups offer one of the best structures for safe sharing, such as support groups without a leader, self-help groups, or therapy groups. (We must be careful, however, to accept ourselves rather than shame ourselves if we aren't ready to share.)

Moving On

As we heal, we often gain compassion for our parents. When we can say, "They made mistakes, but they did the best they could, given our culture and what they got from their parents," we not only enhance our relationship with them, we free up our ability to be compassionate with ourselves, because we, too, make mistakes while doing the best we can.

Out of a fear of disloyalty, sometimes we are afraid to differ from our mothers in the ways we do things. When Margo wouldn't give up her whole weekend for distant relatives, she broke with the family tradition of women putting their needs last. She had to give herself permission *not* to be like her mother.

In moving on, we let go of our parents; then, if possible, we take them back as friends. Since as adults we have less need of our parents, we can lower our expectations of them. They no longer have to be perfect to protect us and nurture us. We can do that for ourselves now. We might even accept them for who they are, flaws and all.

In order to feel good about ourselves, we have to be able to appreciate some good qualities in our parents. Even if we decide it is in our own best interests to limit our contact with them, there is no way we can totally disidentify with them. They live inside us. If we are fully to love ourselves, we must learn to embrace their good parts.

Take me, for example. My mother's abiding interest in her own inner life and her leadership in community mental-health activities not only gave me an interest in psychology but a guiding role model. My father taught me about writing: "Good writing depends on clear thinking," he used to say. My mother was gentle and kind. They both taught me a love of learning. My father was affectionate. He taught me about emotions. Not only could he be angry, he could weep with joy or grief. Although much of my childhood was painful, there were wonderful times too: good jokes, catching trout with Dad, long talks with Mom. It was a home full of music, stimulating conversation, good friends, and great food. I learned about shame, but I also learned how enriching life can be.

And if I hadn't learned about shame, how could I have written a book about it?

Can We Ever Forgive?

Our parents and others we loved and trusted made mistakes, sometimes terrible ones. I believe that forgiveness may be the most difficult choice we are ever called upon to make. But if we can forgive, we free ourselves from the victim role. The ability to forgive releases us from unhealthy attachment to those who have treated us poorly. We don't need to wait for apologies that may never be forthcoming. Forgiving doesn't mean we deny our pain or their mistakes. It doesn't ever mean we *condone* what they did. Or that we must spend time with them. But it does mean we summon enough compassion to let go of blaming them. By transcending the victim position we empower ourselves to take charge of our own lives, to create our own happiness, to heal our shame. Forgiving is a gift we give ourselves.

The need to forgive ourselves is another challenge. Yes, we may have done things we feel bad about. We need to understand the anger, fear, and confusion that may have motivated us to hurt others or ourselves. I believe that we all do the best we can, given our circumstances. If we hurt or shame others, it's usually because of our inexperience or our own hurt and shame. As we heal, we become more loving to others and to ourselves and are able to apologize for the hurts we inflicted and to forgive ourselves.

Healing Our Gender Shame

An essential part of healing our shame is to become aware of the role society has played in our feelings of unworthiness. From birth we are treated differently from little boys. We are encouraged to be "feminine," to be good girls, not to get angry, to take care of others. We learn that our appearance is important and that we please people when we are pretty. We see women being treated as objects in the media. We observe women accommodating and serving men, whether as wives and mothers at home or in the world as nurses, secretaries, bookkeepers, flight attendants. We learn that our needs and wants aren't as important as those of men. As we watch them run our schools, corporations, and government, we conclude that they are more powerful, more entitled, and more knowledgeable. Although we don't consciously say to ourselves, *I'm not as powerful, as interesting, as deserving,* our position in the social hierarchy leaves us believing that we are deficient compared with males.

We need to realize that these feelings stem from centuries of society treating women as second-class citizens, denying us the right to vote, to own property, to determine the course of our own lives, to define ourselves. All this is changing, however slowly. We need to continue to work for accessible and affordable day care, humane working conditions, fair and equal wages, an increased voice in government, business, and other institutions.

As we try to have it all, we need to realize that it is not our inadequacy that leaves us exhausted, frazzled, and overextended at the end of the day. Just because we can't gracefully juggle home, family, job, and outside interests, we needn't conclude there is something wrong with us. We're trying to be superwoman managing two or three jobs at once, often without essential support. We need to let go of the need to do everything perfectly.

We must work toward changing family patterns so that both Mom and Dad participate fully in child rearing, enabling their children to bond with both parents and so develop both "feminine" and "masculine" aspects of their personalities. We can prevent shame by teaching them that it's okay to be both nurturing in relationships *and* powerful in the world.

While we work for equality, both at home and in society, instead of undervaluing or negating our special strengths—acquired as females in a male-dominated culture—let's appreciate our ability to be vulnerable, to ask for support, to have our feelings, to be empathic, to work for relationships that thrive, and to be committed to the growth of others.[1]

At the same time we need to develop our often neglected ability to know our own mind, to act in our own best interests, and to give ourselves permission to compete and succeed without feeling "unfeminine" or undeserving of our accomplishment. *Instead of letting others define femininity, we must define it for ourselves.*

Leaving the Shame Trap Behind

In Chapter One I listed nine characteristics of shame-prone women. When we heal our shame, we discover that these qualities become their opposites:

1. **We no longer feel unworthy and inherently defective as human beings.** We realize we are good enough, that we don't have to measure up to anyone else's standards. We are no longer haunted by a sense of not belonging.

2. **We have an unshakable sense of adequacy and wholeness.** We approach life's problems from a perspective of hope rather than despair. We applaud the changes we have made.

3. **We keep the volume low on our critical inner voice as we turn up the volume on our empathic, self-affirming voice.** We refuse to be ruled by our *shoulds*. We no longer let our Inner Shamer stop us from being ourselves.

4. **We celebrate the vital parts of ourselves, our feelings, our ability to know our own minds.** We know what we need and want. We have our own opinions and trust our independent view of things. We relish our successes.

5. **We become the person we are rather than who someone else wants us to be.** We no longer hide behind a pleasing facade, in constant fear of being exposed. We are able to express ourselves fully and reveal who we are without fear of being rejected.

6. **We appreciate our body in spite of its imperfections. We trust it, listen to it.** We maintain a positive body image. We enjoy our sexuality.

7. **We no longer feel like victims of the circumstances of our lives.** Instead we accept that we are responsible for how we choose to deal with the circumstances. We are able to look at our part in our continuing problems. We know the difference between blaming ourselves and being accountable. We know that being responsible for our own happiness empowers us.

8. **We let go of constantly needing to be in control.** We have learned to trust that we can survive being wrong, making mistakes, not always being prepared. We learn we can tolerate being disappointed or even getting hurt. We take more responsibility for how our lives are working out and less responsibility for others.

9. **We are able to establish and maintain mutually empowering relationships.** We let ourselves become vulnerable. We consider how our actions will affect others and work to resolve conflict in healthy ways. We manage both to take care of our loved ones and to take care of ourselves. When we learn to love and honor ourselves, we become able to give love to others and to accept their love in return, trusting that we are deserving even though we have our human limitations.

The day came when Margo and I said good-bye, after much productive work together. "I'm sad and excited about stopping," she told me. "I can trust myself. I now have a self." Through painstaking work she no longer felt defective being Margo. "I don't need a man to survive. I've learned that I'm enough just as I am. I don't have to be a certain way to please people, to get their approval. I'm glad to be me."

As we work to free ourselves from the shame trap, our challenge is to define and accept ourselves as women committed to maintaining our relationships *while at the same time* maintaining a strong sense of self. We can be both nurturing and powerful, confident that we are most lovable when we are being fully ourselves. We must be gentle and compassionate with ourselves, recognizing that change comes in small—sometimes even backward—steps. In order to become whole, we need to both heal our inner shame and work toward a society that values women as equals.

When we are able to embrace ourselves completely, accepting all parts of ourselves—even those parts that cause us shame—then we can begin to lead lives that are rich, joyous, and fulfilling.

Then and only then will we be free.

The Shame Checklist

Are you stuck in the shame trap? Rate yourself on the following questions to determine your Shame Quotient:

	Usually	Often	Sometimes	Seldom	Never
I feel unworthy and defective.	4	3	2	1	0
I feel like I don't belong.	4	3	2	1	0
I am depressed and/or anxious.	4	3	2	1	0
I have a loud internal critic.	4	3	2	1	0

	Usually	Often	Sometimes	Seldom	Never
I am ruled by a list of *shoulds*.	4	3	2	1	0
I let fear of failing keep me from going after a job, an education, or a relationship.	4	3	2	1	0
I have trouble enjoying my successes.	4	3	2	1	0
I am afraid to speak my mind.	4	3	2	1	0
I have lost touch with vital parts of myself:					
I numb my feelings	4	3	2	1	0
I ignore my needs	4	3	2	1	0
I invalidate my wants	4	3	2	1	0
I postpone my dreams	4	3	2	1	0
I don't think for myself	4	3	2	1	0
I feel like a fraud and am afraid of being found out.	4	3	2	1	0
I have difficulty being myself.	4	3	2	1	0
I hate to make mistakes.	4	3	2	1	0
I dislike my body.	4	3	2	1	0

	Usually	Often	Sometimes	Seldom	Never
I am uncomfortable with my sexuality.	4	3	2	1	0
I feel like a victim.	4	3	2	1	0
I think other people are responsible for my happiness.	4	3	2	1	0
I need to fix others.	4	3	2	1	0
I am shy, easily embarrassed, or self-conscious.	4	3	2	1	0
I try to do things perfectly.	4	3	2	1	0
I have trouble forming or maintaining an intimate love relationship.	4	3	2	1	0
I am afraid to be close to people.	4	3	2	1	0

Add your responses to determine your Shame Quotient (SQ). If your SQ is under 20, you may be in need of more humility or healthy shame. If you scored between 20 and 40, you are doing a good job of not taking on unnecessary shame. If your score was 40 or higher, you may want to look at the shame you are taking on that's not your own. You might talk to a friend or a professional to sort out what is unhealthy shame and what it is costing you.

APPENDIX 2

Some Suggestions
for Further Growth

If you decide shame is keeping you from being fully yourself or having what you want in life, you may want to enter into therapy. Finding an appropriate therapist takes time and effort. The best approach is to ask for a recommendation from someone you know or your doctor. You may want to interview several therapists. Although many women prefer working with a woman, this is not essential.

Questions you may want to ask: If money is a concern, do they have a sliding scale? Ask them to tell you about themselves as therapists. What is their training? How long have they been in practice? What is their philosophy or style of therapy? (If you don't understand the answer, be sure to ask for clarification.) Do they have a specialty? A focus? Are your concerns appropriate for psychotherapy or their areas of expertise?

Then ask yourself, *Do I feel a connection or the potential for connection with this therapist?* Remember, you are empowering yourself to make a wise choice. Trust yourself.

Or join a self-help group such as Alanon, Overeaters Anonymous, or an agency group for survivors of abuse. (Check the telephone directory or with a community agency to find a local group.)

If you don't choose therapy or a group, you may want to try working on your own. Why not begin by sharing your feelings with a close friend? I find that acknowledging the fact that I feel shame about something helps me to let go of it.

Here are a few exercises to move you in the right direction:

Exercise 1: *The Healing Letter*

Write a letter (not to send) to someone who is close to you, pouring out your anger, grief, or resentment. Don't censor anything. Often at the end comes love or forgiveness. Don't worry if it doesn't. Remember, there is no right way.

Exercise 2: *Meeting Your Inner Child—A Visualization*

You may want to make an audiotape recording of this exercise, leaving pauses where I've indicated. It may help to look at a photo of yourself as a child before you start this meditation.

First, get comfortable and close your eyes. . . . Relax all the muscles in your body, including your jaw, shoulders, buttocks, and legs. . . . Focus on your breathing as you quiet your mind. . . . Now, in your mind's eye, picture the room you had as a little girl. . . . Look at the furniture, the decorations. . . . Are there any familiar sounds or smells? . . . Picture yourself as a child. . . . Look at this little girl closely. . . . What name is she called by? . . . What is she wearing? . . . How is she feeling? . . . What are her concerns? . . . What does she need? . . . Take your time. . . . Comfort her. . . . Sit on her bed and pull her onto your lap. . . . Be with her. . . . Tell her that she's important to you. . . . Tell her that you will take care of her, that she is special. . . . When it's time, say good-bye and tell her you will always be there for her. . . . Picture the room you are currently in, and when you are ready, open your eyes.

Exercise 3: *The Dust-Filter Check*

Make a list of your resentments, your regrets, and your worries. Are there any you can do something about? Is there something you need to communicate to someone? Have you been taking care of yourself by saying no when it's appropriate? Have you been letting in compliments, taking time to pamper yourself? Have you remembered to be compassionate with yourself? Have you neglected to apologize to someone? Or forgotten to acknowledge someone?

Now make another list acknowledging yourself for who you are and what you have accomplished.

Exercise 4: *Affirmations*

One way to silence your Inner Shamer is to counter it with self-affirming statements. Make your list in the present tense, positively stated. Say them out loud in your car or quietly in your mind. Write each one at least ten times. Here are a few to get you started. Don't worry if negative responses come up. Write them next to the affirmation until they disappear.

Example:

I am lovable just as I am.	No I'm not. I'm stupid.
I am lovable just as I am.	I'm too selfish.
I am lovable just as I am.	Maybe I'm not so bad.
I am lovable just as I am.	I am lovable just as I am.

Sample Affirmations:
I am normal.
It's okay to make a mistake.
I don't have to do it perfectly or be perfect.
I deserve a good life.
I am enough.
People like to be with me.
I love my body as it is.
I have a right to my feelings.

Write these on a card and tape them to your mirror or carry them with you so that you will remember that you are a beautiful and special person.

ENDNOTES

———— ‖‖‖‖‖‖‖ ————

INTRODUCTION

1. Gershen Kaufman, "The Dynamics of Shame," talk given in Santa Rosa, California, October 11, 1987. (Sponsored by Lodestone).

CHAPTER ONE

1. Helen B. Lewis was the first to point out women's special vulnerability to shame because they care more about others—*Shame and Guilt in Neurosis* (New York: International Universities Press, 1974), p. 151.
2. Andrew Morrison, *Shame: The Underside of Narcissism* (Hillsdale, N.J.: The Analytic Press, 1989), p. 193.
3. Helen Lynd, *On Shame and the Search for Identity* (New York: Harcourt Brace, 1958), pp. 40, 42.
4. Silvan S. Tomkins, "Shame," in *The Many Faces of Shame,* ed. Donald Nathanson (New York: Guilford Press, 1987).

5.   Donald Nathanson, *Shame and Pride: Affect, Sex, and the Birth of the Self* (New York: W. W. Norton, 1992), p. 140.

6.   Ibid., p. 138.

7.   Carl D. Schneider, *Shame, Exposure, and Privacy* (New York: W. W. Norton, 1992), p. xix.

8.   G. Piers and M. Singer, *Shame and Guilt* (New York: W. W. Norton, 1953).

9.   Morrison, *Shame,* p. 82.

10.   John Bradshaw, talk given at Sixth National Conference on Children of Alcoholics, San Francisco, California, February 19, 1990.

11.   Leon Wurmser, "Shame: The Veiled Companion of Narcissism," in *The Many Faces of Shame,* p. 86.

12.   *Shame and Pride,* p. 20.

13.   Ibid.

14.   Jonathan Cheek, *Conquering Shyness: The Battle Anyone Can Win* (New York: Putnam, 1989).

15.   *Shame and Pride,* p. 170.

16.   Ibid., pp. 145, 241, 306.

CHAPTER TWO

1.   See I. Broverman et al., "Sex-Role Stereotypes and Clinical Judgments of Mental Health," *Journal of Consulting and Clinical Psychology* 34 (1970): 1–7; and "Sex-Role Stereotypes: A Current Appraisal," *Journal of Social Issues* 28 (1972): 59–78.

2.   Helen B. Lewis makes this point in *Shame and Guilt in Neurosis* (New York: International Universities Press, 1974).

3.   Betty Allgood-Merten, Peter M. Lewinsohn, and Hyman Hops, "Sex Differences and Adolescent Depression," *Journal of Abnormal Psychology* 99 (1990): 55–63.

4.   Ibid., p. 61.

5.   Helen B. Lewis, "Is Freud an Enemy of Women's Liberation?" in *The Psychology of Today's Woman,* ed. Toni Bernay and Dorothy W. Cantor (Cambridge, Mass.: Harvard University Press, 1986).

6.   Helen B. Lewis was one of the earliest scholars to link shame with depression.

7.   See the work of Judith Jordan, Jean Baker Miller, and Janet Surrey, the Stone Center, Wellesley College, Wellesley, Mass.

8.   Hans Selye, M.D., *The Stress of Life* (New York: McGraw-Hill, 1978), pp. xvi–xvii.

9.   Gershen Kaufman, in *The Psychology of Shame* (New York: Springer,

1989), makes the point that shame, not pride, keeps people from asking for help.

CHAPTER THREE

1.   I. Broverman et al., "Sex-Role Stereotypes and Clinical Judgments," *Journal of Consulting and Clinical Psychology* 34 (1970): 1–7; and "Sex-Role Stereotypes: A Current Appraisal," *Journal of Social Issues* 28 (1972): 59–78.
2.   Rosemary Radford Ruether, *Sexism and God-Talk* (Boston: Beacon Press, 1983), p. 165.
3.   Riane Eisler, *The Chalice and the Blade* (San Francisco: Harper & Row, 1988). This is a fascinating anthropological and historical study of the differences between men and women from the prehistoric time of the Goddess to the present.
4.   Kristin Huckshorn, "Women Olympians in Shadow of Men," *The Press Democrat* (Santa Rosa, Ca.), July 30, 1992.
5.   Jean Baker Miller, *Toward a New Psychology of Women* (Boston: Beacon Press, 1986), chaps. 1–3.
6.   Anne Wilson Schaef, *Women's Reality* (San Francisco: Harper & Row, 1985), p. 27.
7.   Linda Tschirhart Sanford and Mary Ellen Donovan, *Women & Self Esteem* (New York: Viking Penguin, 1984), p. 184.
8.   *How Schools Shortchange Girls* (Washington, D.C.: American Association of University Women, 1992), p. 62.
9.   Sanford and Donovan, *Women & Self Esteem*, p. 181.
10.   *How Schools Shortchange Girls*, p. 7.
11.   Ibid., p. 68.
12.   *Shortchanging Girls, Shortchanging America: A Call to Action* (Washington, D.C.: American Association of University Women, 1991). This nationwide survey reported that while 69 percent of boys and 60 percent of girls in elementary school said they were "happy the way I am," by the time they were in high school, 46 percent of boys and only 29 percent of girls claimed this satisfaction (p. 10).
13.   Cited in Ruether, *Sexism and God-Talk*, p. 170.
14.   Ibid., pp. 171–72.
15.   *Jerusalem Bible* (Garden City, N.Y.: Doubleday, 1968), Lev. 15:19–21, 12:2–5.
16.   *Jerusalem Bible*, 1 Cor. 11: 7–10.
17.   Discussed in Ruether, *Sexism and God-Talk*, pp. 96–97.
18.   1 Cor. 11: 3.
19.   Lucy Komisar provides the "give her a pen" quote in "The Image of Woman in Advertising," in *Women in Sexist Society*, ed. Vivian Gornick and Barbara Moran (New York: Signet 1971), p. 306.

20. Essay on MacNeil/Lehrer NewsHour, October 22, 1990.

21. See Dorothy Dinnerstein, *The Mermaid and the Minotaur* (New York: Harper & Row, 1976).

22. The data about women and management come from Fleming.

23. Jennet Conant, "Broadcast Networking," *Working Woman*, August 1990, pp. 58–61.

24. *Bureau of Labor Statistics* (1991).

25. U.S. Department of Education, Office of Educational Research and Improvement, *Digest of Education Statistics*, 1990, p. 363.

26. Susan Swartz, "You Have to Like Meryl," *The Press Democrat*, September 25, 1990.

27. Miller, *Toward a New Psychology of Women*, p. xiii.

28. Nancy Chodorow, *The Reproduction of Mothering* (Berkeley, Calif.: University of California Press, 1978), p. 213.

29. *New Woman*, February 1992.

30. Emily Hancock, *The Girl Within* (New York: Fawcett Columbine, 1989), p. 30.

31. Ibid., pp. 27–28.

CHAPTER FOUR

1. These needs are similar to those put forth by Linda Tschirhart Sanford and Mary Ellen Donovan, *Women and Self-Esteem* (New York: Viking Penguin, 1984), chap. 3.

2. Irene P. Stiver, "Beyond the Oedipus Complex," in Judith V. Jordan, et al. *Women's Growth in Connection* (New York: The Guilford Press, 1991), p. 109.

3. Jean Baker Miller makes the point that "when a girl's painful feelings cannot be shared with another person there are profound consequences," including "a sense of having no impact on the important people in her life." Irene P. Stiver, "Dysfunctional Families and Wounded Relationships—Part I," *Work in Progress* (Wellesley, Mass.: The Stone Center), audiocassette.

4. Carol Gilligan, Nona P. Lyons, and Trudy J. Hammer, *Making Connections: The Relational Worlds of Adolescent Girls at Emma Willard School* (Cambridge, Mass.: Harvard University Press, 1950), p. 4.

5. *How Schools Shortchange Girls,* p. 70.

6. Ibid.

7. Timmon Cermak, *A Time to Heal* (Los Angeles: Jeremy P. Tarcher, 1988), pp. 52–53.

8. Janet Surrey, "The Mother-Daughter Relationship: Themes in Psychotherapy," *Work in Progress* (Wellesley, Mass.: The Stone Center, 1988), audiocassette.

CHAPTER FIVE

1. Lillian Rubin, in her book *Women of a Certain Age* (New York: Perennial Library, 1990), draws these observations about identity differences between men and women from her studies of women.

2. Erik H. Erikson, "Identity and the Life Cycle," in *Psychological Issues,* vol. 1, no. 1. (New York: International Universities Press, Inc., 1959), p. 118.

3. Erik H. Erikson, *Identity: Youth and Crisis* (New York: W. W. Norton, 1968), p. 265.

4. Carol Gilligan, in *In a Different Voice* (Cambridge, Mass.: Harvard University Press, 1982), points out that Erikson never amended his original model.

5. See Ruthellen Josselson, *Finding Herself* (San Francisco: Jossey-Bass, 1990); Rubin, *Women of a Certain Age;* Gilligan, *In a Different Voice;* Nancy Chodorow, *The Reproduction of Mothering;* (Berkeley, Calif.: University of California Press, 1978); Emily Hancock, *The Girl Within* (New York: Fawcett Columbine, 1990); and Jean Baker Miller and the research from The Stone Center, Wellesley College.

6. Jean Baker Miller, *Toward a New Psychology of Women* (Boston: Beacon Press, 1986), p. xx.

7. Chodorow, *The Reproduction of Mothering,* p. 98. The following discussion on development is based on Chodorow's work.

8. Emily Hancock *(The Girl Within)* and Carol Gilligan, Nona P. Lyons, and Trudy J. Hammer *(Making Connections* [Cambridge, Mass.: Harvard University Press, 1950]) maintain that until about age eleven girls have a solid sense of identity, which they abandon in favor of becoming more focused on others' needs and on gaining others' approval.

9. Hancock, Miller, Gilligan, and others point to approaching adolescence as the time when girls move away from confidence toward greater insecurity.

10. Gilligan, Lyons, and Hammer, *Making Connections,* p. 4.

11. *Los Angeles Times,* February 20, 1992.

12. The anchor metaphor is borrowed from Josselson, *Finding Herself.*

13. Ibid., p. 190.

14. Ibid., p. 185.

15. U.S. Department of Commerce, Bureau of the Census, *Statistical Abstract of the United States, 1990* (Washington, D.C.: 1990), p. 451.

16. Josselson found that 85 percent of the women interviewed remained close to their mothers; nearly half chose her as the person they felt closest or second closest to in the world. Daily visits or phone calls for emotional or logistical support were common (p. 173).

17. Hancock, *The Girl Within,* p. 62.

18.   I. Broverman et al., "Sex-Role Stereotypes and Clinical Judgments," *Journal of Consulting and Clinical Psychology* 34 (1970): 1–7; and "Sex-Role Stereotypes: A Current Appraisal," *Journal of Social Issues* 28 (1972): 59–78.
19.   Ibid., "Sex-Role Stereotypes: A Current Appraisal," p. 75.
20.   See Miller, *Toward a New Psychology*, chap. 4, for a discussion of women's strengths.
21.   Helen Lynd, *On Shame and the Search for Identity* (New York: Harcourt Brace, 1958), pp. 9, 38.
22.   Pauline Bart, "Depression in Middle-Aged Women," in *Women in Sexist Society*, ed. Vivian Gornick and Barbara Moran, p. 185.

CHAPTER SIX

1.   Supporting evidence is found in V. J. Crandall, W. Katkovsky, and A. Preston, "Motivational and Ability Determinants of Young Children's Intellectual Achievement Behavior," *Child Development* 33 (1962): 643–61, as cited in Helen B. Lewis, *Shame and Guilt in Neurosis* (New York: International Universities Press, 1974), p. 161–62. The conclusions about girls' self-worth, fear of failure, and shame are Lewis's.
2.   See Matina Horner, "Toward an Understanding of Achievement-Related Conflicts in Women," *Journal of Social Issues* 28, no. 2 (1972): 157–75.
3.   I have drawn from Arnold H. Modell's work, *Psychoanalysis in a New Context* (Madison, Conn.: International Universities Press, 1985), for the ideas about our fears of having more than others and from personal communication with Lloyd and Catherine Kamins and Michael Sheiner.
4.   Merle A. Fossum and Marilyn J. Mason, *Facing Shame* (New York: W. W. Norton, 1986), p. 72.
5.   I am grateful to J. Keith Miller for the distinction between walls and boundaries made during his talk at the First Annual Conference on Shame, Las Vegas, Nevada, 1991. (Co-sponsored by the John Bradshaw Center at Ingleside Hospital and U.S. Journal Training, Inc.)
6.   It's not only male therapists who view attachment to mothers as unhealthy. Female therapists, as Irene Stiver points out, have had men as teachers and therapists and have had to "adapt to the standards . . . that reflect the masculine model of therapy," *Women's Growth in Connection* (New York: The Guilford Press, 1991), p. 257.
7.   Modell, *Psychoanalysis in a New Context*, p. 76.

CHAPTER SEVEN

1.   I thank David Wallin, Ph.D., for the paint metaphor.
2.   I am grateful to Karen Horney for her ideas, especially those on the role of self-hate, the costs of listening to our inner voice, and the tyranny of the

should. See *Neurosis and Human Growth* (New York: W. W. Norton, 1950), chaps. 3 and 5.

3. Ibid., chap. 5.

4. Talk given at the First Annual Conference on Shame, Las Vegas, Nevada, 1991.

5. Horney, *Neurosis,* p. 125.

6. Ibid., chap. 3.

7. Horney makes this useful observation, but doesn't distinguish between male and female *shoulds.*

8. I am grateful to Matthew McKay and Patrick Fanning, *Self-esteem* (Oakland: New Harbinger, 1987), pp. 114–15, for their ideas about the Inner Critic. They suggested most of these areas for an inventory of *shoulds.*

CHAPTER EIGHT

1. Alice Miller, *The Drama of the Gifted Child* (New York: Basic Books, 1981), p. 16.

2. "The Construction of Anger in Women and Men," in Judith V. Jordan et al., *Women's Growth in Connection* (New York: The Guilford Press, 1991), p. 185.

3. Two excellent books on anger are Harriet Goldhor Lerner's *The Dance of Anger* (New York: Harper & Row, 1985) and Carol Tavris's *Anger: The Misunderstood Emotion* (New York: Simon & Schuster, 1989).

4. Catherine Kamins, in personal conversation, gave me the notion that some parents experience a child's need as criticism.

5. Deborah Tannen, *You Just Don't Understand: Women and Men in Conversation* (New York: Ballantine Books, 1990), pp. 129, 179, 215.

6. Ibid., pp. 91–95, 125–29.

CHAPTER NINE

1. John Amodeo uses the term *natural self* in his book, *Beyond Betrayal,* to be published by Ballantine Books.

2. Alice Miller, *The Drama of the Gifted Child* (New York: Basic Books, 1981), p. 15.

3. Gershen Kaufman, *Shame: The Power of Caring* (Cambridge, Mass.: Schenkman Books, 1985), p. 94.

4. I am indebted to Kaufman for his ideas on conversion. See *Shame,* pp. 101–102.

CHAPTER TEN

1. See Karen Horney, *Neurosis and Human Growth* (New York: W. W. Norton, 1950), chap. 1; and Karen Horney, *Our Inner Conflicts* (New York: W. W. Norton, 1945), chap. 6.
2. Gershen Kaufman, talk given at the First Annual Conference on Shame, Las Vegas, Nevada, 1991.
3. Helen B. Lewis calls this humiliated rage, or shame-rage.
4. Andrew Morrison, *Shame: The Underside of Narcissism* (Hillsdale, N.J.: The Analytic Press, 1989), pp. 124–25.

CHAPTER ELEVEN

1. J. B. Miller makes this point about the importance of being able to care for others, in her paper "What Do We Mean by Relationships?" *Work in Progress,* no. 22 (Wellesley, Mass.: The Stone Center, 1986).
2. Harriet Goldhor Lerner, *The Dance of Intimacy* (New York: Perennial Library, 1990), p. 53.
3. See Arlie Hoschchild, *The Second Shift* (New York: Viking, 1989), p. 8.
4. Donald Nathanson, *Shame and Pride: Affect, Sex, and the Birth of the Self* (New York: W. W. Norton, 1992), p. 241.
5. Irving Goffman, "Gender Display" in *Gender Advertisements,* pp. 1–9, cited in Deborah Tannen, *You Just Don't Understand,* p. 287. The quote is Tannen's.
6. Enid Nemy, "Society Looks Askance at the Family of One," *The New York Times,* February 28, 1991, sec. C discusses psychoanalyst Lawrence Hatterer's ideas on the perceived hierarchy.
7. "Getting Dan Quayle's Goat," *New Woman,* September 1992, p. 50.
8. U.S. Bureau of Census, March 1991.
9. John Gottman and Lowell J. Krokoff, "Marital Interaction and Satisfaction: A Longitudinal View," *Journal of Consulting and Clinical Psychology* 57, no. 1 (1989): 51.
10. See the work of the Stone Center, Wellesley, Mass., for their ideas about mutual empowerment.

CHAPTER TWELVE

1. See Nancy Chodorow, *The Reproduction of Mothering* (Berkeley, Calif.: University of California Press, 1978).
2. Robert Sternberg and Susan Grajek, "The Nature of Love," *Journal of Personality and Social Psychology* 47, no. 2 (1984): 318.
3. A recent study at the University of California at San Francisco analyzed

data on death rates, as reported in *The Press Democrat*, October 6, 1990. The researcher cited is Maradee Davis, primary author of the study.

4.   Deerfield Park, Fla: Health Communications, 1989, p. 28.

5.   Wendy Kaminer, "Chances Are You're Co-dependent Too," *The New York Times*, February 11, 1990. Kaminer credits social-critic Barbara Ehrenreich for the assertion that women are blamed for men's failures.

6.   I am drawing on Jean Baker Miller, who was the first to point out women's relational strengths in her book *Toward a New Psychology of Women* (Boston: Beacon Press, 1986), and on the Stone Center, for their ideas on mutual empowerment.

7.   Lillian Rubin, *Intimate Strangers* (New York: Perennial Library, 1983), p. 169.

8.   This is especially true in happy marriages. For research on male-female differences in handling conflict see John Gottman and Lowell J. Krokoff, *Journal of Consulting and Clinical Psychology* 57, no. 1 (1989): 51.

9.   "Courage in Connection: Conflict, Compassion, Creativity," *Work in Progress*, No. 45 (Wellesley, Mass.: The Stone Center, 1990), p. 4.

CHAPTER THIRTEEN

1.   Gloria Steinem, *Ms.* April 1982, cited in Linda Tschirhart Stanford and Mary Ellen Donovan, *Women and Self-esteem* (New York: Viking Penguin, 1984), p. 384.

2.   *The Mismeasure of Woman* (New York: Simon & Schuster, 1992), p. 34.

3.   Ibid.

4.   *Lear's*, "Lunch," April 1992.

5.   I am grateful to Barbara McFarland and Tyeis Baker-Baumann for their ideas on fleshiness, the feminine principle, and our culture. See *Shame and Body Image* (Deerfield Beach, Fla.: Health Communications, Inc., 1990), p. 71.

6.   Judith Rodin, *Body Traps* (New York: William Morrow, 1992), p. 65.

7.   McFarland and Baker-Baumann, *Shame and Body Image*, p. 69.

8.   Rodin, *Body Traps*, p. 165.

9.   Ibid., p. 171.

10.   Cited in Rodin, *Body Traps*, p. 34.

11.   McFarland and Baker-Baumann, *Shame and Body Image*, pp. 68, 93; and Rodin, *Body Traps*, p. 60.

12.   Simone de Beauvoir, *The Second Sex* (New York: Vintage Books, 1974), pp. 345–46.

13.   Merten, Lewinsohn, and Hops, *Journal of Abnormal Psychology*, p. 61. See also Rodin, *Body Traps*, p. 61.

14.   According to Elly Ryder, assistant director of the American Anorexia and Bulimia Association, 1 to 2 percent of teenage girls are anorexic (and

10 percent of those may die from it), and 5 to 6 percent of college-age girls are bulimic. Personal interview.

15. Rodin, *Body Traps,* p. 159.
16. April Fallon and Paul Rozin, "Sex Differences in Perceptions of Desirable Body Shape," *Journal of Abnormal Psychology* 94 (1985): 30–37.
17. Wayne and Susan Wooley, "Feeling Fat in a Thin Society," *Glamour,* February 1984, pp. 198–201.
18. McFarland and Baker-Baumann, *Shame and Body Image,* p. 82.
19. *Revolution from Within* (Boston: Little, Brown, 1992), p. 224.
20. Ibid.

CHAPTER FOURTEEN

1. Donald Nathanson, *Shame and Pride: Affect, Sex, and the Birth of the Self* (New York: W. W. Norton, 1992), p. 284.
2. Ibid., p. 286.
3. Ibid., p. 301.
4. Sigmund Freud, *Collected Papers,* vol. 4, ed. James Strachey, trans. Joan Riviere (New York: Basic Books, 1959), p. 215.
5. Ibid., vol. 5, p. 257.
6. Mark Belsey, M.D., chief of the Maternal and Child Health Program, World Health Organization. Personal communication.
7. Linda Tschirhart Sanford and Mary Ellen Donovan, *Women and Self-esteem* (New York: Viking Penguin, 1984), p. 390.
8. I am grateful to Deborah L. Tolman for her ideas about adolescent conflict between body and culture. "Adolescent Girls, Women and Sexuality: Discerning Dilemmas of Desire," *Women & Therapy* 11, no. 3/4 (1991): 55–69.
9. I am grateful to Alix Shulman for her ideas in "Organs and Orgasms," *Women in Sexist Society,* ed. Vivian Gornick and Barbara Moran (New York: Signet, 1971), p. 292.
10. See Harriet Goldhor Lerner, *Women and Therapy* (New York: Harper & Row, 1989), p. 33.
11. See Lonnie Barbach, *For Each Other* (New York: Signet, 1984), p. 28.
12. William H. Masters and Virginia E. Johnson, *Human Sexual Response* (Boston: Little, Brown, 1966).
13. Masters and Johnson, *Human Sexual Inadequacy* (Boston: Little, Brown, 1970), p. 240.
14. *Diagnostic and Statistical Manual of Mental Disorders* (Washington, D.C.: American Psychiatric Association, 1987), p. 294.
15. Shere Hite, *The Hite Report* (New York: Macmillan, 1976), p. 154.
16. Sharon Wegscheider-Cruse uses the term *emotional foreplay.* Workshop

given at the Sixth National Convention of Children of Alcoholics, San Francisco, February 19, 1990.

17. Carol Tavris, *The Mismeasure of Woman* (New York: Simon & Schuster, 1992), pp. 158–59.

18. Susan Brownmiller, *Femininity* (New York: Ballantine Books, 1984), p. 212.

19. I recommend Tamara Slayton's excellent workbook *Reclaiming the Menstrual Matrix* (Santa Rosa, Calif.: The Menstrual Health Foundation, 1990).

20. See Gail Sheehy, *The Silent Passage* (New York: Random House, 1992); Sadja Greenwood, M. D., *Menopause, Naturally* (Volcano, Calif.: Volcano Press, 1984); Germaine Greer, *The Change: Women, Aging, and the Menopause* (New York: Alfred A. Knopf, 1992); and Dena Taylor and Amber Coverdale Sumrall, eds., *Women of the 14th Moon: Writings on Menopause* (Freedom, Calif.: The Crossing Press, 1991).

21. See Lillian Rubin, *Women of a Certain Age* (New York: Harper & Row, 1979), p. 74.

22. Ruth Formanek, ed., *The Meanings of Menopause* (Hillsdale, N.J.: The Analytic Press, 1990), p. xii. John McKinlay, Sonja McKinlay, and Donald Brambilla, "The Relative Contributions of Endocrine Changes and Social Circumstances to Depression in Mid-aged Women," *Journal of Health and Social Behavior* 28 (1987): 345–63.

23. Cheryl L. Bowles, "The Menopausal Experience: Sociocultural Influences and Theoretical Models," in *The Meanings of Menopause*, pp. 166, 171.

24. Ibid., p. 168; and Pauline Bart, "Depression in Middle-Aged Women," in *Women in Sexist Society*, p. 176.

25. Linda Ward, psychotherapist, makes this observation.

CHAPTER FIFTEEN

1. Judith Herman, "Sexual Violence," in *Work in Progress*, no. 83-05 (Wellesley, Mass.: The Stone Center, 1984), p. 3.

2. Sigmund Freud, "The Aetiology of Hysteria," (1896) in *Standard Edition of the Complete Psychological Works of Freud*, vol. 3, ed. James Strachey (London: Hogarth, 1962), pp. 191–221.

3. James Strachey, "Further Remarks on the Neuropsychoses of Defence" (1896), in *Standard Edition of the Complete Psychological Works of Sigmund Freud*, vol. 3 (London: Hogarth, 1962), editor's note, p. 160.

4. "For Three Girls, Justice Takes a Holiday," *Boston Globe*, February 11, 1982. Cited in Herman, "Sexual Violence," p. 4.

5. *People*, October 28, 1991, p. 49.

6. For further reading I recommend David Gallen and Martin Eskenzi, *Sexual Harassment* (New York: Carroll and Graf, 1992).

7. "Listen to Us," *The New York Times,* October 9, 1991.

8. Herman, "Sexual Violence," p. 2.

9. *New Woman,* October 1986, pp. 95–102.

10. Cited by Sanford and Donovan, *Women and Self-esteem* (New York: Viking Penguin, 1984), p. 121.

11. Diana Russell, *Rape in Marriage* (New York: Macmillan, 1982).

12. A. M. Freedman, H. I. Kaplan, B. J. Sadock, *Comprehensive Textbook of Psychiatry* (Baltimore: Williams and Milkis, 1975). Cited in Judith Herman, *Sexual Violence,* p. 3.

13. Helen Resneck-Sannes, "Shame, Sexuality, and Vulnerability," *Women & Therapy* 11, no. 2 (1991): 116.

14. I recommend *The Courage to Heal* by Ellen Bass and Laura Davis (New York: Perennial Library, Harper & Row, 1988). However, I don't agree with their assertion that "If you think you were abused and your life shows the symptoms, then you were." (p.22) This is not a foolproof method to determine if one has been abused and may lead to serious damage when unfounded accusations are made. I strongly recommend seeing a therapist who realizes that vague inklings, "intuition," or even dreams don't guarantee that abuse occurred, someone who can assist in clarifying what actually took place. Sometimes we have to settle for not being sure. Nevertheless, this is a useful book for aid in recovering from sexual abuse. I also suggest *The Courage to Heal Workbook: For Women and Men Survivors of Child Sexual Abuse,* Laura Davis (New York: HarperCollins, 1990).

CHAPTER SIXTEEN

1. Jean Baker Miller, *Toward a New Psychology of Women* (Boston: Beacon Press, 1986), chapter 4.

Barbach, Lonnie. *For Yourself: The Fulfillment of Female Sexuality*. New York: Signet, 1976.

————. *For Each Other: Sharing Sexual Intimacy*. New York: Signet, 1984.

Bass, Ellen, and Laura Davis. *The Courage to Heal*. New York: Perennial Library, 1988.

Beauvoir, Simone de. *The Second Sex*. New York: Vintage Books, 1974.

Belenky, Mary, Blythe Clinchy, Nancy Goldberger, and Jill Tarule. *Women's Ways of Knowing*. New York: Basic Books, 1986.

Borysenko, Joan. *Guilt Is the Teacher, Love Is the Lesson*. New York: Warner Books, 1990.

Bradshaw, John. *Healing the Shame that Binds You*. Deerfield Park, Fla.: Health Communications, 1988.

Cermak, Timmon. *A Time to Heal*. Los Angeles: Jeremy P. Tarcher, 1988.

Cheek, Jonathan. *Conquering Shyness: The Battle Anyone Can Win*. New York: Putnam, 1989.

Chodorow, Nancy. *The Reproduction of Mothering.* Berkeley: University of California Press, 1978.

Davis, Laura, *The Courage to Heal Workbook: A Workbook for Women and Men Survivors of Sexual Abuse.* New York: HarperCollins, 1990.

Dinnerstein, Dorothy. *The Mermaid and the Minotaur.* New York: Harper & Row, 1977.

Eichenbaum, Louise, and Susie Orbach. *Understanding Women.* New York: Basic Books, 1983.

Estes, Clarissa Pinkola. *Women Who Run with the Wolves.* New York: Ballantine Books, 1992.

Eisler, Riane. *The Chalice and the Blade.* San Francisco: Harper & Row, 1988.

Fossum, Merle A., and Marilyn J. Mason. *Facing Shame.* New York: Norton, 1986.

Freedman, Rita. *Bodylove: Learning to Like Our Looks and Ourselves.* New York: Perennial Library, 1990.

Gallen, David and Martin Eskenzi. *Sexual Harassment.* New York: Carroll and Graf, 1992.

Gilligan, Carol. *In a Different Voice.* Cambridge, Mass.: Harvard University Press, 1982.

———, Nona P. Lyons, and Trudy J. Hanmer, eds. *Making Connections: The Relational Worlds of Adolescent Girls at Emma Willard School,* Cambridge, Mass.: Harvard University Press, 1950.

Greenwood, Sadja, M.D., *Menopause, Naturally.* Volcano, Calif.: Volcano Press, 1984.

Hancock, Emily. *The Girl Within.* New York: Fawcett Columbine, 1989.

Herman, Judith. *Trauma and Violence.* New York: Basic Books, 1992.

Hoschschild, Arlie. *The Second Shift.* New York: Viking, 1989.

Jordan, Judith, et al., eds. *Women's Growth in Connection.* New York: The Guilford Press, 1991.

Josselson, Ruthellen. *Finding Herself.* San Francisco: Jossey-Bass, 1990.

Kaufman, Gershen. *Shame: The Power of Caring.* Cambridge, Mass.: Schenkman Books, 1985.

———. *The Psychology of Shame.* New York: Springer, 1989.

Lerner, Harriet Goldhor. *The Dance of Anger.* New York: Harper & Row, 1985.

———. *The Dance of Intimacy.* New York: Perennial Library, 1990.

Lewis, Helen B. *Shame and Guilt in Neurosis.* New York: International Universities Press, 1974.

———. ed. *The Role of Shame in Symptom Formation.* Hillsdale, N.J.: The Analytic Press, 1987.

Lewis, Michael. *Shame: The Exposed Self.* New York: The Free Press, 1992.

Lynd, Helen. *On Shame and the Search for Identity*. New York: Harcourt Brace, 1958.

Mason, Marilyn J. *Making Our Lives Our Own*. San Francisco: Harper San Francisco, 1991.

McFarland, Barbara and Tyeis Baker-Baumann. *Shame and Body Image: Culture and the Compulsive Eater*. Deerfield Beach, Fla.: Health Communications, 1990.

McKay, Matthew and Patrick Fanning. *Self-Esteem*. Oakland, Calif.: New Harbinger, 1987.

Middelton-Moz, Jane. *Shame and Guilt: Masters of Disguise*. Deerfield Beach, Florida: Health Communications, 1990.

———. *Children of Trauma*. Deerfield Beach, Fla.: Health Communications, 1989.

Miller, Alice. *The Drama of the Gifted Child*. New York: Basic Books, 1981.

Miller, Jean Baker. *Toward A New Psychology of Women*. Boston: Beacon Press, 1986.

Morrison, Andrew. *Shame: The Underside of Narcissism*. Hillsdale, N.J.: The Analytic Press, 1989.

Nathanson, Donald. *Shame and Pride: Affect, Sex, and the Birth of the Self*. New York: W.W. Norton, 1992.

———, ed. *The Many Faces of Shame*. New York: Guilford Press, 1987.

Piers, G., and M. B. Singer. *Shame and Guilt*. New York: Norton, 1953.

Rodin, Judith. *Body Traps*. New York: William Morrow, 1992.

Rubin, Lillian. *Women of a Certain Age*. New York: Perennial Library, 1990.

———. *Intimate Strangers*. New York: Perennial Library, 1990.

Ruether, Rosemary Radford. *Sexism and God-Talk*. Boston: Beacon Press, 1983.

Sanford, Linda Tschirhart and Mary Ellen Donovan. *Women and Self Esteem*. New York: Viking Penguin, 1984.

Schaef, Anne Wilson. *Women's Reality*. San Francisco: Harper & Row, 1985.

Schneider, Carl D. *Shame, Exposure, and Privacy*. New York: W.W. Norton, 1992.

Sheehy, Gail. *The Silent Passage*. New York: Random House, 1992.

Slayton, Tamara. *Reclaiming the Menstrual Matrix*. Santa Rosa, Calif.: The Menstrual Health Foundation, 1990.

Smedes, Lewis B. *Shame and Grace: Healing the Shame We Don't Deserve*. San Francisco: Harper San Francisco, 1993.

Steinem, Gloria. *Revolution From Within*. Boston: Little, Brown, 1992.

Tannen, Deborah. *You Just Don't Understand*. New York: Ballantine Books, 1990.

Tavris, Carol. *Anger: The Misunderstood Emotion*. New York: Simon & Schuster/Touchstone, 1989.

———. *The Mismeasure of Woman*. New York: Simon & Schuster, 1992.

Taylor, Dena, and Amber Coverdale Sumrall, eds. *Women of the 14th Moon: Writings on Menopause*. Freedom, Calif.: The Crossing Press, 1991.

Viorst, Judith. *Necessary Losses*. New York: Ballantine Books, 1987.

Whitfield, Charles L. *Healing the Child Within*. Deerfield Park, Fla.: Health Communications, 1989.

Wolf, Naomi. *The Beauty Myth*. New York: William Morrow, 1991.

INDEX

————————||||||||||||————————

Exercise, 222–223
  negative view of, 223
Eye contact, of shame-based
    person, 17

False self
  authentic self versus false self,
    156
  effects of, 157–159
  feeling like a fraud, 152–154
  purpose of false self, 154–157
  recognition of, 160–161
  and substitution of feelings,
    159–160
Family
  abuse of child
    forms of, 78
    sexual abuse, 76
  busy parents, effects on
    children, 66–67
  dysfunctional roles
    Daddy's wife role, 76
    scapegoat role, 77–78
    surrogate parent role, 77
  family secrets and shame, 74
  fathers, role of, 65–66
  feelings created by dysfunctional
    family, 72
  and gender-role socialization,
    48–49
  most damaging acts in, 65
  reinforcement of behaviors in,
    49–50
Family shame, 25–26
  characteristics of, 25–26
  as generational experience,
    32–33
Fathers
  and female adolescence,
    90–91
  role of, 65–66
  shame of, 79

Faultfinder, as adaptive role,
    167
Fear of exposure, 21
Fear of failure, 101–102
  areas for, 101–102
  crippling effects of, 104
  protection against, 102
Fear of success, 102–105
  and attitudes of men, 103–104
  crippling effects of, 104
  reasons for, 102–103
  and shame of having too much,
    105–106
Feelings
  ability to feel and healing,
    271–273
  acknowledgment by parents,
    67–68
  anger, 134–137
  competitive feelings, 140
  excitement, 139
  hurt, 138
  lack of feelings, origin of,
    133–134
  needs/wants, 141–146
  and overeating, 229
  pride, 139–140
  related to shame, 16–17
  sadness, 137–138
  shame related to, 133
  stifled with shame, 165
Femininity, 205
Femininity (Brownmiller), 248
Finding Herself (Josselson), 93
Forgiveness
  importance of, 280
  of mother, 114–115
  of parents, 78–79
Freudian theory, penis envy, 46,
    238–239
Freud, Sigmund, 46
Friendships, 202–203
  love in, 202

Gender differences
  body image, 231–232
  communication styles, 146
  identity formation, 87–88
  and importance of relationships,
    191–192
  in response to intimacy,
    201–202
Gender roles, family socialization
  of, 48–49
Gilligan, Carol, 69, 89, 98, 201
Giving/receiving, 106–107
  giving/getting balance, 106–107
Goffman, Erving, 190
Good girl, as adaptive role,
  176
Gottman, John, 196
Greed, and suppressed
  needs/wants, 145, 164
Group therapy, 278
Guilt
  of abortion, 249–250
  nature of, 23
  and sex, 240–241
  versus shame, 23–24

Hancock, Emily, 95
Healing
  and ability to feel, 271–273
  affirmations for, 289
  and care of self, 275–276
  and compassion, 273–275,
    278–279
  confronting defenses, 276
  connecting past and present,
    270–271, 278
  finding source of shame, 269
  and forgiveness, 280
  gender shame, 280–281
  and groups, 278
  healing letter, 288
  and lost child, 273

qualities of healed women,
    282–283
  resistance in, 277
  from sexual abuse, 263–264
  visualization for inner child, 288
Healing the Child Within (Whitfield),
    205
Healing the Shame That Binds You
    (Bradshaw), 23
Health, and shame, 39
Herman, Judith, 253
Hill, Anita, 254–255
Hischchild, Arlie, 110
Hite Report, The (Hite), 244
Homemaker
  lack of husband's help, 110–111
  lack of payment for, 58
  role of women, 47–48, 51, 93
Hopelessness, and shame, 20
Horner, Matina, 103
Horney, Karen, 168
Humble one, as adaptive role,
    174–175
Hurt, 138
  and shame, 28, 138
  and women, 138

Identity
  and autonomy, 85–87
  false self, 152–161
  formation of, 84–85
  gender differences in formation
    of, 87–88
  healthy, requirements for, 86
  and homemaker role, 91–92
  loss of, 96
  and marriage, 95
  and relationships, 94, 182–183
  shame-based, 17–18, 23, 30–31,
    84
  women in adolescence, 88–91
  and work role, 92–94

Indecisiveness, and fear of failure,
102
Individuality, discouragement of,
71
Infatuation
disillusionment, 186–187
versus love, 184
Infidelity, by women, 67
Inner resources, lack of access to,
159
Intimacy
fear of, 196–197
gender differences in response
to, 201–202

Jordan, Judith, 212
Josselson, Ruthellen, 93
Joy
and false-self, 158–159
and self-shame, 125–126

Kaminer, Wendy, 205
Kaplan, Dr. Helen Singer, 257
Kaufman, Gershen, 158

Landers, Ann, 160
Lerner, Harriet Goldhor, 58, 186
Lesbians, 246–247
Lewis, Helen B., 36
Love
acceptance of, 197–198
conditional love, 155
versus infatuation, 184–185
Lynd, Helen, 17

MacKinnon, Catherine A., 253
Manipulation, and women, 60
Marriage
bad marriage

and growth, 195
reasons for, 194–195
death of spouse, 203
dominance/deference in,
190–191
failed marriages, 193–194
false idealization of, 189
and fear of independence,
194–195, 207–208
and female dependency, 95
and identity, 95
impostor marriage, 189
versus singlehood, 192–193
withdrawal in, 195–196
See also Mate selection
Martyr role, of women, 60
Masturbation, 242–243
Mate selection
attraction of opposites, 183
disillusionment in, 186–187
failed expectations in, 188
inequities in marital
relationships, 188–189
and search for happiness,
184–185
and shame, 34–35
Media
and message about body image,
219–220
stereotyping of women by, 55–57
Men
demeaning attitudes about
women, 44
and family socialization, 49
lack of household help from,
110–111, 188–189
myths about male sexuality,
252–253
response to intimacy, 201–202
and shame, 16
Menopause, 248–249
attitudes about, 249
sexuality in, 249

"Should"
  healthy replacements for, 130
  negative aspects of, 127–128
Shulman, Alix, 242
Shyness, nature of, 26
Singlehood, feelings related to, 192–193
Social injustice, and shame, 19
Socialization, and shame, 18–19
Star, as adaptive role, 168–169
Streisand, Barbra, 90
Stress of Life, The (Selye), 39
Surrogate parent role, of child, 77

Tannen, Deborah, 146
Tavris, Carol, 222, 247
Therapy, self-help groups, 288
Thomas, Clarence, 254
Time to Heal, A (Cermak), 72
Tompkins, Silvan, 18
Trivial incidents, and shame, 17
Trust, 73–75
  lack of, origins of, 73–74
  trusting oneself, 74–75

Victim, as adaptive role, 167–168
Visualization, for inner child, 288
Volcano, as adaptive role, 172

Whitfield, Charles, 204–205
Witch-hunts, 53
Withdrawal, as adaptive mechanism, 172–173
Women
  adaptations as second-class citizens, 60–61
  and anger, 135–137

culture and role of, 15–16, 31
demeaning traits attributed to, 44
and depression, 36–38
healing gender shame, 280–281
need for connection, 201–204
relationship skills of, 86, 208–209
response to intimacy, 201–202
and self-shame, 117–118
sex-object role of, 16
societal myths related to, 43–44
Women and shame, 4–9, 15–16, 31–32
  and childhood socialization, 48–49
  and disempowerment, 46–47, 50–51
  and family roles, 49–50
  and homemaker role, 47–48, 51
  and media, 55–57
  and religion, 44–45, 53–55
  and schooling, 51–53
  societal aspects, 44–46
  and workplace, 57–59
Work/workplace
  double standard in, 58
  glass ceiling, 57
  importance to women, 93–94
  and role strain for women, 109–111
  women's earnings, view of, 93
  women's position in, 57–59
  women to women relationships, 58

You Just Don't Understand: Women and Men in Conversation (Tannen), 146

Photo courtesy of Harvey Henningsen

CHRISTINE BRAUTIGAM EVANS has been a therapist in private practice for twenty years. She has led many women's therapy and
support groups and has given successful workshops on a wide
range of topics, including parenting, communication, assertiveness training, marriage enrichment, and most recently, shame.
She lives with her husband and daughter in California.